# Yale French Studies

NUMBER 142


# Lesbian Materialism: The Life and Work of Monique Wittig

**Yale French Studies**



*Editorial office:* Humanities Quadrangle,
320 York Street, 3rd Floor
*Mailing address:* P.O. Box 208251, New Haven,
Connecticut 06520-8251
*Sales and subscription office:*
Yale University Press, P.O. Box 209040
New Haven, Connecticut 06520-0940



Designed by James J. Johnson and set in Trump Medieval Roman by Newgen North America.
Printed in the United States of America.

ISSN 044-0078
ISBN for this issue 978-0-300-26735-8

# A Note from the Managing Editor

With this volume, *Yale French Studies* celebrates its 75th anniversary. No small feat, even for the country's oldest English language journal devoted to French and Francophone literature and culture. For three quarters of a century, this lively and essential presence in the field has been sustained through the unceasing support, ardent intellectual curiosity, and warm community of the French department at Yale University. In marking this *semisequicentennial*, we are grateful to the members of the editorial board over the last twenty-five years, especially the current members: Howard Bloch, Morgane Cadieu, Thomas C. Connolly, Marlene Daut, Jill Jarvis, Alice Kaplan, Pierre Saint-Amand, and Maurice Samuels.

Since *YFS* last took stock of its history, with a double issue retrospective for the fiftieth anniversary in 1998-1999, there have been many more highlights worth revisiting. Over the last quarter century, these pages have seen Tyler Stovall uncover the role of Black American Expatriates in the Algerian War (vol. 98); Michel Butor recollect on his relationship with Jean-François Lyotard (vol. 99); and Jacques Roubaud offer a charming list of "Perec's 17 Extreme Experiences" (vol. 105). Deborah Jenson assembled an impressive collection of voices to examine the 1804 anniversary of Haitian independence (vol. 107) and Lauren du Graf, Julia Elsky, and Clémentine Fauré orchestrated a rich conversation on the legacy of existentialism (including a nod to this journal's role in importing the movement to the U.S.) (vol. 135/136). More recently, Pierre Joris and Habib Tengour surveyed the ends of the Maghreb, and Francophonie itself (vol. 137/138) in a wide-ranging conversation recalling the provocation of Christopher Miller and Farid Laroussi in their own volume, "French and Francophone: The Challenge of Expanding Horizons" (vol. 103).

Entire volumes have been dedicated to vital figures like Emmanuel Levinas (vol. 104), Claude Levi-Strauss (vol. 123), Marie Vieux Chauvet (vol. 128), Jorge Semprun (vol. 129), Patrick Modiano (vol. 133), and more recently, Maryse Condé (vol. 140). We even made "Time for Baudelaire" (vol. 125/126) through the capable hands of E.S. Burt, Elissa Marder, and Kevin Newmark. Ranging restlessly beyond literature, *YFS* has explored Lanzmann's cinematic career after *Shoah* (vol. 141); traced the contours of photography and the body in nineteenth-century France (vol. 139); and enlarged notions of literary studies with volumes on *bande-dessinée* (vol. 131/132) and crime fiction (vol. 108).

Throughout, *YFS* has sought to provide a curatorial response to the words of Christiane Taubira, reflecting on her experience reading her childhood friend, Condé: "There is a standing invitation to travel. . . . An invitation to travel through time and space, through the vastness of History and the most minuscule of lives."

As it happens, the journal's 75th year is my first as its managing editor. I look forward to venturing into a new quarter-century ushering in volumes that match the intellectual depth and creative breadth that have marked the last seventy-five years of work. I am eager to become acquainted with readers, joining them in the powerful potential of the "literary worksite," to borrow a term from the current, inspiring, volume on Monique Wittig. As I embark, I wish to acknowledge the invaluable contributions of my predecessors—especially Alyson Waters, who graciously gave her time and expertise to ensure the continuous forward momentum of *YFS*—as well as the wonderfully kind and knowledgeable team at Yale University Press. *En avant*!

ANNABEL L. KIM

# Preface: Lesbian Materialism in the Life and Work of Monique Wittig

As with so many figures from the second-wave feminist movement of the 1970s, the radical feminist thinker and activist Monique Wittig has often been relegated to the twentieth century, useful for then but not for now. Wittig, an avant-garde writer and heir to the New Novel, wrote novels that, in their formalist experimentation and unapologetic literariness, have been read by relatively few. And yet, the vision of radical equality and freedom that animates the whole of Wittig's literary and theoretical oeuvre remains inextinguishable. After peaking in the 1990s, at the apogee of academic feminism in literary studies, when Wittig's *The Straight Mind* was a feminist reference and a seemingly obligatory touchpoint (especially following Judith Butler's extended engagement with Wittig's work in *Gender Trouble*), interest in Wittig declined in parallel with the decline of French Theory and of the poststructuralist linguistic turn.[1] As the twentieth century, in all its necropolitical violence, came to an end, the humanities turned away from what seemed like a naive faith in representation to attend instead to the material. This materialist turn was defined in opposition to the representational and the discursive and in alignment with the distinctly twenty-first-century project of critiquing the *anthropos* at the heart of the mode of devastation that is the Anthropocene: against this anti-humanist and posthumanist backdrop, Wittig, with her resolute attachment to the human as a cognitive subject and site of political agency, was left behind.

1. Monique Wittig, *The Straight Mind* (Boston: Beacon Press, 1992); Judith Butler, *Gender Trouble: Feminism and the Subversion of Identity* (New York: Routledge, 1990).

**YFS 142,** *Lesbian Materialism: The Life and Work of Monique Wittig,* ed. Cadieu and Kim, © 2023 by Yale University.

However, just as there has been in recent years a renewed interest in second-wave feminism[2] and in re-excavating this heterogeneous political and theoretical moment for its still radical potential, there has likewise been a renewed interest in Wittig, including from somewhat unexpected quarters. This became very clear when Morgane Cadieu and I organized the October 2019 international conference, "Drafting Monique Wittig,"[3] and discovered that there was a strong will not only to reevaluate Wittig's oeuvre but also her life, as evidenced in a roundtable that launched a discussion of what it would entail to write a critical biography of Wittig and thereby cement her status as an indispensable writer and thinker for feminism, and for French literature.

This reconsideration of Wittig coincides with a contemporary desire to push back against dominant feminist and literary historiographies—a position that permits us to work through how Wittig might enable us to rewrite our histories (and thereby our understanding) of 1970s feminism and of twentieth-century French literature. This reconsideration also coincides with a desire to open Wittig's thought up to the queer and trans movements and theories that Wittig's premature death in 2003 prevented her from fully engaging with. The conference was thus marked by a dual perspective, by a renewed retrospective regard and a regard turned fully forward toward the future, toward the prospect of using Wittig to engage with and enrich the political movements of our current moment, which are marked—in contrast to the political context of the turn of the twenty-first century that was the backdrop for the 2001 conference on Wittig, "Parce que les lesbiennes ne sont pas des femmes" (Because lesbians are not women) . . .[4]—by a resolutely intersectional approach to the politics of identity (or politics tout court) and haunted by the shadows of mass

2. See, for instance, "1970s Feminism," ed. Lisa Disch, special issue, *South Atlantic Quarterly* 114, no. 4 (October 2015) and Clare Hemmings, *Why Stories Matter: The Political Grammar of Feminist Theory* (Durham: Duke University Press, 2011), which revisit narratives of feminist history. One can also see engagement with and reconsideration of such controversial second-wave figures as Andrea Dworkin in work such as Leah Claire Allen, "The Pleasures of Dangerous Criticism: Interpreting Andrea Dworkin as a Literary Critic," *Signs: Journal of Women in Culture and Society* 42, no. 1 (2016): 49–70.

3. The conference was held October 3–4, 2019, at Yale University's Beinecke Rare Book and Manuscript Library, New Haven, CT.

4. The conference was held June 16–17, 2001, at Columbia University, New York, NY.

extinction and planetary demise ushered in by the Anthropocene and climate catastrophe. To engage with Wittig now, as opposed to at the beginning of this century, is to do so in a moment where not just the end of history, but the end of humanity itself, is in sight.

The through-line that emerged during the two days of our conference was Wittig's commitment to materialism, which connects Wittig's political praxis and theory to her literary production and theory. It is by focusing on Wittig's materialism in its multivalence and multifariousness that we are able to see how Wittig's radical lesbian feminism and her unending quest for new literary forms are, in fact, two sides of the same coin. Indeed, the materialist ethos of the conference put into relief the irony of Wittig's being cast aside for being insufficiently materialist, when Wittig's entire oeuvre constitutes a materialism.

If the literary is political for Wittig and the political, literary, it is because both are rooted in an unwavering materialist positionality vis-à-vis the world. To understand Wittig's life and work is to conceive of Wittig as a materialist in the most capacious sense of the term. Wittig's materialism is philosophical, political, existential, and aesthetic. If we place this issue of *Yale French Studies* under the sign of not simply materialism, but, specifically, *lesbian materialism*, it is because lesbian materialism, more than either lesbian by itself or materialism by itself, enables us to perceive and apprehend Wittig's literary, theoretical, and political work in its globality, as a whole. Lesbian materialism, by making lesbian the method and materialism the object, allows Wittig's work to realize its full range: it allows us to put Wittig's ecological sensibilities—what some might call a proto-ecocriticism or a proto-ecofeminism—in conversation with a more contemporary theoretical development such as new materialism; it allows us to ensure that Wittig's continued concern with the heteropatriarchal violence of the straight mind remains foregrounded against the backdrop of a recent revival in Marxist and socialist thought and activism; it enables us to shake up traditional historical materialism and its somewhat congealed model of history by forcing it to shed the assumed heterosexuality that undergirds it.

To separate Wittig's radical lesbianism from her equally radical materialism is to subject Wittig's body of work to the analytic violence she describes linguistics as having done to language, transforming an integral, living body into "dismembered, dismantled, reduced, cut up signs," the thus mutilated body being reduced to a "fragmented, meaningless" state.[5] Sappho, this precursor to and guiding light for Wittig, comes to us in fragments, to be sure, but with Wittig, we as readers and interpreters have the ability to find ourselves "situated, confronted, body to body, with this panorama of language"[6]—a panorama and a body that are both made with and in language. Wittig's lesbian cannot exist apart from language just as her materialism cannot, either.

The core principle of Wittig's materialism is that of the materiality of language, of language's capacity to "cast sheaves on the real."[7] It is a principle that brings everything under language's purview and insists on a necessary relation between the abstract and the concrete. If Wittig is a materialist insofar as she is firmly anti-essentialist when it comes to concepts, insisting on breaking any causality that might be asserted between nature and ideas that are supposedly based on it, rejecting the very premise that ideas reflect a pre-existing reality rather than shape it, the different spheres that Wittig's materialism encompasses are in turn marked by language. Any understanding of Wittig's materialism must pass first through language, which is where Wittig's projects start as well as end.

Wittig's lesbian materialism, and the language that permeates every aspect of it, is, like Wittig's oeuvre, informed by the deeply heterogeneous repertoire of texts she frequents, as seen, exemplarily, in the bibliography to be found at the end of *Les Guérillères*, which frames the novel as "the meeting place of some texts,"[8] bringing together Aristophanes, Beauvoir, Confucius, Homer, Mao, Perrault, and the Robert dictionary of the French language, to name a few of the texts summoned to this meeting place. We can thus find in Wittig's lesbian materialism a similarly rich and varied set of sources of encounter, from Rousseau to Sarraute, from Lucretius to Marx and the revisions to Marxian dialectical materialism made by feminist activ-

5. Monique Wittig, *Le Chantier littéraire* (Lyon: Presses universitaires de Lyon; Donnemarie-Dontilly: Éditions iXe, 2010), 95, 43. All translations unless otherwise noted are my own. Lynne Huffer and I are currently translating *Le Chantier littéraire* into English, which will be published by Verso Books in 2024 under the title *The Literary Workshop*, making this seismic text available for the first time to an Anglophone audience.

6. Wittig, *Le Chantier littéraire*, 51–52.

7. Wittig, *The Straight Mind*, 43–44.

8. "Le lieu de rencontre de quelques textes," Wittig, *Les Guérillères*, 209.

ists and theorists such as Christine Delphy, Colette Guillaumin, and Nicole-Claude Mathieu.

In *Le Chantier littéraire*, Wittig's posthumously published ars poetica and most complete elaboration of her materialist conception of language, we find language evoked in a dazzling array of dense, incisive chapters: language as a body that is to be held in the tight embrace of combat, as when a writer struggles to find the words to put on the page; language as a gnomon, a tool that brings disparate bodies into relation (as when the sun is placed in relation to the earth upon whose surface it casts a shadow via the gnomon);[9] language as a Trojan horse, a weapon in a war that is, by necessity, political; language as a social contract; language as a quarry; language as paradise. The analogies abound, and this semiotic abundance is matched by the contributions that make up this volume, which shed new light, thereby casting new shadows with the gnomon of Wittig's own work, which continues, in the twenty-first century, to recast materialism and reconceptualize the lesbian.

This volume's contributions cast the following shadows and fashion the following concepts: Lynne Huffer reveals how a quick doodle, a small ink trace tucked away in the archives, constitutes the cosmology of Wittig's thought in miniature, where archive works its way into the literary worksite and collides with Wittig's geometry; Gina Stamm demonstrates how Wittig's staging of putrefactive and dismembered bodies counteracts the subject-consolidating action of abjection, as theorized by Julia Kristeva; Ilana Eloit lesbianizes the archives of feminism and attends to the lesbian as the ghost of history; Sandrine Sanos offers a much-needed study of Wittig's translation of Herbert Marcuse, showing how translation is as much a part of Wittig's literary worksite and arsenal as is the writing of novels; Katherine Costello affirms the importance of Wittig's work for the project

9. The gnomon is most commonly understood to be the part of the sundial that casts a shadow, allowing one to tell, or measure, time. It is also, according to the *Merriam-Webster Dictionary*, "the remainder of a parallelogram after the removal of a similar parallelogram containing one of its corners—a carpenter's square is this type of gnomon, where a square parallelogram is cut out from another square parallelogram, allowing for the construction of things at right angles." Wittig describes the gnomon in *Le Chantier littéraire* as "a measuring instrument, which, it is said, was the first fashioner of concepts [un instrument à mesurer, qui dit-on a été le premier façonneur de concepts]," (Wittig, *Le Chantier littéraire*, 40). And in *The Straight Mind*, Wittig describes the gnomon as "a kind of carpenter's square," (Wittig, *The Straight Mind*, 50).

of thinking transfeminism and shows how trans bodies are Trojan horses infiltrating the straight mind; Alice Kaplan and Anne Garréta offer reflections on how to write the biography of a lesbian feminist thinker and writer, with Kaplan elegantly elaborating the challenge of how writing a biography for Wittig is to make of Wittig's life a novel, to write Wittig the way Wittig writes, and Garréta delivering a death blow to the death of the author by reminding us that a work is produced by a life; Suzette Robichon reflects on the manifold readerships Wittig's work has had since she first emerged onto the literary landscape in the '60s, Wittig's literary worksite still very much open as a site of experience and of worldbuilding; Sande Zeig takes up *The Constant Journey*, Wittig's theatrical rewriting of *Don Quixote*, taking us behind the scenes of this important staging of Wittig's thought, and calling our attention to how Wittig's work of lesbian materialism is itself a constant journey. Finally, Morgane Cadieu, in an afterword, moves us out of the volume through the archives, transporting us from the cosmic, planetary scale that we find in Huffer's text, to that of the atom, revealing the archives to be "an atomist worksite" that points to the potential inhering in Wittig's lesbian materialism as a kind of atomism, a "site of action"[10] where Wittig's letters, as atoms making up the work, converge and act on each other.

The Wittigian site of action is one where language converges with itself, or, in other words, communicates. And as is articulated in a letter from Christiane Rochefort (also a feminist author informed by Marxism) that we find in Wittig's papers, housed at Yale's Beinecke Rare Book and Manuscript Library, this communication constitutes a utopia. In this letter, Rochefort bonds with Wittig over their shared investment in utopia, and declares, "Gotta start with utopia."[11] Utopia, for Rochefort, consists of two things: breathing, and communicating:

> Breathing, that's part of utopia. (The proof = 'here,' we don't breathe.) Not being afraid any longer to be who we are — in particular, not being afraid any longer to be just ourselves. Not being afraid any longer around others. Communicating. Wanting to communicate. Communicating, that's utopia.[12]

10. Wittig, *The Straight Mind*, 90.

11. "Faut commencer par l'utopie." Christiane Rochefort, letter to Monique Wittig, December 1970–January 1971, Box 21, GEN MSS 1359, Beinecke Library, Yale University.

12. "Respirer, ça appartient à l'utopie. (Preuve = « ici », on ne respire pas). Ne plus avoir peur d'être ce qu'on est – en particulier ne plus avoir peur de n'être que ce qu'on

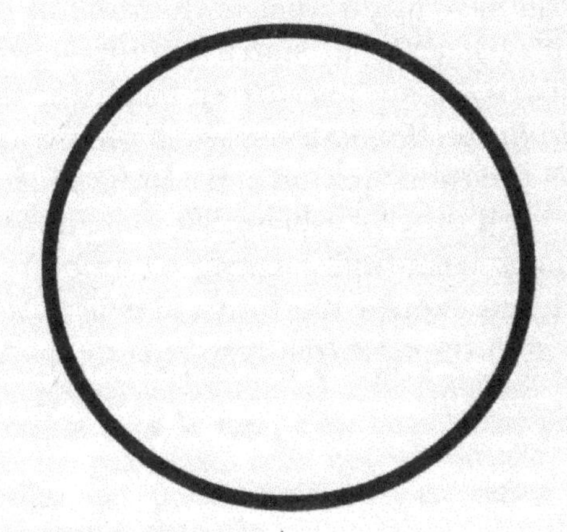

Wittig's lesbian materialism is a text, which is to say a world, which is to say a worksite, where language meets itself, this continual action of contact opening up a space, an interval, where there is room to breathe—to, in freely taking in the atmosphere, claim, through the respiratory act, a place as and for oneself in the world, communicating onto the world in a way that the act of holding one's breath, refusing to let the world inside our lungs, cuts off.

*Respire* breaks down etymologically to *re-* (again) and *spirare* (breathe), the cyclical definition of the breath sending us to the unending circle of *Les Guérillères*, a reminder that the work of utopia, of lesbianizing the world, is never finished but has always begun. *Spirare* is also the root of *spirit*, *spirare* giving us *spiritus*, so that this spirit that signifies both the animating principle of life (as contained in the material, physical support of our body) and the mind (as the container of our immaterial thoughts), is itself caught up in the utopian cycle of re-spiring. The lesbian is a material that is reimagined, recast, and reworked by Wittig as the concrete figuration of the materialism that animates Wittig's oeuvre: a locus of thought and action that conjoins the philosophical, political, existential, and aesthetic through language, which is a kind of spirit, both abstract and concrete. Wittig's lesbian acts as a kind of temporal bridge, able to connect the ancient—*lesbian* comes to us from Sappho of Lesbos—to the

est. Plus avoir peur devant les autres. Communiquer. Vouloir communiquer. Communiquer, c'est l'utopie." Rochefort, letter to Wittig, December 1970–January 1971.

present and to the near future that is the time of utopia, which, as Rochefort exclaims, is also our starting point—our past. Indeed, we could see the potential histories written in Wittig and Zeig's *Lesbian Peoples: Material for a Dictionary* as the building of precisely such a temporal bridge—the transmission and communication of all lesbian temporalities to each other. Lesbian materialism, then, and the language that animates it and the language it animates, as respiration, inspires the past and expires the future, inspires the future and expires the past: a counterpoint that responds to apocalypse now with utopia, now.

LYNNE HUFFER

# This Whispering Skeleton

> Ask the librarian behind the desk for a cardboard box of labeled file folders containing singular whispering skeletons. Place one in my looking-glass hands.
> —Susan Howe, *Spontaneous Particulars*

## 1.

This whispering skeleton, sketched in Monique Wittig's hand, adorns the back page of the Beinecke manuscript of *Virgile, non* (*Across the Acheron*). "On the other side of the sun lies the earth's twin planet. ~~Like the earth~~ It turns around the sun in a gyrating movement symmetrical to that of the earth."[1]

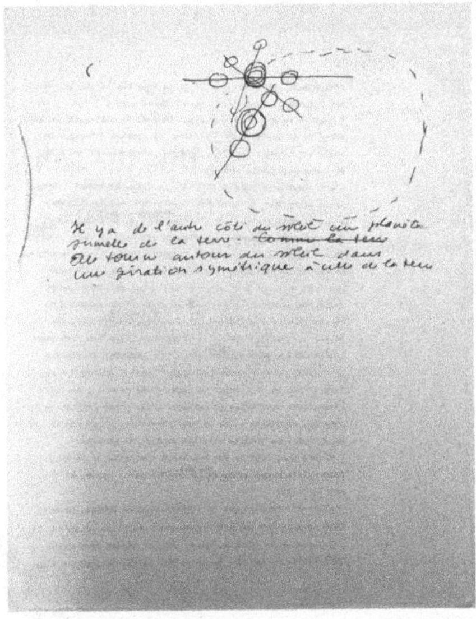


I want to express my gratitude to Morgane Cadieu and Annabel Kim for soliciting this essay. Many thanks to Sande Zeig for her response to my queries about Monique Wittig's sketch. Special thanks to Morgane Cadieu for making this archival object from Yale's Beinecke Library available to me.

1. Monique Wittig, *Virgile, non* manuscript (verso side), Wittig Collection, Beinecke Library, Yale University, translation mine.

**YFS 142,** *Lesbian Materialism: The Life and Work of Monique Wittig,* ed. Cadieu and Kim, © 2023 by Yale University.

I print out a copy of the emailed scan, an electronic copy of a copy placed in "my looking-glass hands."[2] What to make of these lines and circles? I scratch the object's surface with my pen, match shapes with names. Mix my hand with Wittig's, leaving marks.

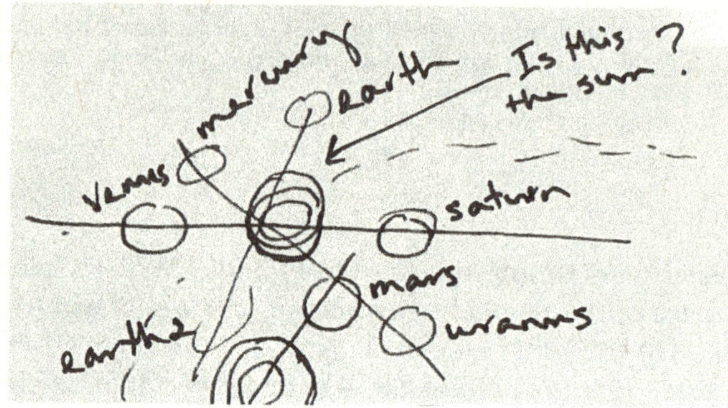


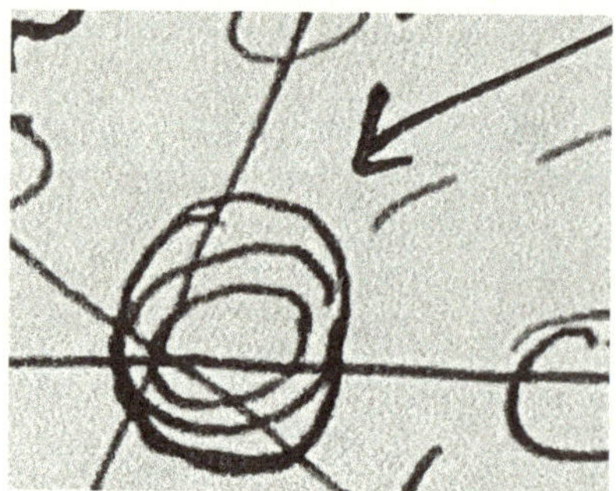

Is this the sun?

Is this the earth?

2. Susan Howe, *Spontaneous Particulars: The Telepathy of Archives* (New York: New Directions, 2014), 41.

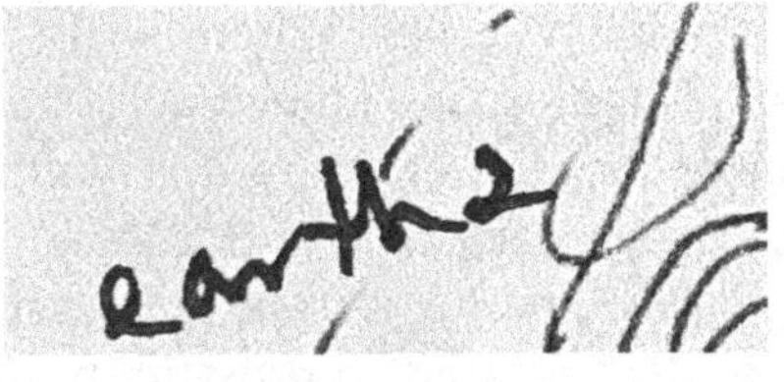

Is this horseshoe shape earth's twin?

I want it to be. Overcome by a memory of reading that is less a thought than the materiality of the page, a mental image of the shape of words in *Les Guérillères*: how black lines emerge against a white backdrop. I remember what they say, "that the most ancient figures depicting the vulva resemble horseshoes."[3] The memory now layered with the doodle's shape:

bonheur. Elles disent que les figures les plus anciennes pour décrire les vulves ressemblent à des fers à cheval. Elles disent

I continue tracking shapes, scanning, copying, printing, scribbling: an arrow, intersecting lines, letters. Trailing movements: archival traces form a palimpsest across memories of reading. Is this the gyrating circle's trail? Is there something new here, or are these the worn-out forms of old struggles?

I send an email to Sande Zeig, Wittig's partner. What is this? Could it be an early sketch of *Virgile, non*?

"Honestly," she says, "I think it is more likely a doodle."[4]

Sande tells me there are diagrams of novels in Wittig's papers, but this is not one of them.

3. Monique Wittig, *Les Guérillères*, trans. David Le Vay (Champaign, IL: University of Illinois Press, 2007), 44–45, hereafter cited as *LGE*. For the French original, see Monique Wittig, *Les Guérillères* (Paris: Minuit, 1969), 61, hereafter cited as *LGF*.

4. Sande Zeig, email correspondence, November 14, 2021.

I love diagrams.[5] But this doodle is what I've got. Where will it lead? I'm seduced by its strangeness. "Doodles don't need a lot of space," Jane Bennett writes. "They make landfall on margin of text, corner of napkin, upside down is fine, though they do like to roam."[6]

To *doodle* is to "scrawl aimlessly," 1935, perhaps from dialectal *doodle, dudle,* to "fritter away time, trifle," related to *dawdle,* perhaps a variant of *daddle,* to "walk unsteadily."

Aimless and unsteady, I follow the doodle's path. Its etymological roots drop me underground to an eighteenth-century track where I trip over a "doodle sack." A doodle sack is a bagpipe. It is also, according to the *Classical Dictionary of the Vulgar Tongue,* 1796, (and *this* is no surprise): "the private parts of a woman."[7] Remembering, again, what "elles" said, "that they have found a very large number of terms to designate the vulva."[8]

> Elles disent qu'elles ont trouvé des appel-
> lations en très grand nombre pour désigner
> les vulves. Elles disent qu'elles en ont retenu

Doodle, dudle, dawdle, daddle, doodle sack. I scramble back up to the surface, lift my gaze to Wittig's celestial bodies, stare at the sun.

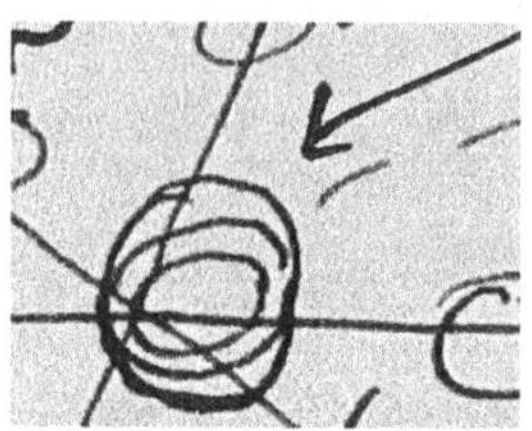

"Lo, a shape!"[9]
this movement, this O

5. For a brilliant defense of radical formalism and an ontology of the diagram that "humiliates metaphysics," see Eugenie Brinkema, *Life-Destroying Diagrams* (Durham: Duke University Press, 2022), 243.

6. Jane Bennett, *Influx and Efflux: Writing Up with Walt Whitman* (Durham: Duke University Press, 2020), x.

7. Online Etymology Dictionary, "doodle," https://www.etymonline.com/search?q=doodle, accessed August 26, 2022.

8. *LGE,* 48; *LGF,* 66.

9. From Walt Whitman, *Leaves of Grass,* in Bennett, *Influx and Efflux,* ix.

o

o

o

O o

O

O

As I scan the heavens I'm recalling again, not only *ce qu'elles disent*, what *les guérillères* say, but also that sound beyond language—O—
"Somewhere there is a siren."[10]

Il y a quelque part une sirène.

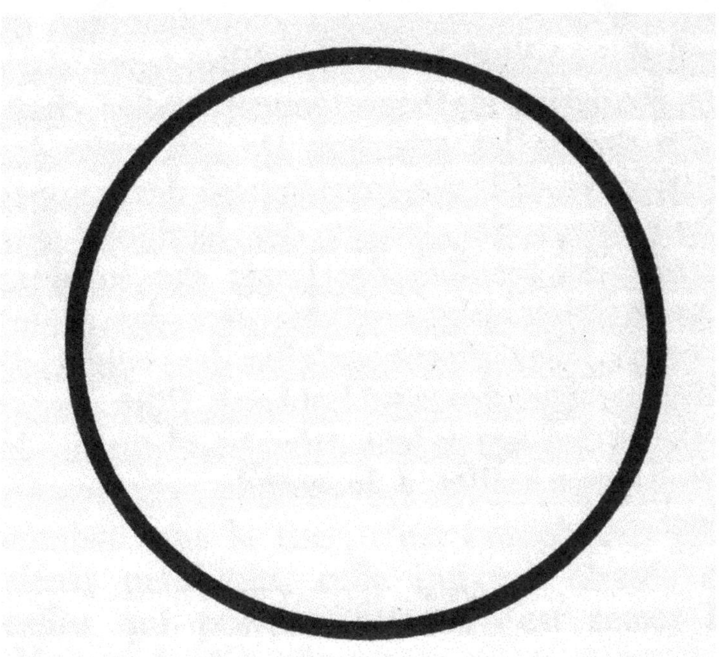

Sometimes she begins to sing. They say that of her song nothing is to be heard but a continuous O. That is why this song evokes for

10. *LGE*, 14; *LGF*, 16.

them, like everything that recalls the O, the zero or the circle, the vulval ring.[11]

> d'incarnat. Quelquefois elle se met à chanter. Elles disent que de son chant on n'entend qu'un O continu. C'est ce qui fait que ce chant évoque pour elles, comme tout ce qui rappelle le O, le zéro ou le cercle, l'anneau vulvaire.

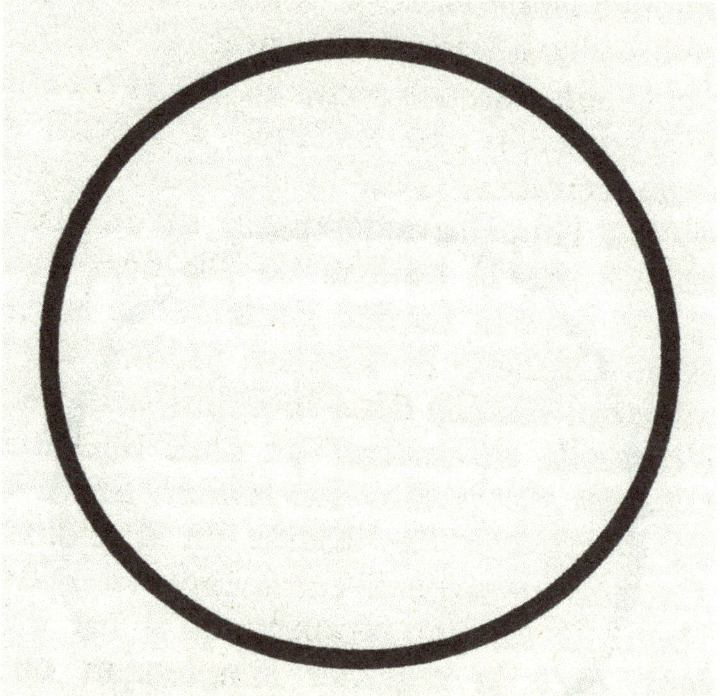

"I," an empty shape-finder, "at once carried along and creative,"[12] nothing more nor less than a relation to a memory of *Les Guérillères* in an encounter with the manuscript of *Virgile, non*.

Standing in the swirl of Wittig's writing, an archival object in my hands, this "I" is carried by the skeleton's murmur, a whisper on the

11. LGE, 14; LGD, 16, translation modified.
12. Bennett, *Influx and Efflux*, x.

edges of speech. The O O O O of *Les Guérillères*, their siren's song, seduces (again)! "I" must learn (again!) what they say: Please, my dear, don't compare vulvas to the sun, to the moon, to the stars. Or vice versa.

> They say that they did not garner and develop symbols that were necessary to them at an earlier period to demonstrate their strength. For example they do not compare the vulvas to the sun moon stars. They do not say that the vulvas are like black suns in the shining night.[13]

> **Elles disent qu'elles n'ont pas recueilli et développé les symboles qui dans les premiers temps leur ont été nécessaires pour rendre leur force évidente. Par exemple elles ne comparent pas les vulves au soleil à la lune aux étoiles. Elles ne disent pas que les vulves sont comme les soleils noirs dans la nuit éclatant.**

"They do not say that gyratory movements are like vulvas."[14] To exult in these gyrations—these O's set in motion as celestial bodies held in these hands—would be to succumb to the habit language of the printer's cast. "Starting with the Cartesian principle that one can only conceive that which exists,"[15] these gyrations keep orbiting clichés and common places, *les lieux communs*.

How to break the conceptual code, make new tracks that flee the rutted path,[16] "crack open the social fabric of the common-place?"[17]

2.

Inside the pages of the doodled typescript another Wittig awaits her companion, Manastabal. In *Virgile, non* (*Across the Acheron*),

13. *LGE*, 57–58; *LGF*, 81.

14. *LGE*, 61.

15. Wittig, *Across the Acheron*, trans. David Le Vay (London: Peter Owen, 1987), 21. For French original see Wittig, *Virgile, non* (Paris: Minuit, 1985), 25.

16. See Annabel Kim on "The Runaway Tropism" in *Unbecoming Language: Anti-Identitarian French Feminist Fictions* (Columbus: Ohio State University Press, 2018), 61–64.

17. "Faire craquer le tissu des lieux communs." Wittig, *Le Chantier littéraire* (Lyon: Presses universitaires de Lyon, 2010), 68, translation mine.

Manastabal is to Wittig as Virgil is to Dante, guiding her descent into hell. And yet here, in Wittig's version, the underworld is already on the earth's surface: "the earth is Hell."[18]

la terre c'est l'enfer

This *terre-enfer* is inhabited by fantastical creatures: *dragons, bourlabadus, ulliphants*. Inside the story, Wittig is herself a strange being with scales on her chest and covered in shiny black fur. As she waits for Manastabal, Wittig listens to a story, told by the *ulliphant*, that mirrors the archival doodle: "The ulliphant then relates how on the other side of the sun there is another planet, a twin to the earth. It is there apparently that Paradise is situated, whereas the earth is Hell."[19]

> L'ulliphant raconte donc qu'il y a de l'autre côté du soleil une planète jumelle de la terre. C'est là qu'à l'en croire se situe le paradis, tandis que la terre c'est l'enfer.

The story doubles the doodle; the doodle doubles the story. The chiasmus is also a mise en abyme. The typescript's insides are its outsides, and vice versa. Words rub against drawing; drawing rubs against words.

What to make of this archival chiasmus, its abyssal mise en abyme? Might it break open the *lieux communs*?

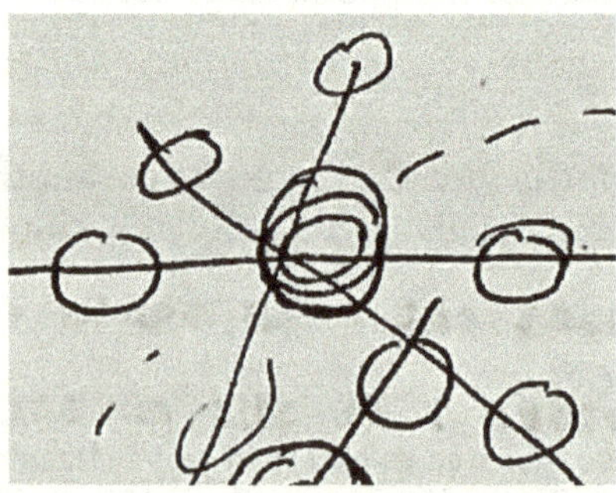

Chiasmus (X)

18. Wittig, *Across the Acheron*, 22; Wittig, *Virgile, non*, 25.
19. Wittig, *Across the Acheron*, 22; Wittig, *Virgile, non*, 25.

3.

Attentive readers will notice the "guideline," the "fil conducteur"[20] of my own mental doodling: "They say that this series of symbols has provided them with a guideline for reading."[21]

> Elles disent que cette série de symboles
> leur a donné un fil conducteur pour lire

Enough said. I've been led by the nose toward vulvular objects. O O O, to say nothing of the doodle sack. "They say that the feminaries give pride of place to the symbols of the circle, the circumference, the ring, the O, the zero, the sphere."[22]

> Elles disent que les féminaires privilégient
> les symboles du cercle, de la circonférence,
> de l'anneau, du O, du zéro, de la sphère.

Let me not turn Wittig's singular writing into ill-digested, chewed-over food.[23] Let me not transform this archive into my own feminary. Let me not be swallowed by my own old words.

4.

> Il y a de l'autre côté du soleil une planète
> jumelle de la terre. ~~Comme la terre~~
> Elle tourne autour du soleil dans
> une giration symétrique à celle de la terre

"On the other side of the sun lies the earth's twin planet. ~~Like the earth~~ It turns around the sun in a gyrating movement symmetrical to that of the earth."[24] Inside the story or out doesn't matter. We Cartesians have this deductive habit. Our methods are analogical. We place existence in our looking-glass hands. Like the earth.

*Comme la terre*

20. *LGE*, 45; *LGF*, 61.
21. *LGE*, 45; *LGF*, 61, translation modified.
22. *LGE*, 45; *LGF*, 61.
23. On writing as "nourritures remâchées" see Nathalie Sarraute, *L'Ère du soupçon* (Paris: Gallimard, 1956), 65.
24. Wittig, *Virgile, non* (verso) ms.

But inside or out, the mirror is not Wittig's tool. In the Beinecke doodle, "Comme la terre" circles back, pauses, puts itself under erasure, *sous rature*:

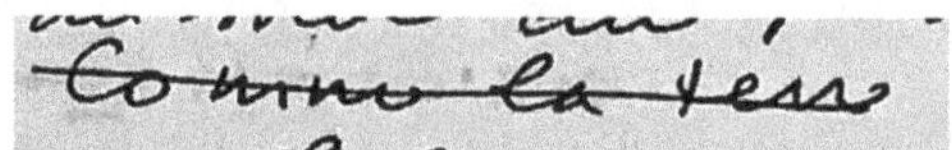

Wittig's tool is a line, a scratch mark over words ————————, ~~Comme la terre~~ or the slashed *j/e* of *Le Corps lesbien* (*The Lesbian Body*).[25] This line is her style, the mark of her gnomon: the rod whose shadow parses slices of sun. (For Wittig, writers are gnomons. Hers is Natalie Sarraute).[26] In Wittig's journey through earth-hell, her guide is this *rature*, this line that writing casts over speech as it falls: a tropistic movement, a Sarrautean rupture. The gnomon fractures language, cracking it open, allowing it to say something new.

Wittig crafts the angles of the gnomon's shadow, her words and sentences blocking out the straight mind's *lux et veritas*. This precise word-crafting of light and shadow places the luminosity of old symbols *sous rature*. The gnomon's line cuts into speech, cuts it off ("lui coupe la parole"),[27] forms the "secant lines"[28] that intersect geometry's circles. Its slashing movement snags our Cartesian thinking, makes our habit words catch in our throat.

## 5.

"Before *I* even know it, *I* is made prisoner."[29] Despite my best efforts, again and again I find myself trapped in this "I." Getting free (no more "I") is not once and for all. Let Wittig's doodle be my gnomon. Again and again, let this gnomon put me under erasure.

25. See Wittig, *Le Corps lesbien* (Paris: Minuit, 1973).
26. See Zeig, "Avant-Propos," in Wittig, *Le Chantier littéraire*, 9.
27. Wittig, *Le Chantier littéraire*, 56.
28. Wittig, *Le Chantier littéraire*, 53, translation mine.
29. "Avant même que *je* le sache *je* est fait prisonnier," Wittig, *Le Chantier littéraire*, 63, translation mine.

6.

"Genealogy is gray."[30] Inside the Beinecke and outside it, this "I" and this "I" imprisoned: this "grayish herd of captives" ("troupeau grisâtre des captifs").[31] But something in the archive flickers.

"Knowledge . . . is made for cutting."[32] "Le savoir . . . est fait pour trancher."[33] Here in the Wittig archive there is a ~~je~~ under erasure, *sous rature*, a slashed lesbian *j/e* who returns after an arduous journey. This "I" *sous rature* holds the same doodled object in her hands: these looking-glass hands now cracked by a gnomon whose shadow cuts me off: *me coupe la parole.*

In that cut between object and speech, line and page, something flickers. Wittig calls that something interlocution, which she defines as:

> what happens among people when they speak. . . . Meaning is derived from interruption, that is, cutting into speech ("couper la parole"), which doesn't exactly mean the actual speech act. I extend this to every action that is linked to language usage, discursive accidents (stops, excess, defect, tone, intonation) and the effects to which they are attached (tropisms, gestures).[34]

In the text-doodle breach there is interlocution: accidents and effects, tropisms in the space we call archive. The interval holds open an invitation into a Wittigian practice beneath the surface of speech: "an immense profusion of sensations, images, sentiments, memories, impulses, little larval actions that no inner language can convey."[35]

30. Michel Foucault, "Nietzsche, Genealogy, History," in Paul Rabinow, ed., *Essential Works of Foucault, 1954–1984*, 3 vols. (New York: New Press, 1998), 1:253.

31. Sarraute, "disent les imbéciles," in Wittig, *Le Chantier littéraire*, 64, translation mine.

32. Foucault, "Nietzsche," 380.

33. Foucault, "Nietzsche, la généalogie, l'histoire" (1971), in *Dits et écrits* 1 (Paris: Quarto Gallimard, 2001), 1016.

34. Wittig, *Le Chantier littéraire*, 56, original emphasis, translation mine. "Ce qui se passe entre les gens quand ils parlent. . . . Son sens dérive d'interrompre, c'est-à-dire, *couper la parole*, ce qui ne désigne pas un acte de parole proprement dit, je l'étends à toute action liée à l'usage de la parole, aux accidents du discours (arrêts, excès, défaut, ton, intonation) et aux effets qui s'y rattachent (tropismes, gestes)."

35. Sarraute, *The Age of Suspicion: Essays on the Novel*, trans. Maria Jolas (New York: George Braziller, 1963), 91. For French original see Sarraute, *L'Ère*, 97: "un foisonnement innombrable de sensations, d'images, de sentiments, de souvenirs, d'impulsions, de petits actes larvés qu'aucun langage intérieur n'exprime."

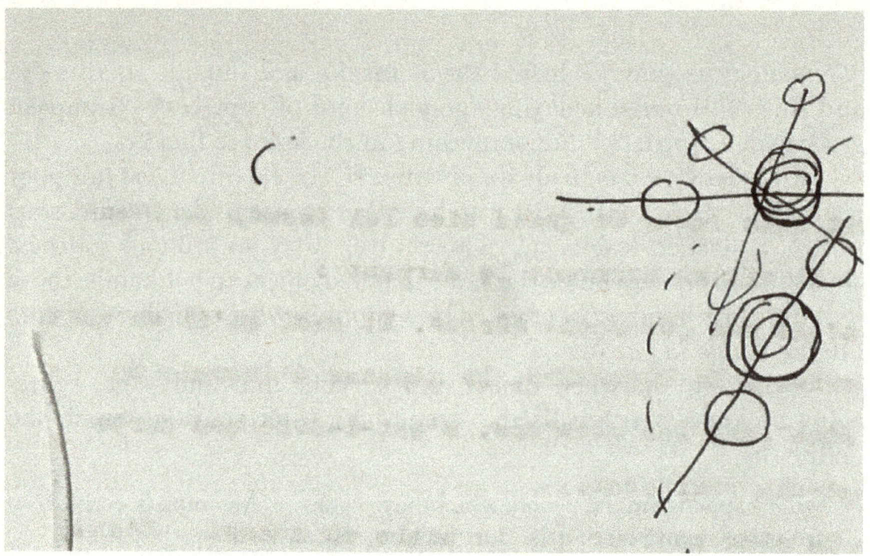

This practice in the archive, "on the threshold of consciousness,"[36] brings new materials to the *chantier littéraire*, the literary worksite: not only words "rubbed against one another"[37] but also a geometrical *frottement* of lines, triangles, angles, dashes, horseshoes, and golden gnomons. Rubbed together, text and doodle spark "a new form,"[38] some other-than-hellish earth—paradise, perhaps—forged in a box, *par éclairs*.[39]

36. Sarraute, *Age of Suspicion*, 91.
37. Wittig, *Le Chantier littéraire*, 61, translation mine.
38. Sarraute, *Age of Suspicion*, 92, translation modified; Sarraute, *L'Ère*, 98.
39. Wittig, *Virgile, non*, 25.

GINA STAMM

# *Le Corps lesbien*: Material without Abjection

Monique Wittig's corpus foregrounds descriptions of the human body, its viscera, and its functions—to a degree, in fact, that often provokes feelings of disgust and revulsion in her readers, and extends to its critical reception. Such imagery is associated in her texts with a wide spectrum of affects—revulsion, but also astonishment and joy. The material body itself is not revolting, but the structural relationship to it determines the emotional response. While the broken bodies of women stuck in the underworld of *Virgile, non* (*Across the Acheron*) provoke horror, the emergence from the underworld at the beginning of *Le Corps lesbien* (*The Lesbian Body*) coincides with a very different feeling for the lovers who tear each other apart: wonder and glee.[1] Repulsion and nausea in response to material phenomena are among the feelings theorized in Julia Kristeva's *Pouvoirs de l'horreur* (*Powers of Horror*). For Kristeva, the porosity and viscosity of the human (and particularly female) body are associated with death and are rejected as "abject." Kristeva uses this analytic lens to characterize twentieth-century literature and examines writers such as Marcel Proust and Louis-Ferdinand Céline as case studies. Abjection has become in many ways a blanket term to refer to texts that engage with these material phenomena, without considering whether the text truly reacts to them as such, or whether the affect associated with them is something else entirely. Wittig, however, explores how, in a non-heteropatriarchal world, the material lesbian body is freed from the

1. Monique Wittig, *Virgile, non* (Paris: Editions de Minuit, 1985) [*Across the Acheron*, trans. David Le Vay and Margaret Crosland (Chester Springs, PA: P. Owen, 1987)] and *Le Corps lesbien* (Paris: Editions de Minuit, 1973) [*The Lesbian Body*, trans. David Le Vay (Boston: Beacon Press, 1986)].

**YFS 142,** *Lesbian Materialism: The Life and Work of Monique Wittig,* ed. Cadieu and Kim, 

affective baggage of disgust. In doing so, she reveals the contingency of Kristeva's analysis of the literary landscape and, I argue, gives us a different way of evaluating both literary and philosophical discourse about the materiality of the body if we can manage to uncouple the body from this horror.

## THE BODY AND ABJECTION

For Kristeva, the abject is associated with certain material phenomena such as dirt and viscosity, with things to which the designations "subject" and "object" cannot be applied with clarity, and, above all, with the affects of disgust and revulsion that accompany the physical response of nausea:

> Food loathing is perhaps the most elementary and most archaic form of abjection. When the eyes see or the lips touch that skin on the surface of milk—harmless, thin as a sheet of cigarette paper, pitiful as a nail paring—I experience a gagging sensation and, still farther down, spasms in the stomach, the belly; and all the organs shrivel up the body, provoke tears and bile, increase heartbeat, cause forehead and hands to perspire. Along with sight-clouding dizziness, nausea makes me balk at that milk cream [. . .]. "I" want none of that element, sign of their desire; "I" do not want to listen, "I" do not assimilate it, "I" expel it. But since the food is not an "other" for "me," [. . .], I expel myself, I spit myself out, I abject myself. [2]

The fragile milk skin is not an "other," but rather the porous borderline between subject and object, as is one's own skin, and nausea is the rejection of the blurring of this border. The subject, assailed by the abject threatening its borders, retreats into what Kristeva refers to as a "château fort" (fortified castle) to separate itself completely from the threat of the abject, to keep itself "pure" and "moral."[3] The fortified castle's rigid walls might otherwise crumble to allow the abject to rush in. If, on the one hand, this subject revels in the fascinating abject, on the other hand, it risks psychosis and death as the result of this dissolution of its borders.

Judith Butler has, in *Gender Trouble*, critiqued the reaffirmation of the patriarchal order present in Kristeva's work, in which the domi-

2. Julia Kristeva, *Powers of Horror,* trans. Leon S. Roudiez (New York: Columbia University Press, 1982), 2–3.

3. Kristeva, 46.

nant structure must exclude the abject to affirm its own identity, and in which an alternative structure is not seriously considered.[4] According to Kristeva, the source of our feelings of body horror, of abjection, is our feelings about the female body and the double stain of menstrual blood and excrement.[5] However, it seems unclear how the abject would obtain in a world where gender difference is no longer valid, or at least where it is no longer seen as a primary lens of differentiation between individuals.

Kristeva, in the second half of *Powers of Horror*, develops abjection not only as a psychoanalytic framework, but also as a tool of literary analysis, which she then uses to make a historical claim about the preoccupations of "contemporary" (twentieth-century) literature:

> Contemporary literature [. . .] seems to be written out of the untenable aspects of perverse or superego positions [. . .] as the sense of abjection is both the abject's judge and accomplice, this is also true of the literature that confronts it. One might thus say that with such a literature there takes place a crossing over of the dichotomous categories of Pure and Impure, Prohibition and Sin, Morality and Immorality.[6]

Authors may reinforce their "fortified castle," or alternatively revel in the "perversity" of abjection as abjection, while not challenging the dichotomy that led to its expulsion from the pure or moral domain. Contemporary literature supposedly then expresses menace of disintegration or the abandon to it, described here as *borderline* conditions.[7]

Kristeva acknowledges in passing the *possibility* of a lack of abjection with these viscous, squishy bits of matter that she calls the "amorale" (amoral).[8] This is a category that cannot be said to revel

4. "'Inner' and 'outer' make sense only with reference to a mediating boundary that strives for stability. And this stability, this coherence, is determined in large part by cultural orders that sanction the subject and compel its differentiation from the abject." Judith Butler, *Gender Trouble* (New York: Routledge, 1990), 182.

5. "These *two* defilements stem from the *maternal* and/or the feminine, of which the maternal is the real support. That goes without saying where menstrual blood signifies sexual difference. But what about excrement? It will be remembered that the anal penis is also the phallus with which infantile imagination provides the feminine sex." Kristeva, *Powers of Horror*, 71.

6. Kristeva, 16.

7. A similar claim, but based on different authors and his own clinical case studies, was made by Kristeva's colleague and training analyst André Green in *La déliaison: Psychanalyse, anthropologie, littérature* (Paris: Hachette, 1998).

8. Kristeva, *Powers of Horror*, 4.

in the impure as does some of the literature of abjection; it does not recognize the legitimacy of prohibition. However, her reference to the amoral is brief and Kristeva does not endow it with the same generative power in literary analysis that she ascribes to the abject. Departing from Kristeva's framework, Hannah Freed-Thall, in her article "Heartsick: The Language of French Disgust," acknowledges the prevalence of abjection in contemporary French literature but opposes it to "base corporeality," an attitude that does not treat the body as the subject of a prohibition:

> Base corporeality is nothing new in French literature—consider François Rabelais's hilarious list of potential "ass-wipes" in *Gargantua* or Michel de Montaigne's philosophical discussion of his kidney stones—but in the post-Cartesian, postrevolutionary age, the porous, mortal body is neither bawdy and carnivalesque nor the object of an edifying humanism. Its decay—now described in the utmost detail—is irreversible, unredeemable.[9]

For Wittig, even a body that has been abjected can in fact be redeemed, its decay no longer inspiring disgust. She acknowledges the existence of the dominant paradigm but then leaves it behind to create a reality in which the body is not proscribed, has no moral content, but is instead material, "base corporeality" in the sense of raw (base) material that can create new meaning.

## FROM ABJECTION TO INTIMACY WITH WITTIG

Monique Wittig does in fact represent abjection at times, in both its material and affective dimensions, but only within the world she has explicitly abandoned. For example, her alter ego narrator "Wittig" is moved to horror by the condition of the abused, broken, and disintegrating bodies of the women damned to suffering in *Across the Acheron*. These women are not abject because they are women, in women's bodies, but they are abject in that they are *abjected* in the system of hell, a system they refuse to leave, even when Wittig offers them the opportunity. They are part of the gender binary that subjects them to patriarchal power and, in fulfilling their role as subjects of domination or oppression, their mutilated bodies inspire the kind of affect associated with abjection (disgust, horror, nausea). "Wittig"'s

9. Hannah Freed-Thall, "Heartsick: The Language of French Disgust," *Modern Language Quarterly* 79, no. 4 (December 2018): 424.

body, on the other hand, may be covered with scales that horrify the women trapped within the system, but she, who can leave and join earth or paradise, finds them beautiful.[10]

In the opening pages of *The Lesbian Body*, "j/e" (*I*) sees herself as abject and describes her own body with words such as *pourri* (rotten), *moisi* (moldy), *infecte* (diseased), *putréfié* (putrefied), a body prone to emitting purulence and fermentations; she does in fact see it as diseased and dangerous, as abject:

> The stink of my bowels surrounds us at m/y every movement. You seem not to notice it, you walk on steadily calling m/e in a loud voice all the love names you were used to call me. From time to time m/y yellow decaying arms from which long worms emerge brush against you, some climb on your back, you shudder, I can see your skin bristle right across your shoulders [...] M/y armpits are musty. M/y breasts are eaten away. I have a hole in m/y throat. The smell that escapes from m/e is noisome. You do not stop your nostrils. You do not exclaim with fright when at a given moment m/y putrescent and half-liquid body touches the length of your bare back. Not once do you turn round, not even when *I* begin to howl in despair the tears trickling down m/y gnawed cheeks to beg you to leave m/e in m/y tomb to brutally describe to you m/y decomposition the purulence of m/y eyes m/y nose m/y vulva the caries of m/y teeth the fermentation of m/y vital organs.[11]

Despite these protests, "tu" (you) removes the narrator from hell, at which point the body, even in pieces, sheds the vocabulary of disgust associated with it. Guided by the Orphic figure of "tu," "j/e" leaves the underworld and is resuscitated at the surface, open to a new range of feelings and able to engage new modes of interaction and exchange marked by a porosity that, in the new order, is no longer threatening.

For the lovers, desire and affection are expressed in and through all organs, breaking down the boundaries among them. Both "j/e" and "tu" at various points experience the dismemberment or decomposition of the other without surprise and even with affection. While we, the reader, may be revulsed, that is not the experience of "j/e" and "tu,"as contrasted to the third party "quelqu'un/une" (someone) who is put off by it. "Tu" "frissonnes" (shudders/shivers) but does not flee.

10. Wittig, *Across the Acheron*, 15–16.
11. Wittig, *The Lesbian Body*, 19–20.

Earlier in the text the Orphic figure spoke to the narrator, telling her what she risked if she stayed in the underworld:

> While you with siren voice entreat some women with shining knees to come to your aid. But you know that not one will be able to bear seeing you with eyes turned up lids cut off your yellow smoking intestines spread in the hollow of your hands your tongue spat from your mouth long green strings of your bile flowing over your breasts, not one will be able to bear your low frenetic insistent laughter. The gleam of your teeth your joy your sorrow the hidden life of your viscera [. . .] all will be equally unbearable to her.[12]

"Pas une" (not one) other would be able to stand the dissection of "tu"'s body in which the eyes, hands, tongue, mouth and breasts are chopped up and mixed with "yellow smoking intestines" and "green strings of bile." Inside and outside become blurred, but rather than being disgusted, "j/e" takes delight in every new part of "tu"'s body exposed by her exploration:

> *I* discover that your skin can be lifted layer by layer, *I* pull, it lifts off, it coils above your knees, *I* pull starting at the labia, it slides the length of the belly, fine to extreme transparency, *I* pull starting at the loins, the skin uncovers the round muscles and trapezii of the back [. . .] *I* reveal the beauty of the shining bone traversed by blood-vessels.[13]

The skin is a thin film here as it is for Kristeva, but instead of being put off by it, the narrator peels one layer after another, associating it not with disgust but with a positive lexicon: "delicately," "beauty," "brilliant." The skinning of the lover is recounted as if the narrator were undressing her, astonished with the beauty, this time not of a naked body, but of its viscera.

As Jean H. Duffy claims, *The Lesbian Body* can be seen as a subversion of (heterosexual) genital sexuality, underlining the polymorphous, reversible nature of the "lesbian" relation as portrayed by Wittig. "Lesbian" has a specific sense for Wittig, who is known for her assertion that "Lesbians are not women." They are not "women who love women," but people who have abandoned the binary system of heterosexuality in which women always exist in relation to, and dependent upon, the category of men. Thus the sexual relationship is transformed:

12. Wittig, *The Lesbian Body*, 15.
13. Wittig, *The Lesbian Body*, 17.

> Here, sexual intercourse involves loving, penetrating and fusing with every organ of the partner's body, not just those which have been culturally designated as erogenous. The point Wittig seems to be making is that the partner is first and foremost a human being, not a man or a woman. The repetitive, over-lengthy and often rather gruesome lists of the essential organs involved drive home relentlessly the point that the human body, whether it is male or female, is composed for the best part in the same way and that genital and reproductive differences are irrelevant.[14]

Wittig's lovers demonstrate a polymorphous, non-hierarchical sexuality. They do not distinguish between characteristics that are historically and socially considered desirable and those that are not; desire is equally oriented toward the dissolving viscera in the lesbian body.[15] It is worth noting that the dominant paradigm infiltrates even this sympathetic reading, with Duffy's use of the pejorative "gruesome."

Transforming women's bodies into "lesbian" bodies, Wittig strips them of the layers of metaphor under which these bodies have existed. At the same time, she succeeds in demetaphorizing the body in another way. It no longer evokes a paradigm under which sexual difference becomes a basis for abjection, and thus it no longer exists as a reference to the other side of the binary, no longer exists in reference to something outside itself. It constitutes its own logic, and we can see this being gradually built in the intervals of the text filled with lists of body parts in block capitals to which Duffy refers. One can see a progression, bookended by iterations of the phrase "the lesbian body" that begins with bodily fluids ("THE JUICE THE SPITTLE THE SALIVA THE SNOT"[16]), proceeds to tissues ("THE PAPILLAE THE NERVE NETWORKS THE NERVE ROOTS THE BUNDLES"[17]), then to visible features and limbs ("THE GROINS THE TONGUE THE OCCIPUT THE SPINE THE FLANKS THE NAVEL THE PUBIS").[18] The lesbian body reconstructed after it emerges from hell has its origin

14. Jean H. Duffy, "Monique Wittig," in *Beyond the Nouveau Roman: Essays on the Contemporary French Novel*, ed. Michael Tilby (Oxford: Berg Publishers Ltd, 1990), 207.

15. Dianne Chisholm, "Lesbianizing Love's Body: Interventionist Imag(in)ings of Monique Wittig" in S. Neuman and G. Stephenson, eds. *ReImagining Women: Representations of Women in Culture* (Toronto: University of Toronto Press, 1993), 196–216 (197).

16. Wittig, *The Lesbian Body*, 28.

17. Wittig, *The Lesbian Body*, 53.

18. Wittig, *The Lesbian Body*, 153.

in fluidity that is celebrated here in a rewriting of the *blason* tradition that enumerates the beauties of the female body. Rather than reducing the object of the *blason* to her individual features, we see how the whole is gradually assembled from its most elementary parts.

Despite this intimate dive into the beauty of the internal organs, however, some have described this very dissolving of boundaries between discrete organs and between persons as an example of abjection. Johanna Dehler provides an example of this reading in her book *Fragments of Desire: Sapphic Fictions in Works by H.D., Judy Grahn, and Monique Wittig*:

> Read from a Kristevan perspective, repugnance and disgust associated with fluids the body expels and the disgust evoked by the decaying corpse, indicate a border, a limit against which the self constantly has to define itself. The abject is what the self refuses to assimilate in order to constitute its identity.[19]

Characterizing Wittig's "fluids the body expels" and "decaying corpse" as abject means that they would need to be excluded or resolved in the construction of subjectivity. It implies that there is an effort to somehow get beyond the details of physical embodiment and the breakdown of the organism. Wittig abandons the hell in which bodies become abject. The abjection is not due to the material nature of those bodies themselves, but to the heteronormative system of hell. The only bodies that can escape hell and its abjection are lesbian bodies, not women's bodies.

Although she uses the pronoun "elle.s" (she/they), Wittig prefers the nouns "lesbienne.s" (lesbian.s) or "amante.s" (lover.s), which are identities without reference to masculinity. Women as such are not exempt from disgust and abjection. Only within the lover.s' relationship does one not turn away from decomposition. The unwillingness of "quelqu'une" (someone) to stand the sight of "tu's" mutilated viscera in *The Lesbian Body*, despite having tried to seduce her, is part of her unwillingness to enter into the lesbian lovers' relationship as Wittig describes it. If we are disgusted by it, if we turn away, we separate ourselves from that relationship and the community it binds together. Wittig challenges readers to take in the text as a whole, not to skip over or grit their teeth through these passages.

19. Johanna Dehler, *Fragments of Desire: Sapphic Fictions in Works by H.D., Judy Grahn, and Monique Wittig*, (Frankfurt: Peter Lang, 1999), 125–126.

## BEAUTY AND DECOMPOSITION

It is not in *spite* of decomposition that the lovers desire each other. The lovers of *Le Corps lesbien* tear through each other's bodies with glee and abandon. In addition, across all Wittig's works, decomposition shows itself to be accompanied with a response typically associated with beauty. Lists of traditionally "disgusting" sights, textures, and odors alternate with conventionally beautiful ones. Bodies dripping with blood and pus coexist with lists of flowers and perfumes. In her début novel *L'Opoponax* (*The Opoponax*), the barrier between customarily good and bad odors is shown to be blurred. Smells of decomposition are associated with a range of objects and experiences—with things as anodyne as cats and dogs and as traumatic as the death of other children. The scents of fresh grass, soil, and rain are accompanied by the smell of rotting vegetation essential to their growth. The "opoponax" itself, indefinable and disembodied within the novel, is, in the world outside the text, part of the experience of death and decay; as it is a resin that is used in embalming, it is like the scent in the church during funerals when one of the children has died. Likewise in this first text, the smells of corruption and incense intermingle and the sources of the scents become unidentifiable for the protagonist Catherine Legrand.

The presumably pleasant images of nature do not define themselves in opposition to death or rot, but exist alongside them. Consider how the children of *The Opoponax* leave flowers to macerate in jam jars:[20]

> You make mixtures: lilac, nettles, apple leaves. In certain cases you soak only flower petals: rose, tulip, peony, to obtain essences. You put them in the sun and every so often you stir them with a stick. After a few hours the water is warm and the liquid has a smell. But leaves and petals are hard to dissolve. No matter how careful you are the liquid has a rotten smell. But if you keep on, if you sniff for a while eventually you can distinguish the good smell—apple, rose, or tulip as the case may be.[21]

20. Maceration as practice also has its own entry in Monique Wittig and Sande Zeig, *Brouillon pour un dictionnaire des amantes* (Paris: Grasset, 1976), loc. 1707, Epub. There is no entry for "maceration" or any other translation of that word in the English edition.

21. Monique Wittig, *The Opoponax*, trans. Helen Weaver (Plainfield, VT: Daughters, 1976), 72–73.

The flowers disintegrating in water hide a sweet smell under the odor of rot. The two elements are inextricably mixed, and rot is accepted or even welcomed as part of the sum of the experience. The flowers go from sweet to rotten, but behind the rot the good smell can be detected again. These odors are not eliminable from the system and not to be eliminated. Wittig's characters do not construct themselves in opposition to them.

This intermingling of beauty and decay, the inability to purify experience, may call to mind Joyelle McSweeney's idea of the "necropastoral,"[22] which also highlights the inevitable pairing of natural (pastoral) beauty with death and decomposition. While McSweeney does indeed focus on the inability to eliminate disgust from any world, no matter how idyllic it may seem, she maintains the affective relationship to it that Kristeva describes. For McSweeney, the "necro" that accompanies the pastoral threatens with the "infectiousness, anxiety, and contagion" lurking at the borders of Arcadia. But even a corpse, for Wittig, is "exquisite" by definition.[23] The vocabulary associated with corpses is purely positive; they are attractive, edible. While dismemberment and decomposition in *The Lesbian Body* are part of the relationship between individual lovers, death, rot, and maceration all seem to be part of collective practices: as seen with the group of children in *The Opoponax* and the community of "lovers" in Wittig's *Lesbian Peoples: Material for a Dictionary.* Ceremonial practices involving these acts contribute not just to the relationship of a couple but to the maintenance of a community over time. Decomposition is actually part of preservation—of flower "essences" but also of the group. Wittig's non-hierarchical system is not interested in judging what is aesthetically undesirable or in elimi-

22. "I give the name 'necropastoral' to the manifestation of the infectiousness, anxiety, and contagion occultly present in the hygienic borders of the classical pastoral. For all the pastoral's shoring up of separations, and despite the cordon sanitaire it purports to erect between unhealthy urban strife and wholesome rural peace, we must remember that the premier celebrity resident of Arcadia is Death." Joyelle McSweeney, *The Necropastoral: Poetry, Media, Occults* (Ann Arbor: University of Michigan Press, 2014), 3.

23. "Cadavers: Since the beginning of the glorious age, whether of animal or companion lover, cadavers are always exquisite. They are either embalmed with spices and aromatic herbs, or they are eaten." Monique Wittig and Sande Zeig, *Lesbian Peoples: Material for a Dictionary,* trans. Monique Wittig and Sande Zeig (New York: Avon, 1979), 25.

nating the elements that have been deemed to be useless, distasteful, or past their prime. The subject in this system does not feel anxiety at their continued presence. All beings within Wittig's fictional world are mixed, but that hybridity is not threatening.

## BEYOND ABJECTION IN LITERATURE

The negative relationship to the material body that we see in the abject is not merely a subjective or even intersubjective phenomenon; Kristeva also applies this category to literature, privileging the abject as part of a set of tropes characteristic of authors she deems significant in the modern landscape: Louis-Ferdinand Céline, Franz Kafka, Antonin Artaud. Where does Monique Wittig stand with reference to literature beyond her own? *Powers of Horror* was written after most of Wittig's published work, and while Wittig, in these earlier works, may seem to be anticipating the categories established by Kristeva, it might be more apt to say that Wittig wrote in response to a current which she also observed in the dominant literature of the time, and which would be later codified by Kristeva. While preoccupation with the breakdown of borderlines may indeed be characteristic of twentieth-century literature, Kristeva's singular focus on the threat of breakdown excludes writers such as Wittig whose works undo these borders. Literature that creates the kind of non-hierarchical relationship of body to body characteristic of Wittig's lesbian couples indicates the limits of abjection as a theoretical tool.

Wittig does not face the same interdictions, the same pressure that makes the abject threatening. Her borders are voluntarily porous, her protagonist alter ego can hold her lover covered with spores, decaying into fluid and odor. When faced by a dominant discourse, by a "fortified castle" that seeks to protect itself from an incursion of the impure into a system of prohibitions, she presents what she calls in an essay of the same name a "cheval de Troie" (Trojan horse), a war machine that will explode the "fortified castle" from the inside, reform it from the raw material of language.[24] As Annabel Kim notes:

> Wittig's metaphor of the Trojan horse explains how literature can act on us to subtly but thoroughly rework our subjectivity so that we

24. Monique Wittig, *Le Chantier littéraire* (Lyon: Presses universitaires de Lyon; Donnemarie-Dontilly: Éditions iXe, 2010), 40.

> can rework, as writers do, the language that built up our subjecthood: contained within the seemingly familiar form of the text, waiting to spring out, is the experience of language in its fullness.[25]

This is language as raw material, but language that must give the appearance both of extraordinary beauty and of belonging to the dominant order to be taken into the "fortified castle" in the first place. The beauty is not hard to find in parts of Wittig's work, but the threat it poses to the dominant order can explain the kind of unease that the writing has provoked. There is, however, an exuberance, a lack of the shame and disgust that dominates the texts put forward by Kristeva, and a desire for language, for contact with the raw and undisciplined matter of language that offers an alternative to the dominant discourse and a way to transform it. *The Lesbian Body* and the lesbian body it creates are Trojan horses that have the power to transform our relationship to the material body, in literature and outside.

25. Annabel Kim, *Unbecoming Language: Anti-Identitarian French Feminist Fictions* (Columbus: The Ohio State University Press, 2018), loc. 2780, Epub.

SANDRINE SANOS

# Monique Wittig's *One-Dimensional Man*: Translation Work and Post-'68 Feminist Utopian Thought

THE WOMEN AFFIRM IN TRIUMPH
THAT ALL ACTION IS OVERTHROW

—Monique Wittig, *Les Guérillères* (1969)

Vietnam 67.
I no longer count how many angels can dance on the head of a pin.

—Colette Magny, "Vietnam 67" (1967)

Civilization has to defend itself against the specter of a world which could be free.

—Herbert Marcuse, *Eros and Civilization* (1955)

In an interview she gave ahead of the 2001 French publication of her political essays, *La Pensée straight* (*The Straight Mind*), Monique Wittig pointed to the temporal correspondence between her 1968 translation of German philosopher Herbert Marcuse's *One-Dimensional Man* and the founding of the Féminisme, Marxisme, Action group, only to add that, "there is *always* some *translation work* going on."[1]

I am indebted to Sung Eun Choi, Brian Connolly, Muriam Haleh Davis, Darcie Fontaine, Peter Gordon, Bruno Perreau, Suzette Robichon, Sarah Salter and especially Joan W. Scott as well as this volume's editors, Morgane Cadieu and Annabel Kim, for their generous comments and critiques. I am also grateful to the participants of the 2018 "Legacies of 1968" conference (Harvard University) and of the 2019 "Drafting Monique Wittig" conference (Yale University) for their insightful suggestions. Last, I am grateful to our Paris feminist collective, the Comères—Catherine Achin, Lucie Bargel, Stéphanie Guyon and others—who read *La Pensée straight* with me twenty years ago.

1. FMA was initially founded in 1967 as Féminin, masculin, avenir (Feminine, Masculine, Future) and was renamed Féminisme, marxisme, action (Feminism, Marx-

**YFS 142,** *Lesbian Materialism: The Life and Work of Monique Wittig*, ed. Cadieu and Kim, © 2023 by Yale University.

With this comment, Wittig implied translation work was never just a linguistic and literary practice. It was a process that brought theory and the political together. It was also a political act at work in the "making of thought." While Wittig is known for her experimental and radical literature and her theorization of the relationship between thought, language, sex, bodies, and the political, little attention has been paid, however, to the "translation work" that she suggests defined her intellectual and political praxis.

For Wittig, translation was a feminist practice. It was also a form of theorizing. After Marcuse, she kept translating. In 1974, she was involved in a collaborative translation of Portuguese writers—a language she apparently did not know or practice.[2] In 1982, she translated Djuna Barnes's *Spillway* into French under the title, *La Passion*. Some of her most important theoretical essays featured in *La Pensée straight* were first written in English and later translated into French.[3] As an author who moved between languages, Wittig believed that the circulation of texts across borders and languages enabled the accumulation of "political density."[4] Translation testified to the deterritorialization and decentering effects of forms of political thought that were "made impossible in one language" and needed another.[5] She held that there never was an "original text" that overshadowed another.[6] Her "translation work" in fact constitutes an undeniable feature of her experimental revision of the literary canon and of language that has marked her entire post-1968 body of work.

I wish to propose a somewhat speculative reading of what has usually been read as a minor detail in Wittig's intellectual biography,

ism, Action) in 1968. This reference to FMA and Marcuse only appears in the English version of the interview. See Marie-Hélène/Sam Bourcier, "Wittig la Politique," in *On Monique Wittig: Theoretical, Political, and Literary Essays*, ed. Namascar Shaktini (Champaign: University of Illinois Press, 2005), 189. Italics are mine.

2. Personal conversation with Suzette Robichon, July 19, 2019.

3. Bourcier translated some of her texts into French (overseen by Wittig) for the publication of *La Pensée straight*, Bourcier, "Wittig la Politique," 187. However, according to feminist scholar Marie-Anne Juricic who had interviewed Wittig in 1999 and 2001, Wittig had ambivalent feelings about Bourcier's desire to author the preface and insisted on including the one written by Louise Turcotte. Email correspondance, June 23, 2002.

4. Bourcier, "Wittig la Politique," *La Pensée straight*, 26.

5. Wittig specifically refers to "délocalisation" (delocalization), a point that deserves greater attention. Bourcier, "Wittig la Politique," 26–27; "Wittig la Politique," 193–95.

6. Bourcier, "Wittig la Politique,"188.

namely her translation of Marcuse's *One-Dimensional Man*.[7] When she came to this work, Wittig had already been awarded the Prix Médicis in 1964 for her first novel *L'Opoponax* (*The Opoponax*), which immediately situated her among a new literary avant-garde. While she was writing *Les Guérillères*, the radical and provocative novel she published in 1969, she was asked to translate Marcuse's influential 1964 text by her publisher, the politically-engaged and anti-colonial Éditions de Minuit, which had championed the nouveau roman since the 1950s.[8] By then, Marcuse's intellectual stature among the New Left had become undeniable. *One-Dimensional Man* offered a scathing critique of the ways "advanced industrial" and capitalist society had produced nothing more than a "totalitarian universe" with "its terrifying harmony of freedom and oppression, productivity and destruction" that "pacified" all resistance "without open terror."[9] Only what he called a "Great Refusal," that is complete and total overthrow by those most excluded from the existing political, social, and cultural order, could bring about complete and revolutionary transformation.[10] The French translation of *One-Dimensional Man* was published in April 1968 in the *Arguments* series directed by non-communist leftist

7. I write "speculative" because of the archival absence at the heart of this paper. The Beinecke Library's opening of the Wittig archives has predictably fueled fantasies of archival plenitude. However, Wittig famously noted that she did not keep notes on her work. Her archives do not seem to contain any "paperwork" related to this work aside from one editorial contract confirming Wittig's future royalties for her Marcuse translation. The COVID-19 pandemic made it more difficult to seek archival traces of the (imagined) correspondence that might have existed between Wittig, Marcuse, philosopher Kostas Axelos, or Jérôme Lindon, editor at Éditions de Minuit. Thinking through archival absence means, as Gary Wilder has so astutely noted, questioning how "historians [. . .] typically move from published texts to archival documents to peek behind the scenes, where 'real' meanings supposedly reside" and instead "search [. . .] writing for potentialities within them that might exceed them." The fantasy of archival revelation should therefore not foreclose the fact that an intellectual history of Wittig's translation(s) can nonetheless be undertaken. See Wilder, *Freedom Time: Negritude, Decolonization, and the Future of the World* (Durham: Duke University Press, 2015), 12.

8. Dominique Samson recalls that her aunt was urgently working on the translation at the same time that she was writing *Les Guérillères*. Personal conversation with Dominique Samson, October 11, 2019.

9. Throughout, I use and refer to the French translation, which I have translated back into English, unless the English is cited. Herbert Marcuse, *L'Homme unidimensionnel* (Paris: Éditions de Minuit, 1968), 148, 9, 7. Marcuse refers throughout to "pacified existence," which he defines on p. 45.

10. Marcuse, *One-Dimensional Man*, 248–49.

philosopher Kostas Axelos.[11] Student unrest soon took over the streets of Paris and beyond. These events swept through France two years before the then-infamous feminist "happening" at the Arc de Triomphe, where Wittig and others brought to life the manifesto for the "liberation of women" she had authored.[12]

There is no evidence that Wittig and Marcuse engaged in a sustained dialogue then or after the work of the translation (though the cover indicates the translation was "reviewed" and presumably approved by Marcuse while the front page explains that the translation was a collaborative effort from both). Until recently, Marcuse has not been included in the pantheon of those who inspired or even influenced Wittig.[13] Neither is Wittig remembered as the one who mediated French readings of Marcuse in the 1970s. She remains strikingly (and bafflingly) absent from considerations of "Sixties Utopianism."[14] Her translation, however, troubles commonplaces narratives and timelines of post-'68 French feminisms (and of "French theory's" transatlantic migration and return) that have marginalized Wittig, turning her into what Ilana Elóit has named the "abject" and "politically inassimilable" lesbian figure of French "heterofeminism," and a historical figure who disappears from view after her departure for the U.S. in 1976.[15] Wittig's translation interrogates the meaning and circulation of texts and their readings in this "'68 moment" and beyond.[16] Taking "translation work" seriously means rethinking, as Wittig did, the meaning of

11. *Arguments* was a political and intellectual monthly periodical, published by Éditions de Minuit, and made up of mostly anti-colonial thinkers who had broken with the Parti Communiste, such as Edgar Morin and Jean Duvignaud.

12. "For a Women's Liberation Movement," in Shaktini, ed. *On Monique Wittig*, 21–34.

13. Émilie Notéris, *Wittig* (Paris: Les Pérégrines, 2022), 47–50.

14. See "Psychoanalysis and Sixties Utopianism," *JPCS* 18, no. 2 (Fall 2003): 263–72.

15. On transatlantic migrations and transformations, see Bruno Perreau, *Queer Theory: The French Response* (Stanford: Stanford University Press, 2016); Anne Emmanuelle Berger and Eric Fassin, eds. "Transatlantic Gender Crossings," *Differences: A Journal of Feminist and Cultural Studies* 27, no. 2 (September 2016); and Ilana Eloit, "Lesbian Trouble: Feminism, Heterosexuality, and the French Nation (1970–1981)" (PhD diss., London School of Economics, 2018): 39, 122, 163, 201, 247, 263, 272.

16. As Bruno Perreau has explained, the transatlantic circulation of "feminist texts" is at once more complicated and transformative since "transatlantic exchanges are the product of cultural fantasies whose effect, if not function, is to mask their original source," *Queer Theory*, 7.

canon(s) and how they are made.[17] It also suggests how we may revise Wittig's place within a genealogy of critical theory—feminist and otherwise—and its utopian impulses. In doing so, we are called upon to rethink the meaning(s) of utopia then and now and how its evocation by Wittig and others defamiliarized the present at the same time that it reimagined that which was assumed to be intractable and impossible. Situating her work in a more expansive genealogy and historicizing her writings restore her foundational place in the emergence of radical feminist politics and in our library of post-1968 utopian thought.

Few have examined the role Wittig's Marcuse translation played in her political theorization during the period when she was both writing fiction and fully engaged in feminist collective mobilization.[18] Because these two figures (Wittig and Marcuse) seem, at first glance, to be an unlikely pairing (unlike Wittig's choice to translate Barnes), the translation has not been understood to be an intellectual encounter. Rather, it is often characterized as accidental paid labor taken on by a Sorbonne student who was, at the time, also a copy editor for Éditions de Minuit. From this perspective, the role of this translation—and "translation work" more generally—in her own biography is rendered even more irrelevant because of "Wittig's intellectual impatience with," and critique of, psychoanalysis, one of Marcuse's theoretical lineages.[19]

It might, nonetheless, be worth exploring the afterlife—if any—of Marcusian ideas in Wittig's "call for epistemological revolution."[20] In their introduction to the 2007 *GLQ: A Journal of Lesbian and Gay Studies* special issue on Wittig, editors Brad Epps and Jonathan Ned Katz argue that "Wittig evinces more than passing resemblance to"

17. See Wittig's interview in Alice Jardine and Anne Memke, eds., *Shifting Scenes: Interviews on Women, Writing, and Politics in Post-'68 France* (New York: Columbia University Press, 1991), 192–95.

18. In keeping with a return to utopian thought, one recent exception calls for a "joint reading" of Marcuse and Wittig in order to "interpret the Wittigian utopian imaginary," but it does not explore this original encounter further, noting their works "meet" on a number of issues: Aurore Turbieu, "Sortir de l'enfer unidimensionnel? L'utopie 'réelle' de Monique Wittig," *Mouvements* 4, no. 108 (2021), 80–81.

19. Though some Wittig scholars suggest she was more anti-Lacanian than anti-Freudian; Alice Jardine, "Thinking Wittig's Differences: 'Or, Failing That, Invent,'" *GLQ*, vol. 13, no. 4 (2007), 456. Wittig criticizes psychoanalysis in "The Straight Mind," in *The Straight Mind and Other Essays* (Boston: Beacon Press, 1992), 31.

20. Monique Wittig, "Preface," in *The Straight Mind*, xvii; on this, see also Robyn Wiegman, "Un-Remembering Monique Wittig," *GLQ* 13, no. 4 (2007), 510, 511, 513.

the Frankfurt School and its "dramatically reconfigured Marxism, the resistant potential of concrete individual subjectivity, fragmented though it may be under capitalism."[21] They point to what they call her "*tense*" but "significant affinities" with Frankfurt School thinkers.[22] For Eloit, too, "Wittig's staunch critique of universalist reason as a tool of domination" confirms their claim for a "little examined, or hushed, even 'unconscious,'" "affinity" with the Frankfurt School.[23] However, Epps and Katz's insight inadvertently elides the ways feminists did in fact engage with, and critique, the Frankfurt School. In the narrative set forth by Epps and Katz, Wittig merely echoes "Frankfurt School criticality."[24]

I propose something different: thinking of Marcuse as a "theorist of sex and power" with a "radical and utopian understanding of the Freudian inheritance" means asking how his utopianism may have resonated with Wittig.[25] Here, the point is not to center Marcuse as an originary source for Wittig. Their encounter remains a limited one, unlike Wittig's encounter with Nathalie Sarraute.[26] Rather, I am interested in exploring the ways this *encounter without dialogue* may have shaped both the French Marcuse and the transatlantic Wittig. Asking how this encounter without dialogue may have left traces in Wittig's critical elaboration of the "straight mind" asks that we read Wittig's post-'68 writings anew so as to reveal the different intellectual and conceptual frameworks and contexts from which her thought emerged.[27] It also means historicizing Wittig's work within the world of late-sixties political imaginaries without reducing it to that particular context.

21. Brad Epps and Jonathan Ned Katz, "Monique Wittig's Materialist Utopia and Radical Critique," *GLQ* 13, no. 4 (2007), 427.

22. Epps and Katz, "Monique Wittig's Materialist Utopia," 430, 436, 437.

23. Eloit, "Lesbian Trouble," 162–63; Epps and Katz, "Monique Wittig's Materialist Utopia," 439.

24. Epps and Katz, "Monique Wittig's Materialist Utopia," 439.

25. Dagmar Herzog, *Sex after Fascism: Memory and Morality in Twentieth-Century Germany* (Princeton: Princeton University Press, 2007), 278; and Herzog, *Cold War Freud: Psychoanalysis in an Age of Catastrophe* (Cambridge: Cambridge University Press, 2017), 134.

26. On Wittig's relation to Sarraute, see Annabel Kim, *Unbecoming Language: Anti-Identitarian French Feminist Fictions* (Columbus: Ohio State University Press, 2018).

27. My aim here is not to foreground a "transnational" understanding of Wittig, but to retain a critical engagement with texts, their contexts, misappropriations, and translations.

## THE WAR MACHINE(S), 1967–1980

> They say, let those who call for a new language first learn violence. They say, let those who want to change the world first seize all the rifles.
>
> —Monique Wittig, *Les Guérillères* (1969)

Vietnam was everywhere in 1967. That is what the politically engaged "chanteuse" Colette Magny reminded her listeners in a spoken-word song from the similarly-titled album.[28] The war focused the revolutionary energies that had emerged and would come together in utopian political imaginaries denouncing colonialism, capitalism, and the forces of repression. Onscreen, the film *Far From Vietnam*, featuring filmmakers such as Agnès Varda, Jean-Luc Godard, Joris Ivens, and Alain Resnais, also protested the war. Grassroots "Comités Vietnam" (Vietnam Committees) were founded to do the same. From 1966 onwards, petitions and manifestos abounded.[29] A younger generation of French antiwar activists looked to the North Vietnamese as the exemplary resistance to Western imperialism.[30] In the spring of 1967, the Russell Tribunal held its first "show trial" designed to ask (and protest) whether the U.S. was guilty of genocidal crimes in Vietnam. Jean-Paul Sartre and Simone de Beauvoir, who had been so vehement in their opposition to the Algerian War, were some of its notable figures. Vietnam haunted many of those who became involved in the May '68 student revolts, just as it troubled the radical feminists who burst onto the scene two years later. Monique Wittig was one of them.

Denouncing imperial and state violence seemed urgent, especially as it appeared to many in France and beyond to be the tragic repetition of not-so-distant conflicts and wars. Marcuse gestured to the

28. When I asked Suzette Robichon about the Vietnam War, she recalls listening to and resonating with this Colette Magny song with other radical feminists. Personal conversation with Robichon, October 10, 2019.

29. See Salar Mohandesi, "Bringing Vietnam Home: The Vietnam War, Internationalism, and May '68," *French Historical Studies* 41, no. 2 (April 2018): 219–51; Boris Gobille, *Le mai 68 des écrivains. Crise politique et avant-gardes littéraires* (Paris: CNRS Éditions, 2018); Julian Bourg, *From Revolution to Ethics: May '68 and Contemporary French Thought* (Montreal-Kingston: McGill-Queen's University Press, 2017); Kristin Ross, *May '68 and its Afterlives* (Chicago: University of Chicago Press, 2002).

30. See Mohandesi, "Bringing Vietnam Home" and my current book project, "The Horror of History: Gender and Violence in Cold War France (1954–1967)" (unpublished manuscript).

relationship of past to present violence. In the 1966 preface to the re-edition of *Eros and Civilization*, he explained that "the price of progress" in "affluent society" "had been frightfully high" and noted that the "photographs that show a row of half-naked corpses laid out for the victors in Vietnam," "resemble[d] in all the details the pictures of the starved, emasculated corpses of Auschwitz and Buchenwald."[31] He pointed again to the ways "Auschwitz haunted" the present and its technological progress in *One-Dimensional Man*.[32] A Jewish German exile who had left Nazi Germany for the U.S. in 1934 along with other Frankfurt School thinkers, Marcuse's evocation of the ghosts and the horror of Nazi crimes was an especially charged comparison in the aftermath of the 1961 Eichmann Trial. He explained how "the same aggressive forces lead from death on the highways and streets to bombings, torture, and burnings in Vietnam."[33] Now came the irrepressible and necessary "protest against neo-colonial war and slaughter" and an "opposition that represents a *more radical potential*."[34] Marcuse never ceased holding fast to the possibility of revolutionary resistance and "the fight for life" against war and imperialism, even if the "historical and material realities of colonialism" remained "repressed" in his writings.[35]

Vietnam also haunted the French far left political imaginary and culture. For most in France, it did not just echo Nazi genocidal horrors but those of the Algerian War of Independence, which had ended only five years earlier. Many of those engaged in the anti-colonial radical left and on the Vietnam Committees had also been involved in denouncing the Algerian War, a fact Wittig was intimately aware of.[36] Vietnam also evoked the specter and muted memories of the "forgotten war" of "Indochina." Marcuse seemed to be aware of these conversations: in his February 1967 preface to *L'homme unidimensionnel*, he made reference to the Algerian National Liberation Front and

31. Marcuse, *Eros and Civilization: A Philosophical Inquiry into Freud* (Boston: Beacon Press, 1966), xxi, xx, xxi.

32. Marcuse, *L'Homme unidimensionnel*, 271.

33. Herbert Marcuse, "Vietnam—Analysis of an example," (May 22, 1966), 2, in *German History in Document and Images*, vol. 9: 1961–1989. Italics are mine.

34. Marcuse, *Eros and Civilization*, xxi; "Vietnam," Italics are mine.

35. Marcuse, *Eros and Civilization*, xxvi; Brian Connolly, "Psychoanalysis," *The Routledge Companion to History Theory* (New York: Routledge, 2022), 189.

36. Bourg, *From Revolution to Ethics*, 25. On Wittig's relation to Jean-Pierre Sergent, who had worked for Joris Ivens and returned for France from Vietnam and Laos during the summer 1968, see Notéris, 59–61.

to the "wretched of the earth" alongside the Vietnam War, though he did not interrogate the imbrication of empire and capitalism (12). Algeria and Vietnam were on May '68 participants' minds, just as they were on radical feminists' minds (who had just witnessed the legalization of contraception the previous year). Following a summer spent "theorizing revolt," the Groupe de Vincennes, that Wittig initiated with Antoinette Fouque in October 1968, continued thinking about feminism, class struggle, and anticolonial revolution.[37] Feminists from the MLF (Mouvement de libération des femmes [Women's Liberation Movement]) invoked "[their] Vietnamese sisters" as models.[38] The oppression and violence of empire provided the context for many of these revolutionary imaginaries.

We may trace some of this context in Wittig's own work: the title of her second novel, *Les Guérillères*, directly references female guerrilla fighters, something she explained years later was on her mind as she imagined feminist collective action.[39] Marxist and feminist rebels and revolutionaries were one of the motifs of the reading "encounters" listed at the end of the novel. Wittig gestured to Bolshevik revolutionary and theorist Alexandra Kollontai, utopian feminist socialist Flora Tristan, as well as strategists of (revolutionary) war such as Carl von Clausewitz and Mao Tse-Tung.[40] Violence against state violence: Wittig insisted that revolution needed nothing less and was its very condition (a position that Marcuse also held as he explained the necessity of a "violence of resistance"[41]). Vietnam, too, figured in her reading list: she cited both a Vietnamese poem and general Vo

37. *MLF psychanalyse et politique 1968–2018, 50 ans de liberation des femmes. Volume 1: les premières années* (Paris: des femmes-Antoinette Fouque, 2018), 18, 23; Eloit, "Lesbian Trouble," 20; Jennifer Sweatman, *The Risky Business of French Feminism: Publishing, Politics, and Artistry* (Washington, D.C.: Lexington Books, 2014), 32–33.

38. First issue of the MLF periodical, *Le Torchon brûle* (cited in Mohandesi, "Bringing Vietnam Home," 244); Audrey Lasserre, "Histoire d'une littérature en mouvement: textes, écrivaines et collectifs éditoriaux du Mouvement de Libération des femmes en France (1970–1981)" (PhD diss., Université de la Sorbonne Nouvelle-Paris III, 2014), 19–20.

39. Notéris, 50, 59; *MLF*, 23.

40. For an insightful analysis of such references, see Aubrey Gabel, "Ludic Intertexts in *Les Guérillères*: Reading as Training in Popular Warfare," (Conference presentation, "Drafting Monique Wittig," Yale University, October 10, 2019).

41. Herbert Marcuse, "The Problem of Violence and Radical Opposition," in Douglas Kellner, ed., *The New Left and the 1960s: The Collected Papers of Herbert Marcuse,* vol. 3 (New York: Routledge, 2005), 62.

Nguyen Giap, who had resisted Japanese, French, and American imperialism. But there were also names that may have surprised readers: she cited Jacques Lacan and Marcuse's *Eros and Civilization*.

Despite Wittig's French translation of *One-Dimensional Man* selling 350,000 copies in two months, it is assumed that few May '68 participants and far left activists and thinkers had read it.[42] French feminists, however, did, in fact, read and engage Marcuse. There are traces of such engagement: historian Audrey Lasserre mentions that the reading group founded by Fouque and Wittig read Marx, Engels, Freud, and Marcuse.[43] She notes that Marie-Jo Bonnet recalled reading the trio "Marcuse-Marx-Freud" in the Perverses polymorphes' Sunday reading group, founded by Margaret Stephenson (later Namascar Shaktini) who had participated in the Arc de Triomphe political action alongside Wittig.[44] The group's name echoed Marcuse's *Eros and Civilization* and his theorization of "sex and power."[45] So did, a few years later, the FHAR (Front homosexuel d'action révolutionnaire [Homosexual Front for Revolutionary Action]), which emerged out of these early initiatives, and claimed that "homosexuality [could be] a revolutionary force," "with the power to dismantle capitalism."[46]

Still, these fragments of information do not reveal *which* Marcuse was being read. It may have been that these feminists were made aware of his work because Wittig was involved in translating him. It may have been that, as they were theorizing patriarchy and feminism, contemporary texts—from the Frankfurt School to Lacan's 1966 *Écrits*—required some form of engagement and critique. It may have been urgent to return to Freud in the midst of the publicity around Lacan's work and structuralist insights over language and sexual difference (his *Écrits* had sold 5,000 copies in less than two weeks).[47] Psychoanalysis was an important intellectual influence at the newly-founded Vincennes University, where a department of psychoanalysis had been inaugurated and Wittig and Fouque began their intellectual

42. See Bourg, *From Revolution to Ethics*, 109, 188; Daniel Gordon, *Immigrants and Intellectuals in 1968 France: May '68 and the Rise of Anti-Racism* (Merlin Press, 2011), 21; Ross, *May '68*, 191, 193.

43. Lasserre, "Histoire d'une littérature," 99–100.

44. Lasserre, "Histoire d'une littérature," 137.

45. Herzog, *Cold War Freud*, 134.

46. Eloit, "Lesbian Trouble," 150; Robcis, *The Law of Kinship: Anthropology, Psychoanalysis, and the Family in France* (Ithaca: Cornell University Press, 2013), 206–207.

47. Gobille, *Le mai 68 des écrivains*, 15.

and political work.[48] Though, as Elisabeth Roudinesco suggests, conflicts emerged between them because, while "Fouque believe[d] herself Lacanian," "Wittig [wa]s Marcusian."[49]

## TRANSLATING TOTALITARIANISM AND REVOLUTION: WITTIG AND MARCUSE

This is the pure form of servitude: to exist as an instrument, as a thing.

—Herbert Marcuse, *One-Dimensional Man* (1968)

This was the context in which Wittig's editor asked her to translate *One-Dimensional Man*. Since literary translation is never just linguistic transposition but, in fact, at the same time, an autonomous and creative activity that involves adaptation and migration of a text to a different cultural space, the question arises as to how Wittig may have shaped some of Marcuse's ideas in translation and what might be the place, *if any*, of Marcuse's theorization of the individual and the social in Wittig's thought?[50] What do we make of her engagement with this text that reworked a Marxist idiom through a psychoanalytic exploration of desire, anxiety, and aggression in the making of the social? Could we think of this "translation work" as taking place at a critical moment in the emergence of Wittig's thought, and trace the ways it coincided with her radical feminist praxis and engagement with language and oppression?

Wittig encountered this "translation work" first and foremost as an experimental novelist. From her first novel, Wittig had envisaged language as a "war machine" that could bring about "a conceptual revolution of the social world, its whole reorganization with new concepts, from the point of view of oppression."[51] Wittig's "epistemological revolution" required interrogating the very ways language itself produced sex and naturalized difference.[52] For her, language bore

48. Antoinette Fouque had "assisted François Wahl, Lacan's editor, in laborious publication of the *Écrits*," in Robcis, *The Law of Kinship*, 201.

49. Elisabeth Roudinesco, *Histoire de la psychanalyse en France. 2: 1925–1985* (Paris: Fayard, 1994), 523.

50. That question is also central to *The Straight Mind*, published in 1992, and its "adaptation" in 2001, *La Pensée straight*, since they are not identical and speak to different contexts. Antoine Berman, *Toward a Translation Criticism: John Donne* (Kent State University Press, 2005), 45–47.

51. Cited in Shaktini, ed., *On Monique Wittig*, 4.

52. Wittig, "Preface," xvii.

the "Mark of Gender"—the title of her 1984 essay.[53] She explained that, "to destroy the categories of sex *in politics and in philosophy* to restore language (at least to modify its use)" was "part of [her] work in writing, as a writer."[54] (These were the very domains in which Marcuse theorized and argued for revolution.) Destruction was necessary because, for her, "language casts sheaves of reality upon the social body, stamping it and violently shaping it."[55] Her fiction attempted such a remaking of the social body, "stag[ing]," as Annabel Kim has explained, "feminist utopias."[56] Wittig's *L'Opoponax* and *Les Guérillères* bookended her translation of Marcuse and provided its "horizon."[57]

Translation is always a "critical act" in both form and content.[58] Despite the "secondariness" of her translation, Wittig's authorial practice and literariness undoubtedly shaped Marcuse's language, "broaden[ing,] "amplify[ing], and enrich[ing]" it.[59] Though Wittig's translation of Marcuse appears at first glance especially faithful, her literary register lends greater lyrical force to Marcuse's abstract and philosophically-grounded German-inflected English, itself already a form of translation. The French text possesses more pessimistic, even melancholic, intonations. In particular, Wittig appears to have shaped the essay's tone through the vocabulary of oppression she chose: her seemingly straightforward translation in fact emphasizes the inescapability of repressive forces. Marcuse's "closing" (19) becomes "enfermement" (45) evoking a carceral regime, while "containment" (xliv, 23) becomes "endiguement" (18, 49) evoking policing methods. The inescapability of totalitarian forces takes on a more menacing character as Wittig translates "cancels" (xlvi, 1) as "escamoter" (to evade) —a verb suggesting more sinister intentionality (20, 27). The "paralysis of criticism" (xli) becomes "engourdissement" (numbing) (15). In the French, "technological reason" (3) produces only "uniformisation" (29) rather than the English "coordination" (3), which

53. Wittig, "The Mark of Gender," 76.
54. Wittig, "The Mark of Gender," 8. Italics are mine.
55. Wittig, "The Mark of Gender," 78.
56. Kim, *Unbecoming Language*, 15.
57. Berman explains every text comes into being in a "translating horizon," *Toward a Translation Criticism*, 58; Kim, *Unbecoming Language*, 82.
58. Berman, *Toward a Translation Criticism*, 76.
59. Berman, *Toward a Translation Criticism*, 29.

"pervert[s]" (*pervertit)* (15) rather than the English "deform[s]" (xli). "Technological society" possesses an "overwhelming, anonymous power and efficiency" (226) that, in French, becomes "écrasante" (crushing) (250). These oppressive forces do not just create "fear" (2) as the original English indicates, but an overwhelming "angoisse" (anxiety) (28). Wittig's adjectives punctuate this philosophical text, adding affective density to Marcuse's demonstration. Meanwhile, the repetition of similarly-sounding nouns (and vowels)—*enfermement, endiguement, engourdissement*—echo throughout in a litany of embodied oppression.

Wittig's *langue*—in her vocabulary, alliterations, use of the negative, and syntactic reorganization (253–54, 277–78)—provides a materiality and visuality to Marcuse's mapping out of a utopian project of emancipation. She translates "living on the brink, [and] facing the challenge," (xli) as "vivre au bord du gouffre [et] défier le danger" (to live at the abyss and defy danger) (15). She also pointedly universalizes his language, ungendering it: "man's body and mind" (9) become "une dimension du corps et de l'esprit humain" (a dimension of the human body and mind) (34). Throughout, Wittig's Marcuse offers a less disembodied analysis: for instance, when Marcuse explains that capitalism's "technological universe breaks the innermost privacy of freedom" (27), the French rendering tells readers that it "détruit ce que la liberté a de secret et d'intime" (destroys what is most intimate and secret in freedom) (53). The translation also adds greater urgency to the need for revolution: the forces constitutive of "technological society" become "explosive" (60) rather than the English "centrifugal" (35). The text's concluding thoughts reiterate this urgency: "libérer l'imagination [. . .] c'est un problème politique" (freeing imagination [. . .] is a political problem) (274). Her syntactic rearrangement turns Marcuse's lengthy injunction (250) into what could have easily been a May '68 slogan. In this translation, revolution was soon to come. Wittig may have suggested as much in her adaptation of Marcuse's text. Marcuse listed the "outcasts and the outsiders, the exploited and persecuted *of* other races and other colors, the unemployed and the unemployable" (256) as those who radically refuse the contradictions of technological society. Wittig modified the list, now a catalogue foregrounding margins and race: "pariahs" and "outsiders," "other races, other colors" (280). She added "les classes exploitées et persécutées" (exploited and persecuted classes) as a separate category of people whose "opposition" might be "revolutionary even if their consciousness was not." In the following years, Wittig argued women were precisely such a class.

Still, *One-Dimensional Man* was a text that did not theorize what Wittig deemed foundational, namely the creation of sexual difference as a naturalized category of oppression. If Marcuse theorized how sex, sexuality, and libidinal energies were harnessed in the service of technological society, he had little to say about the ideological operation of sexual difference and the category of "women" produced by such totalitarian oppression. Indeed, when he authored a short 1966 text about opposition to Vietnam, Marcuse pointed to "women" as one potentially oppositional political force but had little to add.[60] He simply explained that there seemed to be only "housewives" supporting the "door-to-door collecting [of] signatures for petitions against the war."[61] As a category, women remained invisible to him. Though, by 1974, he had changed his mind and wrote that he "believe[d] the Women's Liberation Movement today [wa]s perhaps the most important and potentially the most radical political movement that we have [. . .]."[62] In 1967, however, Wittig translated a text that, in fact, reified the mark of gender and left the category of sex unthought.

## THEORIZING EMANCIPATION AND UTOPIA: MARCUSE AND WITTIG

> For the category of sex is a totalitarian one, which to prove true, has its inquisitions, its courts, its tribunals, its body of laws, its terrors, its tortures, its mutilations, its executions, its police.
>
> —Monique Wittig, "The Category of Sex" (1976/1982)

Some of Marcuse's theorization on aesthetics, the totalitarianism of epistemological categories, and the need for true emancipation undoubtedly echoed Wittig's own preoccupations. Both called for similar utopian revolts and radical reimaginings, as others did too around racism and decolonization then. In his 1955 *Eros and Civilization*, Marcuse had already theorized the possibility of a "Great Refusal"

60. Marcuse, "Vietnam—Analysis of an example," 2.

61. Marcuse, "Vietman—Analysis of an example," 2.

62. "Marxism and Feminism" was the transcript of a talk Marcuse gave at Stanford University on March 7, 1974, reprinted in *Women's Studies* 2 (1974) and a student newspaper *The North Star* 4, no. 15 (April 11–15, 1974), 8, reprinted in Kellner, ed., *The New Left*, 165–72.

to the sublimating injunction of capitalist society. He believed such a refusal could take place in the realm of aesthetics.[63] A decade later, Marcuse concluded *One-Dimensional Man* with a meditation on the role of imagination and aesthetics to resist and undo technological society's "totalitarian tendencies" (271).[64] Gesturing to Samuel Beckett, Maurice Blanchot, and Walter Benjamin, he suggested that the domain of (avant-garde) aesthetics, and especially literature, contained within itself the capacity for a "freedom of expression that allows the writer and the artist to call men and things by their name—to name what, under a different form, might be unnameable" (272). For him, even if "touched by reification" (274), the power of imagination lay in its ability to turn "non-sense into sense" and "sense into nonsense" (272), something that Wittig's own "renversement" (reversal) enacted. Only "reversal" (274) and "refusal" (279, 281) could bring about emancipation. Wittig's *Les Guérillères* certainly embodied such an emancipatory gesture.[65] The erotic charge of signifying bodies in their materiality and viscerality saturates every page. And the proliferation of the plural feminine pronoun did the work of subverting from within the social order that kept women oppressed, secondary, and invisible.

We may trace some of these Marcusian preoccupations further in Wittig's later essays, which reworked and extended notions of repressive power, social alienation, and domestication. In her 1976 essay, "The Category of Sex," Wittig explained that "the ideology of sexual difference functions as censorship in our culture by masking, on the ground of nature, the social opposition between men and women" (2). For sexual division and sexual difference, she writes, are not natural: "It is oppression that creates sex and not the contrary" (2). This is why, she argued, women were not a natural category but a "class" alienated, appropriated, and trapped by the demands of production, reproduction, and the marriage contract since "sex is a category women cannot be outside of" (7). In short, it is "the political category that founds society as heterosexual" (5). She wrote this was a "*totalitarian*" operation: it "shapes the mind as well as the body [. . .].

63. Marcuse, *Eros and Civilization*, 145.

64. Marcuse, *L'homme unidimensionnel*, 279.

65. On *Les Guérillères* as a "textual elaboration of freedom," see Linda Zerilli, "A New Grammar of Difference: Monique Wittig's Poetic Revolution," in Shaktini, ed. *On Monique Wittig*, 89, 90.

It grips our minds in such a way that we cannot think outside of it" (8, italics mine). Marcuse's critique of capitalist "domination" had pointed to a similar operation since, for him, this "domination invades all realms of private and public life, integrating any real opposition and absorbing all historical alternatives."[66] Such "domination," achieved "perfection when it created a truly totalitarian universe in which society and nature, mind and body are kept mobilized in a permanent defense of this universe."[67] For Wittig, however, Marxism had failed to theorize how heterosexuality was a "social system" that was "already within all mental categories."[68] Still, she never ceased theorizing that "truly totalitarian universe" whose truth lay, for her, in the ways "[t]he primacy of difference so constitutes our thought that it prevents turning inward on itself to question itself."[69]

Like Marcuse, Wittig pointed to the ways society always domesticates those it seeks to keep subjugated. She explained that the system of "totalizing" thought that kept women "enslaved" always produced its own assimilation of resistance, echoing Marcuse's description of "a society without opposition" (7).[70] The conditions of subjection preoccupied French feminist materialists just as they had constituted a Marcusian obsession. It is therefore interesting that, in *L'Homme unidimensionnel,* Wittig almost always translated Marcuse's "dependents" (85) as "esclaves" (enslaved) (110) who might one day free themselves from their "maîtres" (85) (masters) (110)—terms that appeared often in her own essays and that emphasized the urgency of revolt—just as she extended the vocabulary of "enslavement" (25, 128) into "asservissement" (54) and "servitude" (152). Marcuse had noted that such "revolts" acted as a "symbolic event," an "instinctual revolt," and the "rebel[lion] of the human body against intolerable repression."[71] Undoing the ways sex functioned as a political regime ordering the world and individuals within it therefore required more than political activism. For her, language and the literary were the site of the political. Wittig always situated her own "Great Refusal" in the space of language because only language could allow a space

66. Marcuse, *L'Homme unidimensionnel,* 42.
67. Marcuse, *L'Homme unidimensionnel,* 43.
68. Wittig, "One is not Born a Woman," 20; "On the Social Contract," 43.
69. Wittig, "The Category of Sex," 2.
70. Wittig, "The Category of Sex,", 2; Marcuse, *L'homme unidimensionnel,* 7.
71. Marcus, *Eros and Civilization,* xix.

for "radical imagination."[72] Wittig's theoretical and literary texts brought about this revolution in the very materiality of language.

## LANGUAGES AND SPACES

> I write because life does not appease my appetites and hunger. I write to record what others erase when I speak, to rewrite the stories others have miswritten about me, about you. To become more intimate with myself and you.
>
> —Gloria Anzaldúa, *A Bridge Called My Back* (1987)

Thinking with Wittig anew about translation work may offer a different genealogy of feminist, utopian, and critical theory. One might find echoes of Wittig's thought in unexpected places.[73] Thinking about her "translation work" may also offer a different Wittigian genealogy. Almost two decades after her post-'68 political and theoretical essays, "translation work" led Wittig to Black and Chicana feminism. Here again, few have interrogated the meaning of Wittig's geographical and political location in the U.S. borderlands, its languages, spaces, and violent histories and legacies of dispossession and settler colonialism. Yet, in her interview for *La Pensée straight*, she gestured to the work of Chicana feminists that "undid a feminism that invited them to an undifferentiated sorority" and theorized the very "delocalization" and "displacement" that she explained had been the "price to pay" for "lesbian politics."[74] She mentioned the Combahee River Collective as well as Gloria Anzaldúa and Cherríe Moraga's *A Bridge Called My Back*.[75] As her colleague Sandra Soto recalled, Wittig "genuinely, in fact *passionately*, seemed to care about the current debates taking place among Chicana feminists."[76] Turning again to "translation work," Wittig explained she was "close to the feminist politics of

72. Zerilli, "A New Grammar of Difference," 89.

73. For instance, Irigaray's brief meditation on the "exchange of women" who are turned into "commodities" and on "female homosexuality" may be read as an engagement with Wittig's thought; notably when Irigaray muses: "what if commodities refuse to be commodified" only to add "Utopia? Maybe. . ." *Ce sexe qui n'en est pas un* (Paris: Éditions de Minuit, 1977), 167–68, 190–93. In an interview on haunting and "other utopianism," Avery Gordon points to Wittig's *Les Guérillères* and her mapping out of "utopian margins," in Brenda Bhandar and Rafeef Ziadah, eds., *Revolutionary Feminisms: Conversations on Collective Action and Radical Thought* (New York: Verso, 2020), 201–2.

74. Bourcier, "Wittig la Politique," 193.

75. These references are to be found in the footnotes of both versions though there are notable differences between the two.

76. Sandra Soto, "Wittig in Aztlán," *GLQ* 13, no. 4 (2007), 535. Italics are mine.

woman and lesbians of color of the 1980s" and their "resistance to "homogenization."[77]

Just as Marcuse had held that theory "is always historical," Wittig never ceased theorizing in relation to the world.[78] Her thought was never static but continually engaged with the ways epistemological categories shape bodies and minds and the materiality of the world. Her engagement with Chicana feminism suggests that she kept on interrogating how sex and race were at work in the forces of domination that mark spaces, borders, and bodies, and how they must be resisted.[79] In her interview, she explained how "feminism" could not just "content itself" with the category of gender and that, "after all these years this is my only political truth: we should rethink transversal differences, sex, gender, class, and race."[80] She pointedly cited Anzaldúa's 1987 *Borderlands/La Frontera*, a work that charted the particular live(s) of languages, places, subjectivities from the point of view of a "lesbian of color," a "Tejana" growing up on the Texas-Mexico border, and a "mestiza" in between languages.[81] Here was another "encounter without dialogue" that echoed her own commitment to revolutions in language and in the material world. Wittig's statement that "there is always translation work"—as act, orientation, and metaphor—may in fact have named her life-long movement between physical and political spaces, between languages, and between her work and others'.

77. Bourcier, "Wittig la Politique," 193–94.

78. Angela Davis, "Preface: Marcuse's Legacies," in Kellner, ed., *The New Left*, xiv.

79. Wittig has sometimes been charged with an essentialist deployment of the category of race, because of her analogizing of sexism and racism and evocation of "lesbians" as "fugitive enslaved peoples." However, as some scholars have shown, this would be a limited view of her thought. For instance, Wittig's theoretical engagement and dialogue with Colette Guillaumin still needs to be explored: Guillaumin published *L'Idéologie raciste* in 1972, revised from her 1969 Ph.D. dissertation. She is explicitly and repeatedly cited by Wittig. On "race" in Wittig's work, see Stéphanie Kunert, "L'Analogie 'sexisme/racisme:' une lecture de Wittig," *Comment s'en sortir*, no. 4 (Spring 2017): 80–99.

80. Bourcier, "Wittig la Politique," 193.

81. Gloria Anzaldúa, *Borderlands/La Frontera: The New Mestiza* (San Francisco: Aunt Luta Books, 4th ed., 2012), 19, 59, 79.

# INTERLUDE I

Le Jury Médicis

Gala BARBISAN, Denise BOURDET, Jean CAYROL, Marguerite DURAS, J.-P. GIRAUDOUX, Francine MALLET, Félicien MARCEAU, Claude MAURIAC, Alain ROBBE-GRILLET, Claude ROY, Nathalie SARRAUTE, Marcel SCHNEIDER

*vous prie de lui faire le plaisir d'assister à son Cocktail annuel, le 19 Novembre 1965 de 18 à 21 heures, chez Denise BOURDET.*

*71, Quai d'Orsay*

Invitation to the annual cocktail of the Prix Médicis (Wittig Collection, Box 21, Beinecke Library, Yale University)

To be summoned after having been judged by a jury of one's peers, or rather, those writers one hopes to be able to count as one's peers. This card has been conserved with care for decades—there is nary a smudge or stain, there is no fading. The only indication of contact —a

**YFS 142,** *Lesbian Materialism: The Life and Work of Monique Wittig,* ed. Cadieu and Kim, © 2023 by Yale University.

crease in the upper left-hand corner where the card might have been held tightly between Monique Wittig's thumb and index finger. What emotion does a young writer feel when this evenly aligned block of literary names, names endowed with cultural capital, requests their presence? When Wittig, this transplant to Paris from Alsace, walks into Denise Bourdet's apartment, where will her eyes turn? Will Wittig scan the shelves of Bourdet's private library or instead become preoccupied with what the jury members are doing (where they stand, how they stand, what they choose to drink), perhaps modeling her choices after those of Nathalie Sarraute, her literary hero? What, physically, sensorially, will it look like for Wittig to be one of them? How does the writer that Wittig wishes to be known as deploy body language? What sort of a text will her body become that evening?

ILANA ELOIT

# Lesbian Paradoxes to Offer: French Heterofeminism and the Erased History of Monique Wittig's Exile to the United States

## INTRODUCTION: "NOBODY HERE"

> Woe betide those who do not howl with the wolves, they find themselves hunted down, chased away, they are charged with every evil, accused of tyranny and so on and so forth. As soon as I see one of those unfortunates, I shout to her from afar: Take care to hide your thoughts. Above all, don't say a word. I tell her: Beware, they will attack you savagely while saying that it is you who are killing them. They will wring your neck with a sob in their throats. And the tears that roll down their cheeks will testify to the maximum that they are the victim and you are the torturer. Then they will shove you into a grave full of shit while pretending it is a bath of rose water, they will drown you in it, stifle you, make you suffocate. Finally, they will shove you deep into the ground, they will make you disappear in it and, still not satisfied, they will plant in the soil which covers you and which they will tramp down with their shoes a sign bearing the words: Nobody here.[1]

It is in those words that French lesbian theorist and writer Monique Wittig described, in the political parable "Paris-la-politique" (Politics-in-Paris) published in 1985, her sorrowful experience in the Parisian Women's Liberation Movement (Mouvement de libération des femmes—MLF). At this point, she had lived in the United States for a decade, following her withdrawal from the MLF in 1976—a movement she had pioneered in 1970.

This excerpt constitutes a precious testimony in which Wittig tells us that something in MLF history was not only actively forgotten but also violently buried. *Nobody here.* What is the antagonistic story that Wittig is trying to tell us about? Who is the "they," claim-

1. Monique Wittig, "Paris-la-politique," *Vlasta*, no. 4 (1985): 24. All translations are mine unless otherwise indicated.

**YFS 142,** *Lesbian Materialism: The Life and Work of Monique Wittig*, ed. Cadieu and Kim, 

Fig. 1. First lesbian march. Paris, June 21, 1980. The banner reads: "Heterosexuality is to patriarchy as the wheel is to the bicycle." Photographer: Martine Laroche.

ing to be the "victim," and who are the "unfortunates" being "savagely attacked"? What is the story of this "grave full of shit" and who has been drowned in it? Could this history have anything to do with Wittig's departure to the U.S. in 1976, and if so, what is the history of this departure, which she herself calls an "exile"?[2] When Wittig's allegorical ghost calls the reader out, as in the excerpt above, it is to tell you that if you are willing to stop for her, take her seriously, and follow her where she wants you to go, you might discover an entirely unknown, disconcerting, and perhaps uncomfortable history of 1970s French feminism, one that has yet to be aired.

Paris, Spring of 1980. A spectacular, yet relatively unknown, conflict around lesbianism erupted in the MLF in the wake of the emergence of a movement of radical lesbians that politicized, for the first time in the history of the movement, heterosexuality as a "strategy

2. Wittig, [Letter to Monique Plaza, Nicole-Claude Mathieu, Colette Guillaumin, and Noëlle Bisseret], (1981), 9. Box 29 "Dossier, Monique Wittig and Colette Monique." Monique Wittig Papers, General Collection, Beinecke Rare Book and Manuscript Library, Yale University.

of patriarchal power exerted against women"[3] and lesbianism as a position of resistance.[4] From their new lesbian political position, lesbian activists organized on June 21, 1980 the first lesbian march in Paris (figure 1). Albeit located in the United States at this point, Wittig inspired radical lesbians with the publication, in February and May 1980, of her paradigm-shifting articles "La Pensée straight" (The Straight Mind) and "On ne naît pas femme" (One Is Not Born a Woman) in the materialist feminist journal *Questions féministes* (Feminist Issues). Challenging the idea of a patriarchal oppression common to all women, on which the MLF had been established ten years earlier, Wittig articulates, in these two pieces, the oppression of women by yet another regime of domination: heterosexuality. Arguing that sexual difference is a by-product of heterosexual social systems, she famously asserts that "lesbians are not women"[5] for "what makes a woman is a specific social relation to a man, [. . .] a relation which lesbians escape by refusing to become or to stay heterosexual."[6]

Wittig's epistemological rupture, alongside the emergence of a political movement of radical lesbians, thus provoked a large schism in the MLF in Paris. On the one hand, woman-identified feminists, who firmly opposed Wittig's lesbian theory and radical lesbianism, accused the latter of "separatism,"[7] that is, of betraying the unity of a feminist stance of "We, women," and of seeking to "eliminate heterosexual women from feminist ranks."[8] Conceiving of "women" as the only universalizable feminist identity, they addressed the visibilization of

3. Icamiaba, untitled, *Nouvelles questions féministes*, no. 1 (1981 [1980]): 80.

4. For more details on the history of this conflict, see Ilana Eloit, "Lesbian Trouble: Feminism, Heterosexuality and the French Nation (1970–1981)" (PhD diss., London School of Economics and Political Science (LSE), 2018).

5. Wittig, "The Straight Mind," in *The Straight Mind and Other Essays* (Boston: Beacon Press, 1992), 32.

6. Wittig, "One Is Not Born a Woman," *The Straight Mind and Other Essays*, 20.

7. Christine Delphy, Claude Hennequin and Emmanuèle de Lesseps, "Éditorial," *Nouvelles questions féministes*, no. 1 (1981): 9; Catherine Deudon, "Radicale-ment, nature-elle-ment," *La revue d'en face*, no. 9–10 (1981): 82; Marie-Jo Dhavernas, "Ah, je ris de me voir si belle en ce miroir (critique de l'idéologie séparatiste)," *La revue d'en face*, no. 9–10 (1981): 85.

8. Delphy, Hennequin and de Lesseps, "Éditorial," 7. The section in which Wittig's excerpt from "Paris-la-politique" quoted at the beginning of this article appears is entitled: "Isolationists or isolated?" ("isolationnistes ou isolées?"). This might be understood as a response to accusations of separatism: rather than being "separatists" (or isolationists), lesbians were "separated" (isolated) *from* feminism *by* those who silenced them.

lesbian difference within feminism as a hostile (if not antifeminist) refusal of the MLF's universality. While Wittig made lesbians unbecome women, for universalist MLF activists, lesbians *had* to identify as women—or to relinquish their lesbian difference—for the MLF to be truly universal. On the other hand, radical lesbians articulated, in an unprecedentedly public way, 1970s feminism's exclusionary operations against lesbians, when they started to call it "heterofeminism."[9] They addressed compulsory woman-identification in the MLF as a strategy to invisibilize lesbians and naturalize the heterosexual norm by which sexual categories are entrenched. This political rift between woman-identified women (whether lesbians or heterosexuals) on the one hand, and lesbian-identified lesbians on the other hand, illustrates the ways in which the conflict around lesbianism was not a conflict between heterosexual and lesbian women but a political and symbolic struggle over what "women" and "lesbians" ought to mean, and a struggle between political (rather than sexual) positions within feminism. These lesbian critical discourses, including Wittig's lesbian theory, were violently disqualified at the time of the controversy as "sectarian," "chauvinistic," "crazy," even "terrorist and totalitarian,"[10] and have long been delegitimized as well in MLF historiography. *Nobody here.*

The current MLF regime of truth (i.e., the dominant and unchallenged MLF historiographical storytelling) erases lesbian exclusion from its history while simultaneously foregrounding the figure of the lesbian in its narrative of feminist liberation. Indeed, official narratives of the MLF recount the story of a revolutionary movement which not only included all women in the name of sisterhood but, most importantly, celebrated lesbianism as the driving force of the movement and the heart of the cultural revolution to come.[11] However,

9. Front des lesbiennes radicales, "Rencontre des lesbiennes radicales. 20–21 juin 1981," *Nouvelles questions féministes*, no. 2 (1981 [1980]): 124.

10. Simone de Beauvoir, "Témoignage de Simone de Beauvoir," *Nouvelles questions féministes*, no. 3 (1982 [1981]): 111; Deudon, "Radicale-ment, nature-elle-ment," 83; Monique, "À propos de l'antilesbianisme des lesbiennes féministes," in *Front des lesbiennes radicales. Textes de la rencontre des 14 et 15 novembre 1981*, ed. Marion Page (self-published, 2010 [1981]), 27; "Éditorial," 7.

11. Christine Bard, "Le lesbianisme comme construction politique," in *Le siècle des féminismes*, eds. Éliane Gubin, Catherine Jacques, Florence Rochefort, Brigitte Studer, Françoise Thébaud and Michelle Zancarini-Fournel (Paris: Les Éditions de l'Atelier, 2004), 111–126; Christine Bard, ed., *Les féministes de la deuxième vague*

although radical lesbian archives have never been taken seriously as a legitimate starting point from which to (re)write MLF history, they in fact provide a vital counter-narrative to the official accounts of homosexual liberation: that lesbian exclusion was constitutive of the MLF. Radical lesbians, as the repressed subjects of an unresolved history, dedicated a great deal of their discussions in the early 1980s to the re-narration of the previous ten years of feminist activism. As one participant in the Front des lesbiennes radicales (Radical Lesbian Front), a movement of radical lesbians which split from the feminist movement in April 1981, explains:

> The feminist movement has long been opposed to political lesbianism. When in 1974 Monique Wittig (co-founder of the MLF and Gouines rouges [Red Dykes]) wanted to create with others a Front lesbien international [International Lesbian Front], she was violently persecuted by [. . .] feminists, who accused her of "separating herself from the mass of women." She was used as a scapegoat, which was even easier as she was isolated.[12]

This testimony is important, not only because it provides a drastic refutation of the narrative of homosexual liberation in the MLF, but also because it points to an alternative empirical history: that of feminist attacks against Wittig's lesbian politics in the MLF. In short, radical lesbian testimonies replace narratives of homosexual liberation with narratives of anti-lesbian violence in the feminist movement.

Following—and trusting—the radical lesbian ghost, which tells us that an erasure took place, I ask in this article: what alternative MLF history emerges when we start not from official MLF archives—the archives of woman-identified women/lesbians—but from the buried traces of lesbian-identified lesbians in the decade of women's undifferentiated unity, and from the perspective of Wittig's exile to the

(Rennes: Presses universitaires de Rennes, 2012); Marie-Jo Bonnet, *Les relations amoureuses entre les femmes du XVIe au XXe siècle* (Paris: Éditions Odile Jacob, 1995); Naty Garcia Guadilla, *Libération des femmes: le M.L.F.* (Paris: Presses universitaires de France, 1981); Audrey Lasserre, *Histoire d'une littérature en mouvement: textes, écrivaines et collectifs éditoriaux du Mouvement de libération des femmes en France (1970–1981)* (PhD diss., Université Paris 3 Sorbonne Nouvelle, 2014); Françoise Picq, *Libération des femmes, quarante ans de mouvement* (Brest: Éditions dialogues, 2011); Colette Pipon, *Et on tuera tous les affreux: le féminisme au risque de la misandrie (1970–1980)* (Rennes: Presses universitaires de Rennes, 2013).

12. Monique, "À propos de l'antilesbianisme des lesbiennes féministes," 27.

U.S. in 1976? What happens to MLF history if we take Wittig's epistemological rupture in 1980 not as the *beginning* of a lesbian story and a separation from feminism (thus placing it outside MLF's history), but rather as the *end point* of a ten-year silencing of lesbian difference? What ghosts and sorrows are we about to encounter? What is "heterofeminism" and how is it inextricably linked, in France, to the universalist discursive practices in which feminist agency is shaped? And finally, how does this critical perspective on the MLF illuminate anew the wounded history out of which Wittig's lesbian theory emerged?

Resisting the violence of erasure, I retrace the story Wittig only alludes to in the passage from "Paris-la-politique" with which I began this article: the story of the prohibition of lesbian visibility in the French Women's Liberation Movement. In *Only Paradoxes to Offer: French Feminists and the Rights of Man*, Joan W. Scott has famously argued that French feminism had been constituted through the paradox of demanding the Rights of Man for woman, thus leading feminists to "[produce] the 'sexual difference' it sought to eliminate."[13] Building on Scott's theorization, I read lesbian agency, in the context of the MLF's female universalism, as constituted by a similar paradox: lesbians needed to speak as lesbians in order to make up for their inconsistent exclusion from the category "women," while simultaneously demanding to be recognized as women to be treated equally. From this perspective, I argue that Wittig's sentence "lesbians are not women" was not so much a separation from feminism than a solution to this unsustainable paradox.

Through the history of the MLF's first lesbian collective, the Gouines rouges (Red Dykes), and of Wittig's failed Front lesbien international (International Lesbian Front), I demonstrate that the history of lesbian difference in the context of 1970s French feminist abstract (or undifferentiated) womanhood is by no means the history of progressive inclusion into the "we" of women, but rather is a discontinuous history of lesbians "grappling repeatedly with the radical difficulty of resolving the dilemmas they confronted."[14] Wittig's departure to the U.S. in 1976 was the price French feminism had to pay for such dilemmas.

13. Joan W. Scott, *Only Paradoxes to Offer: French Feminists and the Rights of Man* (Cambridge and London: Harvard University Press, 1996), 3.

14. Scott, *Only Paradoxes to Offer*, 17.

## THE MLF'S FEMALE UNIVERSALISM AND ITS LESBIAN PARADOX

The historiography of the MLF supports the idea of a grand liberatory homosexuality at the heart of the movement. French historian Christine Bard argues, for example, that MLF lesbians found in the movement's "homoerotic"[15] environment "an atmosphere that protected them from ordinary homophobia" and the "conditions for a new collective existence."[16] Along similar lines, historian Colette Pipon contends that the MLF had a "homosexual dimension" and that the movement's *non-mixité* "encouraged [. . .] the appearance of a form of female cultural behavior outside the world of men," which she names "homo-sensuality" or "homo-intellectuality."[17] However, by repeating the dominant terms in which homosexuality was framed in the 1970s, these narratives fail to historicize the ways in which it was discursively and politically constructed. Indeed, homosexuality was thought to be liberated in the MLF to the extent that it was *universalized to all women*: the MLF was defined as a "homosexual space" where homosexuality was not necessarily "erotically experienced."[18] As such, any woman participating in this new homoerotic culture (as a synonym for sisterhood) could claim to be a "homosexual."

The dilution of lesbian difference into a generalized homoeroticism was instrumental in forging the MLF's "we, women." Repeating the dominant abstract universalist regime in which political subjectivities are structured by the French nation, MLF women represented themselves as female individuals, that is to say as female reiterations of the French citizen, based on a universal abstract sameness. The French model of citizenship, as Scott explains, is one in which "equality is achieved [. . .] by making one's social, religious, ethnic, and other origins irrelevant in the public sphere; it is as an abstract individual that one becomes a French citizen."[19] In a similar manner,

15. Christine Delphy, quoted by Christine Bard, "Le lesbianisme comme construction politique," 114.

16. Christine Bard, "Le lesbianisme comme construction politique," 114–112.

17. Pipon, *Et on tuera tous les affreux*, 171.

18. "Quand nous sommes venues au mouvement, d'où que nous venions, nous savions que c'était un lieu homosexuel," *Des femmes en mouvement hebdo*, no. 42–43 (1980): 28.

19. Joan W. Scott, *The Politics of the Veil* (Princeton and Oxford: Princeton University Press, 2007), 11. See also, among others, Naomi Schor, "The Crisis of French Universalism," *Yale French Studies*, no. 100 (2001): 43–64

the eradication of differences was conceived by MLF women as the condition of possibility of an abstract community of women, based on "the oneness, the sameness of all individuals."[20] In other words, while claiming to liberate homosexuality, the (desexualizing) transformation of lesbianism into a universal homoeroticism performed the eradication of lesbian difference in the MLF.[21]

It was precisely to politicize the antagonism between heterosexuality and lesbianism—an antagonism made strategically unthinkable by the universalization of homosexuality to all women—that a group of MLF lesbians created, in Paris, in 1971, the MLF's first lesbian collective: the Gouines rouges. Wittig was a founder and core member of the Gouines rouges and participated in most meetings throughout the group's two years of existence, "pushing [them] to become more visible."[22] However, as Marie-Jo Bonnet, one of the Gouines rouges, recalls, this desire to form a lesbian group was "extremely contested in the MLF."[23] Indeed, for one of the radical feminists who strongly opposed the creation of the group, the Gouines rouges threatened to undermine the unity of the movement, as she explained during an interview:

> INTERVIEWEE: When did they do this to me, stand up and leave all together, as a block [. . .]? After a general assembly [. . .], we went to a café to discuss. [. . .] We, still caught up in our experiences with men, were new [to the movement]. . . And then we saw two or three of them stand up and say "we're off" and "we have a meeting. . . the Gouines rouges. . ." They did not even say [the Gouines Rouges] but it was clear that we did not belong there. . . We were furious! We were already very, very, very close friends, we had already done loads of things together. . . And they did that to us! [. . .] .
> INTERVIEWER: Why were you furious?
> INTERVIEWEE: Because we loved them![24]

As can be seen here, the fiction of an *original* uncorrupted (feminist) unity, which naturalizes and conceals a preexisting relation of

20. Scott, *The Politics of the Veil*, 11. For more details on the eradication of differences in the MLF, and on the abstract universalist regime in which the movement was established, see Eloit, *Lesbian Trouble.*

21. Eloit, "Lesbian Trouble."

22. Marie-Jo Bonnet, "Les Gouines rouges (1971–1973)," *Ex æquo*, no. 11 (1997), https://mariejobon.net/2009/08/les-gouine-rouges-1971–1973/ (accessed July 16, 2021).

23. Bernadette, Nelly and Suzette, "Au commencement, il y eut les Gouines rouges. . .," *Masques*, nos. 9–10 (1981): 115.

24. Interview, May 12, 2016. The anonymization is my decision.

power between heterosexuality and lesbianism, inevitably produces the Gouines rouges' political gatherings as a (hostile) *separation*. This separation is visually constructed in the interviewee's memory as the disruption of a pure unity around a table ("we went to a café to discuss")—itself a continuation of the unitary general assembly—by a "block." The interviewee's narrative is also particularly compelling insofar as it reveals how feminist feelings of collective happiness and sisterly symbiotic love were abusively used as a performative resource to secure the epistemic violence of the heterosexual/universalist frame that considers the visibilization of lesbian difference a "splitting." Indeed, the "fury" to which the interviewee refers is described not as the effect of a hegemonic resistance against the visibilization of a political minority but as the effect of her "love" for them: "We were furious! [. . .] Because we loved them!"

Therefore, lesbians who wanted to politicize their position were ensnared between two impossible options: either remaining invisible and closeted under the sign of "women" (which means leaving heterosexuality unthought/unexamined as an oppressive regime) or speaking up in a discursive/epistemic context where they were always already read as inaugurating a conflict (since the fiction of sameness continually denied any such antagonism).

This impossible conundrum is exemplified in a tract distributed by the Gouines rouges during one of the movement's general assemblies in early 1971, which reads:

> How, in the Movement, we represent to ourselves
> women:
> having abortions
> performing abortions
> workers
> mothers
> housewives
> wives
> chicks
> always implicitly women in sexual relationships with men. When these are talked about in the movement, it's "we" women. When homosexuals are talked about, it's "them." We lesbians, who say "we" with those who have abortions, the workers, the mothers, etc., we are not others.[25]

25. Les Gouines Rouges, untitled (1971). Reproduced in Cathy Bernheim, *Perturbation, ma sœur: naissance d'un mouvement de femmes 1970–1972* (Paris: Éditions du félin, 2010 [1983]), 198.

In this text, the discursive life of the lesbian paradox is starkly laid out. Speaking on behalf of their difference as "lesbians" ("we lesbians") in order to protest their exclusion from the MLF's "we" of "women," the Gouines rouges simultaneously disavow their very difference: "we are not others." In that regard, the MLF's lesbian paradox reiterates feminism's own paradoxical position in relation to (masculine) liberal individualism. As Joan W. Scott explains, "feminism was a protest against women's political exclusion, its goal was to eliminate 'sexual difference' in politics, but it had to make its claims on behalf of 'women' [. . .]." Consequently, it was constituted through the following "paradox": "the need both to accept *and* to refuse 'sexual difference.'"[26] It is, I argue, the same paradox that confronted the Gouines rouges within feminism. Insofar as the MLF was founded on a heterosexual contract, naturalized by the fiction of women's sameness,[27] lesbians found themselves relentlessly demanding inclusion as lesbians in a collectivity which equated femaleness with heterosexuality. Borrowing Scott's formulation and replacing sexual difference with lesbian difference, we could thus argue that "this paradox—the need both to accept *and* to refuse '[lesbian] difference'—was the constitutive condition" of lesbian political subjectivity in 1970s France.[28] Addressing the irresolvable paradox between "'we are all sisters'" and "'dirty hetero,'" "the '[women's] liberation movement'" and "the [lesbian] 'ghetto'"—or the paradox between (women's) sameness and (lesbian) difference—one Gouines rouges member used the humorous metaphor of an "oscillation [. . .] like the crazy needles of a compass that has lost magnetic north" to describe the collective's position in the MLF.[29]

Through their position as *both* lesbians and women, *both* similar and different, the Gouines rouges did neither seek to abandon a woman subject-position nor to impose a new lesbian subject for feminism but endeavored to expand the borders of the feminist "we." When they spoke at a one-day event organized on May 14, 1972 by the MLF ("The Condemnation of Crimes Committed Against Women"), they defined themselves as "Women who reject the roles of wife and mother" and who "collectively express our rejection of the roles and

26. Scott, *Only Paradoxes to Offer*, 3.
27. Eloit, "Lesbian Trouble."
28. Scott, *Only Paradoxes to Offer*, 3–4.
29. Anon., "Il y a comme ça. . .," *Le Torchon brûle*, no. 5 (1973): 22.

functions that [men] have wanted to impose on Women."[30] Addressing lesbianism as a political position in the service of all women, they not only sought to reconcile the tension between lesbian and woman subject-positions in the MLF, but in so doing, to also resignify what might be the meanings of the category "women." In other words, the Gouines rouges sought to occupy the "we, women" from a lesbian position with a view to displacing its (heterosexual) content (the subject "Women" or "We, Women" is invoked nine times in their text and always capitalized). Their goal thus went beyond being able to speak as lesbians: refusing to abandon a universal speaking position, they seem to argue that if lesbians—as the "'not yet'" and the "'unrealized'"[31]—are recognized as women, they will resignify the universal and therefore help liberate all women from a normative definition of womanhood. I would contend that it is the very failure to convince other feminists of the potential of the lesbian paradox (being both similar and different) to broaden the content of the category "women" that led Wittig and radical lesbians to conceive of lesbians as non-women ten years later—and to mourn the possibility of a more inclusive definition of a woman-identified subject position.

Apart from a few consciousness-raising discussions, the scope of the Gouines rouges' actions turned out to be extremely limited. It is arguable that the reason why "the group was so static,"[32] as Wittig notes, and eventually disbanded, was because of the context in which it had emerged as a symptom of the MLF's paradoxical heterosexual individualism. The "self-canceling"[33] effects of their "oscillating"[34] position—tied to the structural impossibility of being both women and lesbians—led to the Gouines rouges' paralysis, finally pushing them into fully relinquishing their unsustainable position. Asked why the group separated in early 1973, one of the Gouines rouges explains: "in the movement, the divisions were increasing and we felt

30. Un groupe de lesbiennes, "Femmes qui refusons les rôles d'épouse et de mère, l'heure est venue du fond du silence, il nous faut parler," *Archives, recherches et cultures lesbiennes*, no. 6 (December 1987 [1972]): 9.

31. Judith Butler, *Excitable Speech: A Politics of the Performative* (New York: Routledge, 1997), 90.

32. Christine Delphy and Monique Wittig, "International Interview: French Feminists' Interview," interview by Carol Anne Douglas. *Off Our Backs* 10, no. 1 (1980): 26.

33. Wendy Brown, "Suffering Rights as Paradoxes," *Constellations* 7, no. 2 (2000): 239.

34. Anon., "Il y a comme ça. . .," *Le Torchon brûle*, no. 5 (1973): 22.

more [. . .] woman than lesbian."[35] In other words, the Gouines rouges ended up privileging their "woman" identification in a renewed fusion with "all" women, an identification that could not help but lead to the dissolution of the group.

On the Gouines rouges, author and journalist Frédéric Martel writes:

> After the first years of battle, however, visibility had become more possible—and more desirable. [. . .] With the first public appearances of the Gouines Rouges, homosexual women became more prominent in the MLF.[36]

While the visibilization of MLF lesbians in the Gouines rouges was indeed an important coming out, it is difficult to consent to the narrative that presents this visibilization as having "finally" liberated lesbianism in the women's movement. Such a narrative does not fit with the future conflicts over lesbianism in the MLF (which remain untold in the historiography) that would arise and forecloses critical inquiry into the heterosexual foundations of the MLF. There was no real change of perspective after the Gouines rouges, who chose to "re-become" women when the group disbanded; rather, there was a fiction of progress that was conveniently used to further silence lesbian voices later in the decade by claiming that the issue had already been resolved. Thus, the Gouines rouges mark not the end of the story, as Martel suggests, but rather the very first manifestation of the awkward lesbian paradox that spanned the decade of the 1970s.

## MONIQUE WITTIG'S FAILED *FRONT LESBIEN INTERNATIONAL*

Shortly after the demise of the Gouines rouges, Monique Wittig tried to re-energize lesbian visibility in the MLF through her project of a Front lesbien international. It was at the International Feminist Conference in Frankfurt, in which 600 women from eighteen countries participated from November 15–17, 1974, that Wittig began rallying people around her plans for a lesbian front. The only archival trace of the Front lesbien international on which I could lay my hands was a single sheet bearing the title "Contacts Lesbian Front (November

35. Anon., "Il y a comme ça. . ." 22,

36. Frédéric Martel, *The Pink and the Black: Homosexuals in France since 1968*, trans. Jane Marie Todd (Stanford: Stanford University Press, 1999), 46.

1974)" at the Marguerite Durand Library in Paris.[37] Typed during or immediately after the Frankfurt conference, the document provides a list of thirty-three representatives of the Lesbian Front in eleven countries (Germany, Italy, England, France, Denmark, New Zealand, Holland, the U.S.A., Switzerland, Sweden and Norway). However, if the Lesbian Front visibly triggered highly positive responses in Frankfurt—as is suggested by the number of people listed on the contact sheet—reactions in France turned out to be drastically different.

Back from Frankfurt, Wittig and other activists raised the topic of the Front lesbien international at a winter 1974 meeting of MLF radical feminists, hoping they would be willing to develop a branch in Paris with them. However, it appeared that Wittig's demands were immediately interpreted as aggressive, if not incomprehensible, by her feminist peers. As one woman who had been present at the meeting and opposed to the Front lesbien recalled during our interview:

> We were waiting for Wittig, who was supposed to present her lesbian front to us. [. . .] We were waiting for her, we were all sitting in a circle in the room, and she turned up with a certain forcefulness, very determined. [. . .] It turned me off. . . So I didn't really get her Front lesbien international. . . I was wondering what she was talking about.[38]

I would suggest that as a "space invader"[39] seeking to address an issue—lesbianism—that fundamentally upset the universalist and heteronormative arrangements of the MLF, Wittig was always going to be perceived as disruptive before she even spoke. The memory of Wittig's physical interruption (by arriving late) of a seamless unity ("we were all sitting in a circle in the room") reiterates the previously mentioned narrative of the feminist according to whom the Gouines rouges "[left] all together, as a block" to attend a separate meeting while the feminists were all in "a café to discuss." Those visual memories materialize the normative effects of the MLF's (heterosexual) universalism, which refused to address differences by presupposing a neutral unity in the present moment of "sisterhood." Since this universalism necessarily reads lesbians' visibilization as producing

37. "Contacts Lesbian Front (November 1974)," folder "Bonnet, Marie-Jo," Bibliothèque Marguerite Durand, Paris.

38. Interview, June 24, 2016. The anonymization is my decision.

39. Nirmal Puwar, *Space Invaders: Race, Gender and Bodies Out of Place* (London: Bloomsbury Academic, 2004).

an antagonism, it is therefore not surprising that both the Gouines rouges' and Wittig's position at that meeting are remembered as hostile interruptions of a previously flawless unity. As a result of this framing, which treats Wittig as the aggressor, what she had to say inevitably became incomprehensible: "I was wondering what she was talking about." These memories figure the impossibility of a lesbian speaking position in the context of the MLF's discursive/epistemic arrangements.

Another of my interviewees made a stunning comment: "It's true that we did not delve any further into the issue, we refused to delve further because of the way it had been brought up, aggressively. They were real bitches."[40] In fact, I suggest a different interpretation: the perception of the group who supported the Front lesbien as "very determined," "forceful," "aggressive," even "bitches," was precisely meant to *prevent* the issue from being delved into. Against the "evidence of [women's] experience"[41] in the MLF—which purports to make Wittig and her group's alleged hostility to be the "truth"—I make the case for a genealogical reading that seeks to ask what political antagonism was being unacknowledged, avoided, and displaced through the perception of violence, as well as what *other* kind of violence was being authorized by the perception of lesbians (who sought to politicize/visibilize lesbian difference) as aggressive and of the other MLF women as overflowing with love. Feminism's lesbian paradox appears insurmountable: calling upon lesbian difference to make up for the inconsistent exclusion of lesbians from the category "women" appears as a violent and irrational gesture legitimizing in return the status quo.

As Wittig herself asserted, her departure from France in 1975—first to Greece, then to Italy, and finally to the U.S., where she permanently settled in 1976—is directly tied to her failure to establish a lesbian position *within* the French feminist movement:

> After [the Gouines rouges], several [lesbian] groups have started and tried to constitute and they had internal fights. This disintegrated all of them. Finally, the situation was so bad that I left France.[42]

40. Interview, May 3, 2017. The anonymization is my decision.

41. Joan W. Scott, "The Evidence of Experience," *Critical Inquiry* 17, no. 4 (1991): 773–797.

42. Delphy and Wittig, "International Interview: French Feminists' Interview," 26.

Wittig's archive provides a drastic counter-narrative to the dominant narratives of affective success and hospitality in the MLF. Regarding the "'Front lesbien international' affair," she speaks about the "worst attacks"[43] perpetrated by the group of radical feminists who opposed her and whom she dubs "oppressors and liquidators."[44] Describing the situation as "dramatic," she concludes: "I have been used as a scapegoat, a fact that perfectly led to my own personal destruction and the destruction of the group."[45] According to Wittig, radical feminists used "authoritarian methods" to "prevent [. . .], paralyze and destroy lesbian groups." She continues: "frankly, and between you and me, they almost succeeded in completely destroying me, and they have, yes, chased me out of Paris."[46] Looking back in 1999 on her experience in the MLF, she revealed the subtext of the situation depicted in "Paris-la-politique":

> In all political groups, whatever they are, there is a way of functioning, always the same, one does not attack the enemy but those closest to one, and it hurts, it can kill. It is a parable about all that, about what it can do to people. The whole time I was immersed in this political matter, I dreamt about this, I was taken to the guillotine, my head cut off. It was horrible.[47]

If, in "Paris-la-politique," Wittig alludes to the act of being buried alive, fourteen years later, when commenting on the situation, she speaks about being decapitated. While the will to kill is common to both metaphors, the first one still let us hear the cries, the tears and the frenetic gestures of the living body resisting elimination. In the guillotine metaphor however, the body is now irrevocably silent: no voice resonating from the depths of the "grave full of shit" can bear

43. Wittig, untitled [Letter to Monique Plaza, Nicole-Claude Mathieu, Colette Guillaumin and Noëlle Bisseret], (1981), 6. Box 29 "Dossier, Monique Wittig and Colette Monique." Monique Wittig Papers, General Collection, Beinecke Rare Book and Manuscript Library, Yale University.

44. Wittig, untitled [chronology of lesbian groups in the MLF], (n. d. [circa 1981]), 2. Box 29 "Dossier, Monique Wittig and Colette Monique." Monique Wittig Papers, General Collection, Beinecke Rare Book and Manuscript Library, Yale University.

45. Ibid.

46. Wittig, untitled [Letter to Monique Plaza], (1980), 2. Box 29 "Dossier, Monique Wittig and Colette Monique." Monique Wittig Papers, General Collection, Beinecke Rare Book and Manuscript Library, Yale University.

47. Wittig, "J'ai connu la guillotine," interview by Claire Devarrieux, *Libération* ("Livres"), June 17, 1999, iii.

witness to the killing anymore. The absoluteness of the guillotine, which is absent in the earlier burial moment, reflects how Wittig sees herself in the late 1990s: not only was her "head cut off" (an image which hints at the severing of exile), but the very traces of active silencing, and resistance to it, were altogether effaced.

In contrast to MLF activist Christine Delphy's recollection of her experience in the MLF as "a romantic passion" endowed with a "kind of magic,"[48] Wittig speaks about "an explosion of hatred toward me from people I believed were not only sisters politically but also friends."[49] At odds with the dominant MLF archive, Wittig's own private archive—the archive of a lesbian-identified lesbian in the decade of women's sameness—replaces ecstatic affects of love and happiness with backwards affects of extreme anger, loneliness, depression, resentment, and bitterness. Following Heather Love, we could argue that Wittig's trajectory in the MLF is illustrative of the "tradition of backwardness in queer representation and experience."[50] As such, Wittig's archive turns the traditional triumphalist history of the MLF's political and affective success into a dark history of injuries and losses. In a picture from 1979 taken in Berkeley, California (figure 2), we can recognize Wittig—alongside her partner Sande Zeig, and two French lesbian activists—wearing a t-shirt that bears the inscription "Front lesbien international." As the melancholic subject of a prohibited and lost history, Wittig did not only refuse to mourn the impossibility of the Front lesbien in France but also to forget its elimination, thereby pleading allegiance to the "lesbian bodies"[51] of the Front lesbian international there against the erasure of the "nobody here."

Wittig's trajectory is illustrative of a ruined lesbian future for French feminism—a future critical of the universalist and heteronormative regime on which the whole semiology of the MLF rested. This potential future was actively disqualified, refused, and forgotten.

48. *Les Temps des femmes*, "Je ne vois pas pourquoi un mouvement s'arrêterait de grandir. . ." (interview with Christine Delphy), no. 12 (1981): 19.

49. Wittig, [Letter to Monique Plaza, Nicole-Claude Mathieu, Colette Guillaumin, and Noëlle Bisseret], 7.

50. Heather Love, *Feeling Backward: Loss and the Politics of Queer History* (Cambridge and London: Harvard University Press, 2007), 146.

51. "Lesbian bodies" is a reference to Wittig's *The Lesbian Body*, published in French in 1973 (Paris: Éditions de Minuit) and in English in 1975 (New York: William Morrow and Company, Inc.).

Fig. 2. From left to right: Monique Wittig, her partner Sande Zeig, and two friends, Christine L. and Martine Laroche. Berkeley, California, August 1979. Photographer: Martine Laroche.

French feminism's lesbian history is the history of a political elimination: feminists never wanted to have anything to do with lesbian Wittig, and they got rid of her—leaving unfinished business and an irredeemable void for French feminism.

## CONCLUSION

On the rare occasions in MLF historiography when radical lesbianism is addressed, it is always from a derogatory perspective that reads their critique of "heterofeminism" as a feminist-corrupting separation from the MLF's universality, or as an extremist obtrusion that sealed the decline of the feminist movement after a heroic ten-year battle. Yet, if we follow the history of the MLF's lesbian paradox I have retraced in this article, the emergence in 1980 of radical lesbianism—and of Wittig's lesbian theory—is not the expression of lesbian separatism or radicalization, but rather the historical moment when lesbians succeeded, after a ten-year failure, in putting into discourse, or intelligibilizing, the MLF's naturalized heterosexual norm as the particular yet dominant standpoint from which feminists spoke.

When Wittig wrote in 1980 that "lesbians are not women," she put a definitive end to lesbians' aporetic demands for inclusion in the "we" of "women" and provided them with the theoretical foundations they needed to withstand their universalist/heterosexual reabsorption into (woman-identified) French feminism. In that regard, her statement was itself the way out of an epistemic violence which had hurt her badly, a *solution* to the MLF's lesbian paradox forged through stubborn refusal and exile. Against naïve (and heteronormative) readings of MLF history, uncritically repeating the ways in which 1970s feminists idealized female homosexuality, my own historiographical intervention seeks to render visible again the (buried) lesbian antagonism at the heart of the MLF. It is thus a profoundly materialist reading which conceives of sexuality—in the direct lineage of Wittig's materialist lesbian theory—as a political regime of domination through which social, political, and symbolic inequalities are entrenched. Against MLF women's appropriative female homoeroticism, Wittig sought to intelligibilize what the lesbian can do when she is not absorbed and neutralized within a (heterocentric) female-identified feminism.

From the standpoint of lesbians' paradoxes to offer to the MLF, the dramatic controversy over radical lesbianism that occurred in the wake of the publication of Monique Wittig's articles "La Pensée straight" and "On ne naît pas femme" in 1980 appears to be haunted by its own "retrospective urgency" and the many (lesbian) "'historical alternatives' that could have been"[52] had MLF women reckoned with the losses and traumas their (universalist) feminist utopia entailed.

52. Avery F. Gordon, "Some Thoughts on Haunting and Futurity," *Borderlands* 10, no. 2 (2011): 5. Gordon borrows the expression "historical alternatives" from Herbert Marcuse's *One-Dimensional Man: Studies in the Ideology of Advanced Industrial Society* (Boston: Beacon Press, 1964, xi). Marcuse's *One-Dimensional Man* was translated into French by Wittig in 1968.

KATHERINE A. COSTELLO

# The Cishetero Mind, or Monique Wittig's Queer and Transgender Lesbianism

The figure of the lesbian appears in feminist, queer, and transgender theory and activism as a naïve, doughty, unfashionable, sexless, politically unsophisticated, anachronistic, transphobic, and decidedly unqueer woman; she is a drag on the radical politics of the present and future.[1] Of course there are excellent reasons to be critical of certain lesbian cultural and political formations. Some lesbian feminism has been largely White, biologically essentialist, sex negative, and violently transphobic.[2] But whereas the terms feminist, queer, and transgender seem to be able to withstand critiques of racism, essentialism, sex negativity, and transphobia, among others, lesbian has for the last several decades become a seemingly irreversibly contaminated identity and political affiliation to be avoided in the name of revolutionary, or even simply contemporary, gender and sexual politics—something to be left behind and with which to disidentify, if not disavow. Thus, for example, queer theory has privileged gay male sexuality as an object of study, transgender activism has constituted itself outside of, and often in direct opposition to, lesbian politics and culture, and there has been a general decline in lesbian identification and spaces. This article does not emerge out of a nostalgic desire to

1. See among others, Elizabeth Freeman, *Time Binds: Queer Temporalities, Queer Histories* (Durham: Duke University Press, 2010) and Kyla Wazana Tompkins, "Ball Busters and the Recurring Trauma of Intergenerational Queer/Feminist Life," *Bully Bloggers*, February 20, 2016, https://bullybloggers.wordpress.com/2016/02/20/ball-busters-and-the-recurring-trauma-of-intergenerational-queerfeminist-life/.

2. For examples of transphobic lesbian feminism, see Janice Raymond, *The Transsexual Empire: The Making of the She-Male* (Boston: Beacon Press, 1979) and Sheila Jeffreys, *Gender Hurts: A Feminist Analysis of Transgenderism* (London: Routledge, 2014).

**YFS 142,** *Lesbian Materialism: The Life and Work of Monique Wittig*, ed. Cadieu and Kim, 

mourn or reinstate lesbian identities or political formations, but out of a concern over the political underpinnings of the narrative at work in the disidentification of queer and transgender theory and activism with lesbianism.

The rejection of lesbianism by queer and transgender movements is largely generational. In the imaginary at play, lesbian belongs to the 1970s and '80s, while queer emerges in the '90s and transgender takes flight in the 2000s. Such a mapping turns generations into coherent units, essentializing them and enabling younger generations (queer and transgender) to blame political shortcomings on the previous generation (lesbian). The younger generations thereby perversely empower themselves to inhabit a fantasy of perfect politics.[3] This relational structure collapses into a familial one in ways that prove problematic. In *Not My Mother's Sister* (2004), Astrid Henry shows that third-wave feminism of the 1990s represents 1970s lesbian feminism as a mother, which "requires that she [the figure of the lesbian] be stripped of her sexuality."[4] Henry notes that the tropes of third-wave feminism's rejection of lesbian feminism closely track that of its broader rejection of second-wave feminism. Lesbianism seems to become the ultimate scapegoat for the most problematic elements of feminism (namely its investment in the category of woman as a normative, essentialized identity lacking intersectional analysis) so that feminism itself can survive, albeit in a tenuous manner—as evidenced in the way feminism is still undergoing a process of reclamation (see, for example, books such as *I Call Myself a Feminist* [2017]).[5] The framing of lesbianism as a desexualized mother by her metaphorical children, her simultaneous positioning as a figure of reproductive sexuality and intellectual sterility, is so pervasive in queer and transgender theory that it prompts Kyla Wazana Tompkins, in a 2016 article on intergenerational clashes between lesbian, queer, and transgender politics, to ask "is it possible to relate to lesbian [. . .] history without deploying the basic Oedipal (Electra?) drama [. . .]? Do

3. Elliot Evans, "'Wittig and Davis, Woolf and Solanas (. . . ) simmer within me': Reading Feminist Archives in the Queer Writing of Paul B. Preciado," *Paragraph* 41, no. 3 (2018): 285–300.

4. Astrid Henry, *Not My Mother's Sister: Generational Conflict and Third Wave Feminism* (Bloomington: University of Indiana Press, 2004), 14.

5. Victoria Pepe, Rachel Holmes, Amy Annette, Martha Mosse, and Alice Stride, eds., *I Call Myself a Feminist* (London: Virago, 2017).

we always have to murder our mothers?"[6] By disavowing lesbians' contributions, and by reducing the multiplicity of possible relations with women to that of mother-child, the (often violent) disidentification with lesbianism reproduces misogyny, lesbophobia, and cis-heteronormative models of kinship. It also appears to be coterminous with the necessary critiques of certain lesbian formations. But does it have to be? Can we, those of us engaged in intellectual and activist work around gender and sexuality, recognize our entanglements in the legacies we need to critique and avoid reproducing the very forces from which we seek to disidentify? Can we create different forms of intergenerational relating—ones that might be more feminist, more queer, more trans and, yes, more lesbian? To put it another way: can we do critique differently?

In both France and the U.S., a number of scholars have tried to rewrite the relationship between queer and transgender theory and lesbianism by turning to Monique Wittig. In *Why Stories Matter: The Political Grammar of Feminist Theory* (2010), a book that has become essential to rethinking intergenerational relations within feminist theory, Clare Hemmings proposes to put Wittig back into the intellectual genealogy of queer theory through citational practice. Her strategy of recitation—renarrating intellectual history by pointing out Wittig's absence in queer theory's genealogies and reintroducing her there—situates Wittig as a "precursor" to queer theoretical approaches to sex, gender, and sexuality rather than as "antithetical."[7] This kind of recitation has also proven to be a common strategy in scholars' efforts to rethink the relation between transgender theory and lesbianism. In *Living A Feminist Life* (2017), Sara Ahmed cites Wittig as a radical lesbian who makes possible a coming together of these intellectual currents.[8] Karine Espineira and Sam Bourcier assert in "Transfeminism: Something Else, Somewhere Else" (2016) that the Zoo seminars of the 1990s that generated the first articulations of both queer and transgender theory in France were very much inspired by Wittig,[9] and Paul B. Preciado, the most prominent scholar of

6. Tompkins, "Ball Busters."

7. Clare Hemmings, *Why Stories Matter: The Political Grammar of Feminist Theory* (Durham: Duke University Press, 2010), 187.

8. Sara Ahmed, *Living A Feminist Life* (Durham: Duke University Press, 2017).

9. Karine Espineira and Sam Bourcier, "Transfeminism: Something Else, Somewhere Else" *TSQ: Transgender Studies Quarterly* 3, nos. 1–2 (2016): 84–94.

transgender theory in France today, relies heavily on Wittig throughout his work.[10]

All these scholars assert that there is a lesbian history to queer and transgender theory. However, they either stop short of reading Wittig, relying instead on citing her, or read her outside the context of her materialist lesbianism.[11] Thus, although Wittig appears in both queer and transgender theory as a reconciliatory elder, her theoretical framework of materialist lesbianism and consequent elaboration of the lesbian as an emancipatory figure has been further erased or deliberately set aside. Wittig then has been reclaimed as a lesbian ally to queer and transgender theory by being paradoxically "de-lesbianized" as a consequence of being "de-materialized," and confined to the past. In "Becoming Lesbian: Monique Wittig's Queer-Trans-Feminism" (2018), Kevin Henderson argues for the relevance of Wittig's figure of the lesbian to contemporary queer and transgender politics.[12] Like Henderson, this article seeks to bring the Wittigian lesbian into the present as a figure that has something to offer queer and transgender theory, but whereas he emphasizes how Wittig helps problematize the term cisgender, I look at what she has to offer intergenerational models of relating. Furthermore, while he focuses on Wittig as a neglected figure who can be brought into queer and transgender theory by rethinking her opposition with Luce Irigaray, I show how queer and transgender works that already claim Wittig but abandon her theoretical framework paradoxically participate in creating an opposition between queer and lesbian, and lesbian and transgender. It is remembering her materialist lesbianism that allows the lesbian to get unstuck from the past and form new relations with queer and transgender that escape the mother-child bind.

10. See for example his first book, Paul B. Preciado, *Countersexual Manifesto*, trans. Kevin Gerry Dunn (New York: Columbia University Press, 2018), which is dedicated to Wittig. This dedication functions similarly to recitation as it inscribes her as a major influence on his work. Wittig also features prominently in the bibliography of Preciado's *Testo junkie: sexe, drogue et biopolitique* (Paris: Grasset, 2008). More recently, *Je suis un monstre qui vous parle: rapport pour une académie de psychanalystes* (Paris: Grasset, 2020) can be read as an extension of Wittig's critique of psychoanalysis in "The Straight Mind," in *The Straight Mind and Other Essays* (Boston: Beacon Press, 1992).

11. While this volume has excellent reasons to opt for the term "lesbian materialism," I keep Wittig's original "materialist lesbianism" in order to maintain lesbianism as a noun and thus center it as an object of study and a political intervention.

12. Kevin Henderson, "Becoming Lesbian: Monique Wittig's Queer-Trans-Feminism," *Journal of Lesbian Studies* 22, no. 2 (2018): 185–203.

## MATERIALIST LESBIANISM

Like other French materialist feminists of the 1970s, Wittig extends Marxist class analysis to sex in order to show the social origins of women's oppression, thus denaturalizing it and opening up the possibility of change. However, she breaks with the likes of Christine Delphy by following the logical consequences of this materialist critique of sex all the way into the realm of sexuality and inaugurating materialist lesbianism.[13] If materialist feminism agrees that compulsory reproduction and the appropriation of women's labor and personhood constitute the material bases of women's oppression by men, materialist lesbianism further asserts that these also constitute the economic and political basis of the "heterosexual regime" and that the ideology of the "straight mind" masks this material cause of women's oppression. According to the straight mind, heterosexuality is foundational to society and a natural outcome of the indisputable existence of two biological sexes with evidently differing functions. Wittig reverses this accepted teleology and posits instead that heterosexuality produces men and women as classes and then naturalizes them to create the self-legitimizing illusion of an always already there of the sexes. Following the work of Colette Guillaumin, she posits sex as a mark:

> This mark does not predate oppression: Colette Guillaumin has shown that before the socioeconomic reality of slavery, the concept of race did not exist, at least not in its modern meaning [. . .]. However, now, race, exactly like sex is taken as an "immediate given," a sensible given, "physical features," belonging to a natural order. But what we believe to be a physical and direct perception is only a sophisticated and mythic construction, an "imaginary formation," which reinterprets physical features (in themselves as neutral as others but marked by a social system) through the network of relationships in which they are perceived.[14]

13. On the place of lesbian feminism in French feminism of the 1970s, see Ilana Eloit in this volume, "Lesbian Paradoxes to Offer: French Heterofeminism and the Erased History of Monique Wittig's Exile to the United States."

14. Wittig "One is Not Born a Woman," in *The Straight Mind and Other Essays*, 11–12. The French materialist feminists and Wittig homologize the logic of slavery (and serfdom) and their critical notion of sex. This homologization has been criticized and proven problematic for U.S. feminists, though it bears striking similarity to the development of materialist feminism in the U.S., which was itself deeply influenced by and tied to the Civil Rights Movement. On the importance of the relation between materialist feminism and the Black feminist movement in the United States, see Teresa De Lauretis, "Eccentric Subjects: Feminist Theory and Historical Consciousness,"

This process of construction, imaginary formation, and reinterpretation—the marking operation—is called "sexage."[15] Labor and ideology are intertwined in sexage: a certain division and alienation of labor shapes the body into sexual difference, and ideology consequently imagines this difference as natural. In order to free women of the oppressive consequences of sexage (one would add today that men as well suffer from sexage even while they also benefit from it), one must "destroy politically, philosophically, and symbolically the categories of 'men' and 'women'"; which is to say then, that one must also destroy heterosexuality.[16]

Against the heterosexual regime and its categories of sex, Wittig deploys lesbian society because it eliminates the "economic, political, ideological order"[17] of sex: "lesbian society destroys the artificial (social) fact constituting women as a 'natural group.'"[18] Lesbians escape *sexage*, thus Wittig can (in)famously claim that "lesbians are not women."[19] Because in the heterosexual regime identity requires sex, a lesbian society without sex is also an anti-identitarian society. Within this society, lesbians function as emancipatory subject positions rather than as beings distributed and assigned to an identity category by the binary operations of sex and sexuality. Lesbianism then cannot be homosexuality since that concept also relies on the categories of sex; lesbianism's erotic expression might be more accurately described as anti-identitarian desire. In *Lesbian Peoples: Material for a Dictionary*, the "amantes" (the lovers who make up the lesbian peoples) are defined as ones who feel "a violent desire for each other."[20] Underscoring the plurality of "each other" ("les unes pour les autres" rather than "l'une pour l'autre" [one another]), Anne F.

---

*Feminist Studies* 16, no. 1 (1990). On the connection between materialist feminism in the United States and the Civil Rights Movements, see Donna Landry and Gerald MacLean, *Materialist Feminisms* (Cambridge, MA: Blackwell, 1993). For a critique of arguments that homologize race and sex, see Janet E. Halley, "'Like-Race' Arguments," in *What's Left of Theory? New Work on the Politics of Literary Theory*, eds. Judith Butler, John Guillory, and Kendall Thomas (New York: Routledge, 2000), 40–74.

15. Colette Guillaumin, "The Practice of Power and Belief in Nature," in *Sex in Question: French Materialist Feminism*, eds. Lisa Adkins and Diana Leonard (London; Bristol, PA: Taylor & Francis, 1996), 72–108.

16. Wittig, Preface to *The Straight Mind*, xiii–xiv.

17. Wittig, "The Category of Sex," in *The Straight Mind and Other Essays*, 2.

18. Wittig, "One is Not Born a Woman," 9.

19. Wittig, "The Straight Mind," 32.

20. Wittig and Sande Zeig, *Brouillon pour un dictionnaire des amantes* (Paris: Grasset, 2011), 24, trans. mine.

Garréta, in her preface to the French edition of the book, remarks that "no doubt it is because of that that they live not in couples, but in immediately political and plural formation (peoples)."[21] The inextricable link between lesbian desire and lesbian society is what allows the former to operate the economic, political, and ideological shifts necessary to escaping sexage. The entry on desire further asserts that there isn't "anything in the world more mysterious than desire in its manifestations, its appearances, its disappearances."[22] Wittig, in collaboration with Sande Zeig, thereby defines desire as something opaque—never fully knowable—and transitory, something radically heterogeneous to the knowability and fixity of identity. Sexuality creates sexed identity whereas desire undoes it. The point of lesbianism then is to defy and escape the categorical, identitarian logic of heterosexuality that creates men and women as classes. When Wittig writes about lesbians in her essays, she is not theoretically elaborating an empirical existence so much as describing and creating a de-alienated subject position that both anticipates the dissolution of the categories of sex and suggests an already realized possibility of overcoming the alienation of sex, which she further explores in her novels.

The potential of lesbianism to undo sexage is perhaps nowhere more explicitly developed than in *The Lesbian Body*, which stages and deploys desire against sexuality to create a process of subjectivation without sex. Wittig's 1973 novel stages a relationship between two lovers, "*I*" and "you" that creates a new body, one that is not symbolically organized, charged, and eroticized into and along the heterosexual categories of sex. In keeping with figuring the lesbian as a subject, not an identity, "*I*" and "you" cannot be said to be characters in any traditional or novelistic way; they defy the logic of individuality and identity, as signaled for example by their lack of (proper) names: they are subjects without identities. If sexage is the process of gendering anatomy, *The Lesbian Body* outlines a process for ungendering it. The desire between "*I*" and "you" displaces the genitals as a primary erotogenic zone and eroticizes the entire body, thus divesting

21. Anne F. Garréta, preface to *Brouillon pour un dictionnaire des amantes*, 7, trans. mine. The plural dimension is lost in the English version, which defines the companion lovers as those "violently desiring one another" (Wittig and Sande Zeig, *Lesbian Peoples: Material for a Dictionary* [New York: Avon, 1979]). Garréta pursues the anti-identitarian conception of lesbian desire opened up by Wittig in her novel *Pas un jour* (Paris: Grasset, 2002).

22. Wittig and Zeig, *Lesbian Peoples*, 42.

sex of its supposedly necessary and causal link to desire. Wittig's destruction of the primacy of genitals through a material work with language is most explicit in the ten bold lists of body parts and bodily secretions. The "VAGINA" is no more or less symbolically charged than "THE DIAPHRAGM," "THE ANUS," "THE SOFT PALATE," and/or "THE CONNECTIVE TISSUE."[23] While there are no parts of the body associated with men in the list (according to the logic of the straight mind), the "male body" is not replaced by a "female body," or the phallus by the vagina. The lesbian body has a vagina but it is no more important than other body parts and does not make the lesbian a woman. Whereas for the straight mind, which, it becomes clear, is also the cisgender mind and might thus be renamed the cishetero mind, the vagina is synecdochically and causally related to women, in Wittig's work, or in materialist lesbianism, the vagina and other so-called sex characteristics exist outside the categories of sex. These physical traits are returned to being neutral since they have no inherent meaning outside of sexage. Just as the lesbian is beyond identity and the categories of sex, so the lesbian body does not subscribe to and in fact undoes the binary physical sex of the cishetero mind. A lesbian body then is any body that undoes sexage.

If this new body is (partially) created through a listing of body parts that fragments and proliferates the body into multiple and equally valued pieces, the desire between "*I*" and "you" also allows for their creative reunification as one new whole ("THE LESBIAN BODY"): "*I* speak to you. *I* am seized by vomiting, *I* choke, *I* shriek, *I* speak to you, *I* yearn for you with such marvelous strength that all of a sudden the pieces fall together, you don't have a finger or a fragment missing."[24] It is through their desire that lesbians remake each other beyond the cisheteronormative categories of sex. Wittig also includes in one of the ten lists of words the equation "THE REPRODUCTION [XX + XX = XX]."[25] Lesbian desire, the "want" between "*I*" and "you," is explicitly beyond the reproductive logic of the cishetero regime of sexuality, and productive of new subjects. Wittig posits this creative model in direct opposition to that of motherhood. In the entry on

23. Monique Wittig, *The Lesbian Body*, trans. David Le Vay (Boston: Beacon Press, 1986), 101.

24. Wittig, *The Lesbian Body*, 113–114.

25. Wittig, *The Lesbian Body*,128.

"mother" in *Lesbian Peoples*, Wittig and Zeig elaborate a golden age of lesbianism in which there was no division between mothers and daughters: all were "amazons."[26] But, "then came a time when some daughters, and some mothers did not like wandering anymore in the terrestrial garden. They began to stay in the cities and most often they watched their abdomens grow. This activity brought them, it is said, great satisfaction. Things went so far in this direction that they refused to have any other interests."[27] By becoming exclusively defined by motherhood, some amazons became women. The advent of motherhood is thus coextensive with that of the cishetero regime, ushering in the demise of lesbian society. In *The Lesbian Body*, *I* somatizes this painful betrayal:

> *I* am at the Golgotha you have all abandoned [. . .] now *I* shriek fit to burst m/y lungs, not one of you awakens, yet m/y voice issues so powerfully from m/y throat that it injures m/e in passage, *I* do not recognize it, a red mist comes before m/y eyes, a bloody sweat traverses m/y pores, suddenly it covers m/e entirely, m/y very tears dripping in great drops on m/y arms stain them with blood, bloody m/y saliva falling in strings from m/y mouth, red the moon when she appears in the sky red the earth red the night red *I* see red all around m/e, *I* cry out in m/y great distress, mother, mother, why have you forsaken m/e.[28]

"You all" refers to those amazons who became women, just as the mother has forsaken *I* by becoming precisely that, a mother. However, the suffering undergone by *I* promises to be regenerative. The passage is a rewriting of the biblical scene of Christ's crucifixion. *I* appropriates His words ("My God, my God, why have you forsaken Me?" [Mark 15:34 and Matthew 27:46]) and *I*'s blood is thereby likened to that of Christ. Moreover, violence in the Wittigian universe is indicative of the energy and strength of the amazons; it is mothers who have distorted the word to mean aggression and destruction.[29] It is the desire to be reunited with *you* that generates *I*'s lament and it is *I*'s voice which causes the bleeding that will result in resurrection.

26. Wittig and Zeig, *Lesbian Peoples*, 5.

27. Wittig and Zeig, *Lesbian Peoples*, 108.

28. Wittig, *The Lesbian Body*, 122.

29. See the entry on "violence" in *Brouillon pour un dictionnaire des amantes* and, to a lesser extent, in *Lesbian Peoples*.

Born out of desire, lesbian speech is creative violence.[30] To the cishetero mind's question of how a lesbian society can reproduce itself, Wittig answers: through the generative force of lesbian desire. Lesbian desire—desire between any bodies that are neither women nor men—replaces motherhood as that which creates new beings, thus offering a new model of kinship. Given the queer and transgender possibilities opened up by Wittig's materialist lesbianism, why do queer and transgender theorists turn away from it?

## LESBIANISM'S QUEER SUBJECTS

Judith Butler's 1990 *Gender Trouble*, a canonical text considered foundational to queer theory, elaborates its main argument on anti-identitarianism through a rejection of lesbianism, represented by Monique Wittig. Hemmings also points out that it is Michel Foucault who is consistently cited as the direct and exclusive intellectual influence on *Gender Trouble*, despite the fact that Butler engages Wittig as much as she does Foucault. Wittig's disappearance in existing accounts of Butler's intellectual genealogy defines queerness as male and poststructuralist. Within this framework the "representation of Butler as feminist queer, indeed *lesbian* queer, remains a contradiction in terms."[31] To argue that the association of Butler with Foucault rather than Wittig separates queer theory from feminist theory and poststructuralism from materialism, as Hemmings convincingly does, is to claim that the contradiction between "lesbian" and "queer" that subtends queer theory depends upon the erasure of the particular materialist lesbianism represented by Wittig. Yet it is this very framework that is expunged in Butler's critique of Wittig. *Gender Trouble* participates in, perhaps even inaugurates, the queer theoretical rejection of the lesbian as insufficiently politically sophisticated. Given Butler's reading of Wittig, it seems unlikely then that the genealogical, "corrective" approach of recitation suggested by Hemmings will suffice to dissolve the contradiction between lesbian and queer.

Wittig's theoretical works provide the basis for two of *Gender Trouble*'s most famous claims: that sex is always already gender and

30. The passage is also of course an insertion of a lesbian subject into a foundational text of Western cishetero ideology and thus an extension of the book's project of "*I*" assuming subjectivity.

31. Hemmings, *Why Stories Matter*, 175.

that the binary identity categories of sex and gender are the naturalizing and self-legitimizing effects of what Butler, drawing on Wittig's theorization of the heterosexual regime, calls the heterosexual matrix. These insights opened up by Wittig's materialist lesbianism have in turn led to one of queer theory's most defining paradigms: anti-identitarianism. However, while Butler develops queer theory's foundational political commitment in large part from a reading of Wittig, that reading rejects Wittig's deployment of lesbian subjectivity as an anti-identitarian strategy for undoing the categories of sex and the heterosexual regime.

Butler presents two main objections to Wittig's turn to lesbianism. First, she argues that the category of lesbian breaks solidarity with heterosexual women in the same way that the saying "feminism is the theory, lesbianism the practice" does; it amounts to "separatist prescriptivism."[32] Second, defining lesbianism as the exclusion of heterosexuality makes lesbianism dependent on heterosexuality for its definition, foreclosing the possibility of resignification and thus ultimately consolidating heterosexuality as oppressive:

> Wittig appears to believe that only the radical departure from heterosexual contexts—namely becoming lesbian or gay—can bring about the downfall of this heterosexual regime. But this political consequence follows only if one understands all "participation" in heterosexuality to be a repetition and consolidation of heterosexual oppression. The possibilities of resignifying heterosexuality are refused precisely because heterosexuality is understood as a total system that requires a thoroughgoing displacement.[33]

Butler's critique of prescriptive lesbian separatism and the perception of heterosexuality as wholly and invariably oppressive presupposes that heterosexuality refers, at least in part, to a form of desire. Heterosexuality is indeed inherently oppressive for Wittig, but as a political regime of domination to be escaped, not as desire. "[B]ecoming lesbian or gay," in the traditional meaning of those terms, is neither the only nor even a guaranteed mode of departure from heterosexuality. For Wittig, the only way to escape heterosexuality is to break with the economy of sexage.

32. Judith Butler, *Gender Trouble* (New York: Routledge, 1990), 173.
33. Butler, *Gender Trouble*, 164–165.

Butler explicitly acknowledges that Wittig is a materialist, but she nonetheless quickly translates Wittig through Foucault: heterosexuality becomes an "obligatory or presumptive" "norm" rather than a regime of power, and sex slips from an economically mandated and generated category to a purely discursive function of naming.[34] Whereas for Wittig discourse is one of the ways in which heterosexuality legitimizes, naturalizes, and sustains itself, in Butler's reading it becomes heterosexuality's only mode of operation. Within this landscape of heterosexuality as desire and discursive norm, lesbian becomes just another normative identity. Butler then proposes to undo the normative effects of the binary categories of sex not through the wholesale destruction of heterosexuality, and hence sex, but, through a "thoroughgoing appropriation and redeployment of the categories of identity themselves, not merely to contest 'sex,' but to articulate the convergence of multiple sexual discourses at the site of 'identity' in order to render that category, in whatever form, permanently problematic."[35] Butler promotes parody, or subversive mimesis, as a strategy for problematizing identity because of its ability to reveal the performative aspects of sex and gender. What Butler's analysis misses is not only that the Wittigian lesbian is already an anti-identitarian subject of desire, but also that there is a material dimension of sexuality beyond discourse that is unlikely to be changed by discursive resignification alone.

Recognizing her "mistaken formulations," Butler does rework her reading of Wittig in a 2007 essay entitled "Wittig's Material Practice: Universalizing a Minority Point of View."[36] But not only had her reading in *Gender Trouble* already become field-forming by then, her rereading continues to elide the full force of Wittig's materialist lesbianism, even as it tries to do justice to it. Amending her earlier interpretation, Butler underscores that Wittig's lesbians are not "women who more or less conduct their sexual lives with other women" and that a lesbian is "one who conducts the nullification of the category of gender." However, according to Butler it is exclusively by "universalizing her perspective as a minority" that the lesbian does this.[37]

34. Butler, *Gender Trouble*, 165–166.

35. Butler, *Gender Trouble*, 174.

36. Judith Butler, "Wittig's Material Practice: Universalizing a Minority Point of View," *GLQ: A Journal of Lesbian and Gay Studies* 13, no. 4 (2007), 518.

37. Butler, "Wittig's Material Practice," 518.

She situates this practice as materialist insofar as it shows truth to be the effect of relations of power and insofar as it is underpinned by a recognition of language's action on the body, but she loses sight of the social body, as evidenced by her focus on the singular lesbian. For Wittig, rendering gender obsolete is not only a matter of universalizing a lesbian point of view and in so doing producing different discourses that affect the body; it is and must also be a practice of extracting oneself from the economic and political order of sexage, not just its ideological order, no matter how material the latter may be. Butler's ongoing failure to attend to those dimensions of the heterosexual regime leads her to again argue that Wittig asserts a false binary between homosexuality and heterosexuality. She once again collapses the utopian subject position of lesbian with the everyday meaning of lesbian as homosexual, and fails to separate sexuality and desire. Ultimately, Butler, and after her, queer theory, refuses to divest from identity as radically as Wittig demands.

In Butler's 1990 reading, the naïve, dogmatic, and unsophisticated lesbian, incapable of accepting desire in all its multiplicities and distinguishing pleasure from oppression, must be passed/past in order to make way for a queer future. In her 2007 reading, the lesbian remains inextricable from identity formations. However, attending to Wittig's framework of materialist lesbianism makes it evident that she develops the figure of the lesbian not in the common sense of the term but as a political subject position that eludes the categories of sex by escaping heterosexuality understood, crucially, as a political and economic, as well as ideological order. Materialist lesbianism offers then a much more capacious understanding of sexuality, sex, and anti-identitarianism that opens up queer theory to a reconsideration of its rejection of materialism in favor of poststructuralism. In the Wittigian landscape of subjects without sex, there can be no heterosexuality or homosexuality, only embodied subjects desiring other embodied subjects. How queer!

## LESBIANISM'S TRANS-FORMATIONS

Preciado, the scholar of queer and transgender theory the most directly indebted to Wittig, elaborates his understanding of the transgender body through an engagement with her work. Yet, despite a deep affinity with her writing, he deliberately leaves Wittig's materialist lesbian framework behind. In "Gare à la gouine garou! Ou comment se faire un corps queer à partir de la pensée straight?" (Beware of the Were-Dyke! Or How to Make a Queer Body Out of the Straight Mind?), his text that takes up Wittig in most detail, Preciado aims to show the "fundamental differences" between a "radical lesbian" and "queer" reading of Wittig, as well as what can be gained from the latter and "not being constrained by the materialist feminist framework."[38] He explains: "In order to proceed with the queer reading that interests me, I will need to read Wittig outside of the strict Marxist materialist framework [. . .] because this [. . .] framework effaces dyke and transgender sexuality and embodiment."[39] Preciado moves seamlessly between the terms dyke, queer, and transgender, understanding them to be part of a common intellectual, cultural, and political project, one predicated on a mutual rejection of "lesbian." In this mapping, Wittig's materialist lesbian framework, which he collapses with radical lesbianism, materialist feminism, and Marxist materialism, cannot account for transgender embodiment because it advocates abolition and normative separatism. Similarly to Butler, he argues that "it seems not only incoherent but politically naïve to confine lesbian politics to a pure outside, beyond sex and gender, a negative paradise (*defined by the rejection of sex and gender rather than the production of new codes of signification*), absolutely independent (linguistically, visually, technically) from the dominant heterosexual culture."[40] The abolition of the categories of sex and gender and the well-meaning intention to efface the mark of gender "in language" may be "revolutionary" but they are ultimately "sterile."[41] For Preciado, transgender embodiment disrupts cisheteronormative embodiments, whether heterosexual or homosexual, through a process of non-normative (queer) bodily "transformation."[42] He belongs to a strain of transgender theory that understands itself to be closely related to queer theory; the distinction between the two lies in the object of study rather than in differing theoretical underpinnings or political investments. Crucially, the disruptive bodily transforma-

38. Paul B. Preciado, "Gare à la gouine garou! Ou comment se faire un corps queer à partir de la pensée straight?" in *Parce que les lesbiennes ne sont pas des femmes: Autour de l'œuvre politique, théorique et littéraire de Monique Wittig*, eds. Sam Bourcier and Suzette Robichon (Paris: éditions gaies et lesbiennes, 2002), 182.

39. Preciado, "Gare à la gouine garou," 182.

40. Preciado, "Gare à la gouine garou," 187, emphasis mine.

41. Preciado, "Gare à la gouine garou," 187.

42. Preciado, "Gare à la gouine garou," 181.

tions taken up by Preciado are framed as a process of becoming other; they imply a starting point, which is the cisheteronormative body, hence the title of his essay, "How to Make a Queer Body *Out of* the Straight Mind?" (emphasis mine, "à partir de" in the original French). According to Preciado, figuring heterosexuality as a closed and totalizing system of oppression that requires complete escape—as Wittig does—forecloses the possibility of recognizing transgender embodiments since these are produced through subversions; they exist in relation to the heterosexual regime rather than wholly outside of it.

Preciado is also concerned that Wittig's figuration of lesbianism as a pure outside amounts to masking its constitutive relations of power, making it unable to remain critical of its own abjections and thus susceptible to the same kinds of trans-exclusions seen in so many lesbian political formations and epitomized by the Michigan Womyn's Music Festival.[43] This critique stands only if one collapses the radically anti-identitarian meaning of lesbian in Wittig's work back into its everyday meaning as sexual identity. Preciado cannot conceive of the existence of a world in which there are no categories of sex or sexual identities whatsoever, meaning not that the cishetero regime's operations of power are made invisible but that they have ceased to exist. Preciado's inability to hold on to Wittig's theorization of the lesbian as a subject position and not an identity is evident when he rhetorically states that "since the sexes are defined as the products of this totalizing heterosexuality, it is hard to imagine what is left of 'the lesbian' once she reaches this 'outside.'"[44] Preciado, like Butler, refuses to fully let go of identity. Queer theory may then perhaps be redefined as problematizing identity's normalizing operations rather than as truly anti-identitarian.

Yet Preciado does not wholly abandon Wittig; instead he turns to her novels. This engagement with her literary oeuvre is what allows him to ultimately articulate his understanding of transgender embodiment with Wittig, as opposed to Butler who remains primarily focused on Wittig's essays and finds she must leave her behind in order to develop her theory of gender performativity. While Preciado

43. An annual event held from 1976 to 2015, the Michigan Womyn's Music Festival was a landmark of lesbian culture in the United States. It came to epitomize transphobic lesbianism when in 1991 the organizers asked a trans woman to leave the premises and the festival subsequently instituted a "womyn-born-womyn" policy.

44. Preciado, "Gare à la gouine garou," 185.

agrees with much of Butler's critique of Wittig, and while he acknowledges the significant performative dimension of statements such as "lesbians are not women" and "I don't have a vagina," which Wittig is said to have pronounced at Vassar (Preciado temporarily assumes authorship of this sentence because Wittig claims never to have said it), he nonetheless importantly departs from Butler. Butlerian performativity, epitomized by the figure of the drag queen, rests on a binary between gender performance and sexual anatomy that runs the risk of positioning biology beyond the reach of performativity. Butler's framework cannot then properly account for transgender embodiment.[45] Jettisoning Wittig's materialist lesbianism and Butlerian performativity, Preciado offers a Deleuzian reading of *The Lesbian Body* as a guide on how to produce queer, transgender bodies. He argues that the "lesbian fucking" ("la baise lesbienne")[46] of *The Lesbian Body* deterritorializes the straight body and produces a new form of embodiment because "the 'straight' use of sexual organs is diverted and re-appropriated" within a new economy of pleasure and sensibility.[47] The vagina, uncoupled from the reproductive function to which it is assigned by the cishetero mind, becomes something else. In what amounts to an extension of the paradox "lesbians are not women," and in accordance with Wittig's and his assertion, lesbians can no longer be said to have vaginas. *The Lesbian Body* interrupts the assigned labor of the cishetero body and offers news uses of the body that lead to a transformed body, a "re-incorporation."[48] If Preciado frames this transformation as being unreadable within Wittig's materialist lesbianism because the latter's focus on abolition is incompatible with appropriation and subversion (incompatible with the "re" of "re-incorporation and the "trans" of "transformation"), he claims that her novels have a more poststructural bent, which is why they are amenable to a queer, transgender reading. The binary opposition between abolition and subversion—a common tenet of transgender theory[49]—is thus doubled by one between materialist lesbianism

45. Preciado's essay predates Butler's 2007 essay, but as seen above even Butler's reworking eludes a full account of the ways in which the body is shaped by material forces.

46. Preciado, "Gare à la gouine garou," 214.

47. Preciado, "Gare à la gouine garou," 209.

48. Preciado, "Gare à la gouine garou," 211.

49. In their essay reconciling feminist and transgender theory, Espineira and Bourcier state: "transfeminism's political horizon is not abolitionist; rather, it is counter-

and queer poststructuralism, and by one between Wittig's essays and novels.

A closer look at Wittig and the relation between her theory and fiction challenges such a mapping. Her materialist framework itself in fact refuses a strict division between materialism and poststructuralism. Working against a vulgar division between economic base and ideological superstructure, Wittig establishes the materiality of ideology and inscribes discourse, language, and concepts as objects of political intervention:

> We must produce a political transformation of the key concepts, that is of the concepts which are strategic for us. For there is another order of materiality, that of language, and language is worked up from within by these strategic concepts. [. . .I]n the systems that seemed so eternal and universal that laws could be extracted from them [. . .] thanks to our action and our language, *shifts* are happening. [. . .W]e break off the heterosexual contract. [. . .T]he straight concepts are *undermined*.[50]

Action and language contribute to shifts, permutations, subversions, which bring on a rupture, the end of the heterosexual contract, the abolition of its political, economic, and ideological regime. In Wittig's universe, abolition and subversion are not mutually exclusive; on the contrary subversion is an abolitionist practice, which she undertakes in her novels. For example, if Wittig wants to destroy the mark of gender in language, she does not therefore refuse to use gendered language. She does not resolve herself to only write in a gender-neutral way or set out to invent new pronouns, words, or grammatical structures in order to create a realm of existence purely outside of the cishetero mind. Instead, she attempts to subvert the use of existing pronouns and to thereby jam the cishetero mind. The italicized *I* in *The Lesbian Body* (the slashed "j/e" in French) signals the appropriation of the language of desire by a subject meant to only be its object. Similarly in *Les Guérillères*, she does not reject the plural feminine pronoun "elles" in order to escape the mark of gender but rather gives it new meaning by strategically universalizing it ("elles" contains "ils").[51] If ideological subversions can contribute to abolishing

productive: a material proliferation of new femininities and masculinities" (Espineira and Bourcier, "Transfeminism," 89).

50. Wittig, "The Straight Mind," 64–66, emphasis mine.

51. Wittig, *Les Guérillères* (Paris: Editions de Minuit, 1969). Her strategy gets muddled in the English edition, which translates "elles" as "the women:" Wittig, *Les*

sexage and, with it, the cishetero regime, it is because "language casts sheaves of reality upon the social body, stamping it and violently shaping it. [. . .] There is a plasticity of the real to language."[52] Thus, undoing the primacy of the vagina in *The Lesbian Body* undermines the process of sexage, and makes possible the emergence of a new kind of body that destabilizes the cishetero regime. In other words, it is possible to read *The Lesbian Body* as a strategy for bodily transformations by reading it within the context of materialist lesbianism.

So does the lesbian have a vagina as in *The Lesbian Body*, or not, as Wittig's and Preciado's statement asserts? The lesbian body has a vagina only insofar as the latter is given new meaning outside of the cishetero mind, that is, insofar as it ceases to be a mark of sex. The lesbian does not have a vagina in the cishetero meaning of that word. What is important from a materialist lesbian perspective is that the body part in question escape the process of sexage and thus disrupt the cishetero regime. Whether or not it does so by remaining a vagina in name is a question of literary strategy. Both the production of a new kind of vagina in *The Lesbian Body* and the use of the paradox affirming that lesbians do not have vaginas work toward the same end of jamming the machinery of sexage, which is why it is conceivable that Wittig is the author of both. In other words, there is more than one strategy for abolishing the categories of sex.

But what about the fact that materialist lesbianism's end goal is this abolition of the categories of sex, whereas transgender theory and activism include claiming the terms of men and women? Is the Wittigian lesbian who is not a woman or a man only compatible with non-binary forms of transgender subjectivity? In the context of Wittig's materialist lesbianism, transgender investitures of "man" and "woman" can be read as operating like a war machine on the cishetero regime. In her essay "The Trojan Horse," Wittig describes how the Trojans accepted the object built by the Greeks as a horse, which then turned out to be a war machine. While the Trojan horse is recognizable as a horse—is a horse—it "pulverize[s] the old forms and formal conventions."[53] Wittig is talking about the revolutionary po-

*Guérillères*, trans. David Le Vay (Urbana and Chicago: University of Illinois Press, 2007).

52. Wittig, "On the Social Contract," in *The Straight Mind and Other Essays* (Boston: Beacon Press, 1992), 43–44.

53. Wittig, "On the Social Contract," 69.

tential of literature, but her emphasis on the materiality of language, her literary efforts in *The Lesbian Body* to produce bodies that undo sexage, and her refusal of a strict division between ideology and structure, allow one to loosely extend the Trojan horse analogy to bodily assaults on the cishetero regime.[54]

Like lesbians, trans men and women jam the operation of sexage. The cishetero regime marks bodies as (cis) men and (cis) women in order to legitimize (cis) men's appropriation of (cis) women's bodies and labor. The parenthetical use of (cis) in the previous sentence denotes that the cishetero regime exclusively marks bodies as cis men and cis women (trans bodies are not a part of its operations) but that it naturalizes itself by making the cis quality of those marks invisible. Taking into account the existence of trans men and women disrupts this naturalized cishetero regime; it highlights the fact that cis bodies are constructed as such, not natural or inevitable, and that it is possible to produce other kinds of bodies. From this perspective, a woman is no longer necessarily someone subject to compulsory reproduction and whose reproductive labor and personhood is to be appropriated by men, as the cishetero regime would have it. This reality dissociates the mark of sex from its causal relation to the class positions of men and women as oppressor and oppressed. The mark of sex thus dissolves, and lacking marks, domination cannot be naturalized.[55] Whereas French materialist feminists accuse transgender movements of being complicit with sexism because they maintain the categories of sex, and of being idealist and failing to act on material reality, Wittig's framework makes visible the fact that trans men and women undermine sexage; they precipitate the downfall of the cishetero regime by directly attacking its material basis—the economic, political, and ideological order of sex.[56]

54. To be absolutely clear, I understand trans men and women to be just as much men and women as cis men and women; my point pertains to cis and trans men and women's differing relations to the cishetero operation of sexage.

55. In a similar move, Espineira and Bourcier note that reclaiming "'unproductive' bodies capable of becoming bodies of pleasure dedicated to nonreproductive forms of sex" "makes visible the lie of sexual dualism" ("Transfeminism," 89).

56. See for example: Nicole-Claude Mathieu, "Dérive du Genre/Stabilité des Sexes," in *Lesbianisme et Féminisme: Histoires Politiques*, ed. Natacha Chetcuti and Claire Michard (Paris: L'Harmattan, 2003): 291–310. Delphy has also explicitly stated that she sees trans identities as antithetical to feminism (Christine Delphy, "Rencontre avec Christine Delphy au Lieu-Dit," September 28, 2013. Lieu-Dit, 6, rue Sorbier 75020 Paris. Personal recording of a live performance). My point here is not to predicate

Like Wittig's use of gender in language, transgender investitures of man and woman are forms of subversion that work toward the materialist lesbian project of abolishing men and women as classes. Men and women are sexed identities that create classes in so far as they are produced and defined by a material relationship of domination. Just like the use of "vagina" outside of the cishetero mind allows the term to be reclaimed beyond the operations of sexage, so the use of the terms men and women outside of the relations of oppression of the cishetero regime turns them into subject positions rather than sexed identities. In a Wittigian framework, the emphasis on gender identity within transgender movements may be better understood as an emphasis on gender subjectivity. Just as producing a lesbian body with a new kind of vagina or stating that a lesbian does not have a vagina are two different strategies for disrupting sexage, so the production of a lesbian subject position outside of the categories of men and women or the transgender investiture of those categories are also two different ways of attacking the cishetero regime. Writing against the heteronormativity of the women's liberation movement in France and the essentialism of difference feminism (as exemplified by *écriture feminine*), at a time when there was little transgender awareness, it is unlikely Wittig could have imagined such revolutionary reworkings of the terms men and women. Yet, "lesbians are not women" can be seen today to mean "lesbians are not cis women," thus opening up a convergence of lesbian and transgender subjectivities.

## LESBIANISM'S GENERATIONS

Remembering the materialist specificity of Wittig's theory of sexuality shows lesbianism to have been queer all along, or conversely, and somewhat perversely, queer theory as having been lesbian all along. It also establishes a lesbianism of the 1970s that was engaged in a subversion of cisheteronormativity by attacking the cishetero mind and producing bodily trans-formations. The figure of the lesbian, as seen through Wittig's materialist lesbianism, then exceeds her confinement to the past and invites a different form of intergenerational relating among lesbian, queer, and transgender than that of the les-

---

the legitimacy of trans identities on their political positioning but rather to show that becoming allies to the trans movement would in fact be consistent with the overall theoretical premises and political aims of certain heretofore transphobic genealogies of radical feminism and lesbianism.

bian mother and the queer and transgender child, and its problematic disidentifications. In *Lesbian Peoples*, Wittig and Zeig elaborate a model of intergenerational relating that escapes the traps of misogyny, lesbophobia, and cisheteronormative kinship. In the lesbian societies described in their co-authored dictionary, there are no mothers and daughters since mothers are those who are fully defined by their reproductive role and are thus part of the cishetero regime. In lesbian societies, those who have a genetic link are not defined by it. "Mothers" and "daughters" are all amazons and collectively engaged in listening to one another and joining one another in limitless travel and adventure. What if lesbian, queer, and transgender cultural and political formations listened to each other better and became fellow travelers in the raucous terrain of gender and sexual theory and activism, rather than exiling one another to separate lands? What new horizons might emerge?

ALICE KAPLAN

# A Biography for Monique Wittig

*On Friday, October 11, 2019 the colloquium "Drafting Monique Wittig" closed with a plenary session devoted to the question of how to write the life of a feminist writer and thinker. The participants were Anne Garréta, Suzette Robichon, Sande Zeig, and myself. The questions, from the speakers and from the audience, were profound: what kind of biography would suit a writer as playful and iconoclastic as Monique Wittig? Would a biography risk betraying her commitments? On the other hand, would the failure to produce a biography deprive Wittig of her place in literary history? My intervention at the roundtable is followed here by a postscript, bringing the question of Wittig's biography into a hopeful present.*

* * *

Biography is the least experimental literary form—biography as we know it. Its structure is almost always chronological, from birth to death, lighting on the significant events. That's why it's especially interesting to have this opportunity to theorize a biography of Monique Wittig that hasn't yet come into being. To workshop the story of her life, in her sense of a "chantier" (workshop). *Un chantier biographique* (a biographical workshop).

The outliers in biographical form are few and far between. In *Roland Barthes par lui-même* (*Roland Barthes by Roland Barthes*), the author disguises his autobiography as a biography.[1] Or you might as easily say that he's disguised his biography as an autobiography.

1. Roland Barthes, *Roland Barthes par lui-même* (Paris: Éditions du Seuil/Écrivains de Toujours, 1975).

**YFS 142,** *Lesbian Materialism: The Life and Work of Monique Wittig,* ed. Cadieu and Kim, 

Barthes found a unique way to destabilize both genres: he contributed to the Édition du Seuil's "par lui-même" series of books about canonical writers, which includes volumes such as Francis Jeanson's *Sartre par lui-même* (1955) and Chris Marker's *Giraudoux par lui-même* (1952), with the subtitle, each time, at the bottom right hand of the cover: "écrivains de toujours," which I'm tempted to translate, in the spirit of the series, as "immortal writers." The contemporary writers authoring the biography choose passages from the "écrivain de toujours" and supply guiding commentary varying in intent from simple guideposts (Marker on Giraudoux: "We're in Munich"), to full-fledged interpretation (Jeanson on Sartre: "Now we will attempt to extract something like 'the features' of the Sartrian attitude"). The form varies as well. Marker intervenes in italics in discrete sentences or paragraphs, giving Giraudoux's texts in roman letters, while Jeanson does the opposite, putting Sartre's language in italics inside his own analyses in roman type.

Barthes took the series at its word. He chose himself, *lui-même,* as the writer. His book is willfully subjective, theorizing, and mocking: "To write by fragments: the fragments are then so many stones/ on the perimeter of a circle: I spread myself around: my whole little universe in crumbs: at the center, what?"[2] This much-quoted line is usually understood as proof that Barthes thought his task was doomed to failure. When I read it, I'm reminded instead of Wittig's *Les Guerillères*—its circular logic, its mineral qualities, and I imagine her sitting in the amphitheater of Barthes' course on *S/Z* as she was creating her warrior "elles."[3]

We associate Barthes more generally with the theory of the "biographeme"—units of biographical meaning—and with the use of

2. *Roland Barthes by Roland Barthes,* trans. Richard Howard (New York: Hill & Wang, 1977), 92–93.

3. Josiane Chanel and Antoinette Fouque, in *Génération MLF,* place Wittig in Barthes's course on Sarrasine (Josiane Chanel, Antoinette Fouque and Marie-Catherine Marchini, *Génération MLF 1968–2008* [Paris: Des Femmes, 2008]); "It's more than likely," concludes Emilie Notéris cautiously, "that Monique Wittig would have attended at least one session of this seminar" (Notéris, *Wittig* [Paris: Les Pérégrines, 2022], 80). Wittig's critical reflections on Barthes's semiology are certainly well documented, notably in *The Literary Workshop,* trans. Annabel Kim and Lynne Huffer (London: Verso Books, forthcoming, 2024) and *The Straight Mind and Other Essays* (Boston: Beacon Press, 1992). The more interesting question for our purposes goes in the other direction: how could a reader as assiduous as Barthes not have been aware of Wittig's books?

images, and fragments, with the glossary or the primer, where amorous discourse is laid out alphabetically—and that abecedarium is an appealing one for thinking about the author of *Brouillon pour un dictionnaire des amantes* (*Lesbian Peoples: Material for a Dictionary*).[4] It's hard to imagine a straightforward life to death narrative (with apologies for the double meaning of "straight") that could capture the spirit of Monique Wittig. How many scholars and readers of Wittig wonder if a book faithful to her life must be, by necessity, formally playful?

In looking for models, I think of Frances Kiernan's *Seeing Mary Plain: A Biography of Mary McCarthy,* the rare biography in any language to eschew the linear narrative.[5] McCarthy, unlike Wittig, was not an avant-garde writer. She is best known in the U.S. as the author of the bestseller *The Group,* from 1963, a landmark novel of sexual frankness at a time when the absence of legal birth control and abortion drove the heterosexual plot lines of so much women's fiction. McCarthy is also one of the best memoirists of the last century, the author in 1957 of *Memories of a Catholic Girlhood,* an unsentimental vision of her coming of age in Seattle and Minneapolis, following the death of her parents during the 1918 influenza epidemic. An early review of the book praised her for deploying the techniques of the biographer and the sensibility of the autobiographer.[6] The flash points of McCarthy's life are well-known: she was married briefly to Edmund Wilson; she was a regular contributor to *The New York Review of Books*; she had a famous feud with Lillian Hellman. And she spent the later years of her life, the Vietnam war years, as an exile in Paris.

In *Seeing Mary Plain,* Kiernan establishes the periods of McCarthy's life in headnotes. Then she steps back and orchestrates conversations. We hear from McCarthy's friends and colleagues, from writers with a keen sense of the era. Kiernan provides other "voices" that are actually documents from the archives. Into this mix of commentary, she inserts Mary McCarthy's own autobiographical voice. So, for example, a letter of recommendation to Vassar College by her high school Latin instructor describes McCarthy's strong will, while,

4. Monique Wittig and Sande Zeig, *Brouillon pour un dictionnaire des amantes,* preface by Anne Garréta (Paris: Grasset/Cahiers rouges, 2011).

5. Frances Kiernan, *Seeing Mary Plain: A Life of Mary McCarthy* (New York: Norton, 2000).

6. Charles Poore, "Books of the Times: Memories of a Catholic Girlhood," *New York Times,* May 18, 1957.

in the next passage, Kiernan quotes a passage from McCarthy's memoir *How I Grew,* where she claims ruefully that her Latin teacher knew her better than she knew herself.[7] Kiernan's mix of documents gives us a constantly shifting point of view, like a novel where no single character can know what the other characters are thinking.

One of the voices orchestrated in *Seeing Mary Plain* is Monique Wittig's. Wittig met McCarthy through their mutual friend Nathalie Sarraute—Sarraute, who as we know, in 1964, championed *L'Opoponax* for the Médicis prize and admired Wittig's writing enormously.[8] Sarraute, McCarthy, Wittig: all three were producing stories of childhood during the years of their friendship.

In the space of a paragraph, Wittig reveals herself in *Seeing Mary Plain* as a brilliant biographer, an inspiration to any future biographer. Listen to what she says about McCarthy—and the way she says it. The scene is lunch. Wittig is remembering the famous lunches to which she was invited during the 1960s with McCarthy and Sarraute. Just the thought of these lunches makes me want to write a play!

> At lunch she did not speak much. She was not someone who would put herself forward. She did not like to speak French at all. She would sit there with a funny look in her eyes. She was amused by me and I was amused by her. She was conducting herself as though she were a queen, but she had also this shyness. Mary knew I was a feminist from the start. She would push me into a group of men, introduce me, and watch me fight battles that she would not have fought but she was not in disagreement with. When her support became too public, I told her I was a lesbian. I didn't want her to find herself in a false position. As an answer, two weeks later she invited me over and there was Marie-Claire Blais, the girlfriend of Mary Meigs.[9]

A talented biographer can narrate her subject through a scene: Wittig gives us the look in McCarthy's eyes and her queenly shyness. In a single paragraph, she sets up a conflict, creates an expectation that she proceeds to dash with a surprise ending that is also an homage to McCarthy. And along the way she tells us something important about straight women and lesbians, mistrust and trust, in that dark

7. Kiernan, *Seeing Mary Plain*, 59.

8. See Annabel Kim, *Unbecoming Language: Anti-Identitarian French Feminist Fictions* (Columbus: Ohio State University Press, 2018), on the chain of influence leading from Sarraute to Wittig to Garréta, and why it matters.

9. Kiernan, *Seeing Mary Plain*, 564.

era of intellectual France in the 1960s. We learned something else during the "Drafting Monique Wittig" conference about McCarthy's role in Wittig's career: Abigail Fields showed us the American edition of *Les Guerillères* with McCarthy's imprimatur on the cover: "A delectable epic of sex warfare."[10]And here, in an anecdote from real life, it's McCarthy who orchestrates sex warfare, by setting up Wittig to spar with her male friends. Wittig had the last word. At a 1993 conference devoted to McCarthy's work, shortly after the writer's death, she delivered a brilliant reading of *The Group*, entitled "The Fourth Sex," in which the mysterious and beautiful Elinor Eastlake returns with the Baronness d'Estienne to upset the entire sexual apparatus of the novel, and the reader is obliged to queer the plot of everything that has come before. "My friend," Lakey explains in passing, "loves American women. She says American women are a fourth sex."[11] If the "third sex" described by Laure Murat in *La Loi du genre. Une histoire culturelle du troisième sexe* (Gender Laws: A Cultural History of the Third Sex) moves historically between androgyny, sexual neutrality, and inversion, this fourth sex, as imagined by the European outsider and underlined by Wittig, herself a European outsider, grants American women a special lesbian mystique.

Would there then be a "brouillon/draft" for a biography of Monique Wittig that would combine textual fragments and life narratives like these? Wittig sets a high bar.

I'd like to mention another tendency in contemporary literary biography: biography as social network analysis. The metaphor belongs to our current moment, but it lends itself easily to the way we understand lives from the past—as if Bourdieu, not Zuckerberg, invented Facebook. One of the strengths of Ann Jefferson's captivating biography of Nathalie Sarraute, *Nathalie Sarraute: A Life Between,* is the light she sheds on the domination of the literary field by Sartre and Beauvoir circa 1945 to 1960.[12] This is a story we know well; it's been

10. Abigail Fields, "Le pouvoir au bout du pronom: For a reconsideration of *Les Guerillères* in translation" (conference presentation, "Drafting Monique Wittig," Yale University, New Haven, CT, October 10, 2019).

11. Wittig, "The Fourth Sex," unpublished typescript of a paper given at the conference "Truth-Telling and Its Cost: Mary McCarthy, Writing, and Intellectual Politics" at Bard College, October 22, 1993, Monique Wittig Collection, Box 24, Beinecke Rare Book and Manuscript Library, Yale University.

12. Ann Jefferson, *Nathalie Sarraute: A Life Between* (Princeton: Princeton University Press, 2020).

told by Anna Boschetti among others,[13] and it has proven to be a kind of test case for a Bourdieusian school of literary sociology. In an original and politically meaningful intervention in literary history, Jefferson shows Sarraute, over decades, patiently constructing a powerful alternative network, and gradually building an intellectual life outside the existentialist frat house. The lunches with Wittig and McCarthy are one example. This alternative network was key in taking the spotlight off Beauvoir and Sartre and moving it to Duras, Sarraute, Wittig, Cixous, Rochefort; to writers engaged, as Lynne Huffer told us, in a material struggle with words; to writers who were remaking the world through language.[14] I think it's no accident that a critic like Germaine Brée, alert to formal achievement in literature, began her career as a champion of Camus—who also struggled to differentiate himself from the existentialists and who was keenly attuned to the sensuality of language, and to myth—and ended it as a champion of Wittig.

Live with a writer long enough and their story will show up in the most unexpected places. Biography happens sometimes by design, sometimes by accident. When I was working in the Germaine Brée archives at Wake Forest University, in Winston-Salem, North Carolina, I found a letter from poet Yves Bonnefoy to Brée about Monique Wittig. It's exactly the sort of letter Mary McCarthy would write for Wittig much later.[15]

> Dear Germaine Brée,
>
> I'm taking the liberty of writing you not really knowing if it's appropriate, or if it doesn't double up some other request made to you. Still, I'm doing it, because you must know the academic situation in the U.S. well, and especially, because you must also have a precise idea of what I want to talk to you about. You have probably read Monique Wittig's *L'Opoponax,* one of the best novels published in recent years. Monique Wittig, who is absolutely charming and intelligent, is our friend, and before our departure in September, told us that she would very much like to come to this country to teach for a while, perhaps for two years. She is not a professor in France (in fact she's still very young, no more than 25 years old, I suppose) but she's deeply cultured

13. Anna Boschetti, *The Intellectual Enterprise: Sartre and Les Temps modernes,* trans. Richard C. McCleary (Evanston: Northwestern University Press, 1988).

14. Lynne Huffer, "Wittig's Sapphic Body" (conference presentation, "Drafting Monique Wittig," Yale University, New Haven, CT, October 10, 2019).

15. Sophia Wilson Niehaus, "The Discreet Friendship of Mary McCarthy and Monique Wittig," *Women's Studies* 49, no. 4 (2020): 360–373.

and could make the liveliest of contributions. So, I don't hesitate to recommend her, in case, on your end, you have an opening, or hear about some possibility of this kind. [. . . .][16]

At the time of this letter, Brée was teaching at the University of Wisconsin in the mid-'60s, in a career trajectory that had led her from Oran, to Bryn Mawr, to NYU, where she founded the Maison Française. Along with Henri Peyre at Yale, but in a very different mode, she was the unofficial dean of French Studies in the U.S. for a generation. In 1973, she moved to Wake Forest University, and after retiring in 1984, she assembled her archive for the university's special collections. This is a rare personal letter from the 1960s, the only one of its kind. At first you think it couldn't be more ordinary—a piece of academic business, a request for employment, so common in American academic life—yet she clearly felt it was important enough to save.

There is much to say about the letter: about Bonnefoy's confidence in Wittig, about a poet's recognition of Wittig's achievement in *The Opoponax*, and about a friendship between Wittig and Bonnefoy that prompted him to write in her favor to the person he assumes has enough professional clout to find her work in the American academy. The letter leads us to believe that Wittig may have wanted to come to the United States to teach earlier than we imagined—perhaps shortly after the success of *The Opoponax* and before her break with the MLF (Women's Liberation Movement). It is tempting to conclude that if Bonnefoy's letter didn't get Wittig an immediate job in a U.S. college or university, then it did draw Brée's attention to an important new writer and spark her own signal engagement with Wittig's work.

By 1990, Wittig and Brée were corresponding. Brée wrote to Wittig to rejoice in plans for a conference celebrating the work of Nathalie Sarraute in which she intended to participate despite her advanced age. "More and more," Brée wrote, "it's clear to me that it's women writers in France: Nathalie, Marguerite Duras, you (Cixous less so—too influenced by the grand rhetoric) who have oriented French literature to today's world."[17] From Bonnefoy to Brée, from Brée to Wittig,

16. Yves Bonnefoy to Germaine Brée, November 19 [no year given], Germaine Brée papers, Box 8, Wake Forest University Library Special Collections. Unless otherwise indicated, all translations provided in this article are my own.

17. Germaine Brée to Monique Wittig, November 13, 1992, Monique Wittig Collection, Box 24, Beinecke Rare Book and Manuscript Library, Yale University, New Haven, CT.

there's a happy ending to be gleaned here—a sense of community, at last.

Part of the biographer's job consists in tracking down two sides of a correspondence, putting the pieces of a puzzle together. Wittig wrote to Bonnefoy in 1967 to thank him for writing on her behalf: "You're writing letters, you shouldn't have. I never would have allowed you to help me if I had known in advance that it would obligate you to make this kind of effort."[18] And so we gather assumptions, build meanings, and conclude that Bonnefoy, who had a job as a visiting professor at Brandeis, wanted to use his influence and his knowledge of the American scene to support a young writer whom he and his wife admired, for whose support Wittig was both grateful and embarrassed.

Whoever takes on a biography for Monique Wittig will have to explore a cascade of questions provoked by this letter: Why did Wittig come to the United States? How did she come? How did her exile change her vision? And finally, in what tradition do you place the writer who straddles two countries, two languages, and as many networks?

* * *

There was a tangible excitement in the room after the roundtable on biography. Many of us wanted to believe that "Drafting Monique Wittig" had produced a new consensus, and that the leading scholars and readers of Wittig were ready to embrace the project of a life story. There was a sense, not just of a biography of Wittig in the making, but of a biography for Wittig—a book written in deep sympathy, with the goal of restoring her rightful place in literary history, between France and the United States. There was whispering about next steps: what if we, participants in the conference, wrote the biography ourselves as a collective, each person taking an angle, an episode, a text. I remember thinking that this was a noble idea, and a pretty bad one. That an experimental approach could work but would need a guiding hand; that she needed the intelligence of a single biographer, willing to cast a critical eye as well as a loving one, upon whatever style or structure they chose.

18. Yves Bonnefoy to Monique Wittig, November 1967, in Yves Bonnefoy, *Correspondance*, t. 1, ed. Odile Bombarde and Patrick Labarthe (Paris: Belles Lettres, 2018), 1109.

In the spring of 2021 came the news that a biography is under contract with Le Seuil, and that its author will be Laure Murat.

If a biography is a dance between two partners, it's difficult to imagine a better matched pair than Wittig and Murat. The three decades that separate them in age make their common ground all the more striking. After early careers as critics and writers, both completed PhDs at the École des hautes études en sciences sociales (EHESS); both left France to teach at universities in the United States. Both of them, consequently, have a double point of view on French and American intellectual life and a critical perspective that travels in both directions; both write out of a keen awareness of—I believe that Murat coined this phrase—the French "surmoi grammatical" (grammatical superego). Each is committed, in their own way, to resisting the mark of gender.

Murat will bring to her biography of Wittig her important contributions to several aspects of cultural history: the phenomenology of the archive, the study of non-normative identities in both the nineteenth and twentieth centuries, and an understanding of the roles of intermediary figures (psychiatrists, editors) in the transmission of culture.

In *Passage de l'Odéon* (Odeon Street), the book that first took her to Yale's Beinecke Rare Book and Manuscript Library, Murat captured the making of literature between the wars through her exploration of the braided French and American lives of Sylvia Beach and Adrienne Monnier. In *The Man Who Thought He Was Napoleon,* she combed through nineteenth-century medical records to analyze how history informed patients' delusions: guillotine trauma after the Revolution; fantasies of being Napoleon after the return of his ashes to France in 1840; and, more broadly, madness linked to the revolutions of 1830 and 1848, and to the Commune of 1870. Murat gives new poignancy to the problem of distinguishing between what patients say and how their doctors represent their voices, and she makes her own process in the archives part of the story she is telling. Her ability to represent multiple voices makes her uniquely qualified to take on the complexity of Wittig's thought. She will narrate the troubles within French feminism in the 1970s, as well as Wittig's departure from the French scene. She will explore what American campus life did to enable and to complicate Wittig's career—how it freed her from French intellectual life and exiled her from the world she challenged, and at the same time, separated her from the context in which her writing had its most urgent meaning.

A French acquaintance remarked to me in passing a few years ago that his mother had been friends with a "crazy French writer, a feminist." He thought they might have met in Isle-sur-la-Sorgue. The writer in question was Monique Wittig. His mother had even gone to her funeral. I bristled: "Actually she's one of the most important writers of the mid-twentieth century." I wondered, would my acquaintance have said the same of the famously eccentric Alain Robbe-Grillet, who gave his papers to the Institut mémoires de l'édition contemporaine (IMEC) on the condition that they also look after his cactus collection?[19] What are we to make of a reader who follows the literary pages of *Le Monde*, *Le Figaro*, and *La Quinzaine Littéraire* and still knows nothing about Monique Wittig? You start to wonder how reputations are built and how legacies are constructed; how one writer is remembered as a "chef de file" and another as a crazy person. In the case of Wittig, it's paradoxically her own heirs, her most supportive readers, who believed in her right to privacy and guarded her "intimate" exchanges. But in the case of a writer, the intimate is inevitably literary. Olivier Wagner, editor of *Nouveau Roman: Correspondance 1946–1999*, wrote me that he wanted to include Wittig's exchanges with Sarraute and Claude Simon in his book, but couldn't get permission.[20] He was also unable to include several letters in the Beinecke collection from Jérôme Lindon, who was the publisher and mentor at Éditions de Minuit, both to Wittig and to the more recognizable *nouveaux romanciers*— it was Lindon's heirs who felt strongly that the letters shouldn't appear. The wunderkind author of the prize-winning *The Opoponax*, celebrated by Sarraute and Duras, was welcomed onto the literary scene in 1964 as a New Novelist. But Lindon's letters to Wittig tell the story of an unraveling. What happened? She emerged as a radical lesbian and left for the United States, where her concerns went deeper than the deconstruction of narrative

19. Albert Dichy, "The Literary Archive Today: Tales from an Extraordinary Institution," (lecture, Yale University, November 10, 2011).

20. *Nouveau Roman: Correspondance 1946–1999*, ed. Olivier Wagner et Jean-Yves Tadié (Paris: Gallimard, 2021). Email message to the author from Olivier Wagner, October 20, 2021: "For Wittig it's really too bad because her correspondence with Sarraute directly concerns the subject that interests you, the transition from France to the United States."

that is the trademark of the New Novel. She questioned the very core of language and its entanglement with gendered ideologies.

"Three books in twenty years," Lindon complains in a 1990 letter to Wittig. He reminds her that her last novel, *Virgile, non* (*Across the Acheron*) had almost no reviews and had sold only 1,385 copies in five years. As for her request that Minuit publish *Le Chantier littéraire* (The Literary Workshop), her ars poetica, he could do it, he sighs, but doesn't think it would be a good idea: "I fear that today the problems of literary theory and technique are no longer of much interest." What should she expect "after such a long absence," by which he means a long absence from the only literary scene that matters.[21] A long absence from Paris.

Literary history is a series of overlapping misunderstandings. The biographer's task is to uncover the delusions, to reconstruct the puzzle of a life, to question what is assumed, and to welcome what is least expected. Inside the life of Monique Wittig is a literary history that France ignores. That is one reason, among many, why we need Laure Murat's biography.

21. Jérôme Lindon to Monique Wittig, January 24, 1990, Monique Wittig Collection, Box 24, Beinecke Rare Book and Manuscript Library.

# INTERLUDE II

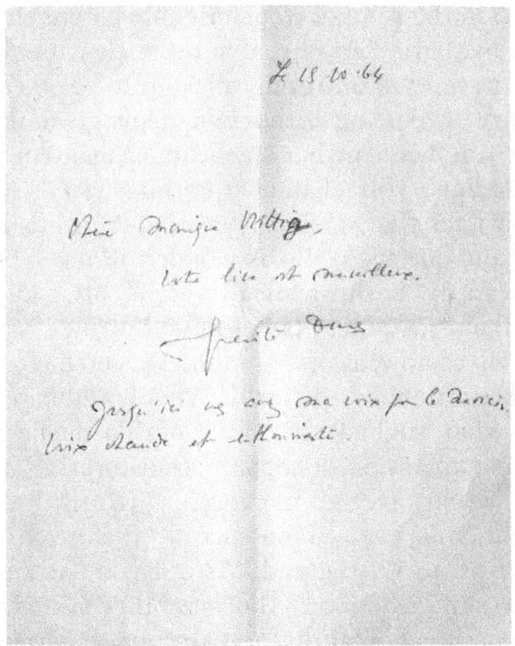

Le 15.10.64

Chère Monique Wittig,

Votre livre est merveilleux.

Marguerite Duras

Jusqu'ici vous avez ma voix pour le Médicis.
Voix [illegible] et [illegible].

Letter from Marguerite Duras to Monique Wittig about *L'Opoponax* (Wittig Collection, Box 21, Beinecke Library, Yale University)

In the middle of the plain white sheet of paper is Marguerite Duras's familiar signature with its outsized M: M for Marguerite, M for *moi. . . moi,* Marguerite. The date is mid-October 1964: the jury for the Médicis is in the middle of its deliberations. Duras, the prima

**YFS 142,** *Lesbian Materialism: The Life and Work of Monique Wittig,* ed. Cadieu and Kim, 

donna of French literature in that moment, has hastily penned this note to Monique Wittig (was it mailed? was it passed from hand to hand, like what Catherine Legrand et al. might have done in the world of *L'Opoponax*?), the *g* in Wittig messy from being passed over multiple times—Duras, either from haste or from lack of familiarity, has made a mistake in writing Wittig's last name. But the name is inconsequential, in a certain way. What matters is Duras's judgment of *L'Opoponax*, summed up in one compact line that comprises the entire body of the message, incarnating the kind of heavy economy we find in Duras's work: "Votre livre est merveilleux." Your book is marvelous. But, in the kind of tropismic movement that we can find in the work of Nathalie Sarraute, that other jury member, where all judgments, all gestures of outreach, turn out to be on thin ice, fragile, subject to change or to being withdrawn at any given moment, Duras writes another line beneath her signature: "Jusqu'ici vous avez ma voix pour le Médicis. Voix chaude et enthousiaste" (As of now, you have my support for the Médicis. Warm and enthusiastic support). For all intents and purposes, this is wonderful news: Duras supports *L'Opoponax*, warmly, enthusiastically—it is, after all, a marvelous book. But. . . that "jusqu'ici" (as of now) burrows its way into the reader's mind. Up to now, as of this moment, you have my support. . . the twinge of conditionality disturbs. What could happen, what text could be read, what might Wittig do or not do that might modulate that conditional expression of support, transforming it into the past tense: "Jusque-là vous avez eu ma voix. . ." (Until then, you had my support). "Avant, vous avez eu ma voix. . ." (Before, you had my support). Duras writes to Wittig, and Wittig has a Sarrautian response, perhaps—a tropismic reaction to the variability of this *voix*, or voice, to the underlying threat of falling out of her grace. Sarraute will trump Duras, in the end, when it comes to what kind of writer Wittig will be. The wavering uncertainty of the author of *Tu ne t'aimes pas* (*You Don't Love Yourself*) will take primacy over the extravagant *moi* of the author of *L'Amant* (*The Lover*).

ANNE F. GARRÉTA

# No Biography for Dead Women

1. Monique Wittig is rumored to have said: *no biography*. The statement is here reported in substance, and not as a quotation, for we have no way, in the absence of a biography which would have referenced and cross-examined available sources, to verify its precise wording and context of utterance. It remains hearsay. And to whom was it addressed? On what occasion or occasions? Prompted by what question, what event?
2. We have multiple attestations of Wittig reading and quoting Émile Benveniste, the man heralded by Roland Barthes as the *linguiste de l'énonciation par excellence* (preeminent linguist of enunciation).[1] Wittig knew that no *énoncé* or statement (such as "no biography") can hold meaning in a void, but can only be interpreted in context, be it that of its utterance or that of its reception, should such reception be disjoined (by time, space, translation. . .) from its utterance.
3. *No biography*. Was it a fear Wittig expressed? Was it a prohibition as absolute as a biblical commandment? Could it have been a blanket condemnation of the genre of biography itself? Or a mere reaction of disgust occasioned by some sorry example of it? Could it have been the product of unease at the sight of the shape her

1. See Yannick Chevalier, "Wittig et Benveniste," in *Le Chantier littéraire* (Lyon: Presses universitaires de Lyon; Donnemarie-Dontilly: Éditions iXe, 2010), 191–200 and Roland Barthes, "Pour Émile Benveniste," in *Langue, discours, société* (Paris: Éditions du Seuil, 1975), collected in Barthes, *Œuvres complètes*, tome IV, 514. Benveniste's two volumes of *Problèmes de linguistique générale* were published by Gallimard in 1966 and 1974. The first volume contains two key chapters for Wittig's practice: on the nature of pronouns (chapter 20, first published in 1956), and on the subject in language (chapter 21, originally published in 1958).

**YFS 142,** *Lesbian Materialism: The Life and Work of Monique Wittig,* ed. Cadieu and Kim, © 2023 by Yale University.

own trajectory was taking, or the turns that her will to a radical life had experienced? Could it have been a test of her audience's blind faith? Or more paradoxically, a test of their capacity to see, through an ostensible injunction, her desire for public recognition?

4. We are left facing an aporia: we would need a biography to understand Wittig's position on the question of writing and life. But *no biography* seems to preclude the establishment of the context which would allow us to elucidate what Wittig meant and intended by it. *No biography* is a self-cancelling utterance, a critical and hermeneutical catch-22.
5. When, again, would Wittig have said *no biography*? In what decade of the last century did she come to the position entailed, prima facie, by the propositional content of this utterance? For it will not resonate identically if proffered in the heyday of structuralism (the French '60s and the proliferation of *procès sans sujet* or process without subject),[2] in the groundswell of '70s feminist struggles (when the personal became the political), or in the '80s as subject, self or ego return, first on the sly, then with a vengeance, onto the literary scene from which Wittig herself seems to be fading.
6. We could articulate our inquiry more closely with Wittig's bibliochronology, with the rhythm that writing and publishing lends a life. Would she have enjoined against biography before or after *Virgile, non* (*Across the Acheron*), the text in which the strategic play with pronouns that undergirds most of her work is bisected for the first time by the appearance of the proper name 'Wittig' within the text? Would she have pronounced this *no biography* verdict even later, during her long literary *traversée du désert*, in exile, and in doubt about her place on the French literary landscape and in the official historiography of the 1970s struggles within the field of sexual politics?
7. What is the point of a writer's biography? Of any biography? Why write one? Why read one? Classically, biographies hold out a promise: they will tell how someone became a warrior, a mathemati-

2. For the most compact articulation of this Althusserian idea, see: "History is a process without a Subject or a Goal where the given circumstances in which 'men' act as subjects under the determination of social *relations* are the product of class struggles. History therefore does not have a Subject, in the philosophical sense of the term, but a *motor*: that very class struggle," "Remark on the Category: 'Process without a Subject or Goal(s)'" collected in Louis Althusser, *Essays in Self-Criticism* (London: New Left Books, 1976), 99, and reprinted as Chapter 11 of *On Ideology* (New York: Verso, 2008).

cian, a tyrant, a ruler, a writer, a killer, a dancer. . . Biographies belong to the useful genres. They purport to elucidate for the aspiring citizen, artist, scientist, arsonist, spectator, autocrat, what it took, at a given moment in history, to become what they aspired to become, the virtues, the skills, the circumstances required to uphold the vocation, and the obstacles along the road. Alternatively, they warn readers, propounding cautionary tales of evil ascendant and of the intricacies of plots against common humanity.

8. Biography is the most exemplary of narrative genres; readers are supposed to learn from them. The subjects worthy of a biography hold public relevance if not public office, and their existence calls for imitation, or thwarting. Biography is indeed the most rhetorical of genres. The Althusserian process without subject or end is the exact negative of the classical ideal of emplotment, since for readers to learn from stories, as Aristotle long ago ruled, a distinct logic and necessity must undergird the events recounted: the plotting of the tale highlights the concerted, purposeful nature of the life led. Alice Kaplan reminds us of exactly these features: "Biography is the least experimental literary form—biography as we know it. Its structure is almost always chronological, from birth to death, lighting on the significant events."[3]
9. This Aristotelian poetics of writing, this rhetorical drive of narrative is exactly what modern (and most determinately modernist) writing has striven to escape. And it is in this vein that Wittig, quoting from Barthes's essay, "Littérature et discontinu" ("Literature and discontinuity") reads Jean-Luc Godard in a 1966 article.[4] Godard's 'lacunary films,' she says, "[turn] discontinuity into a way of working and this way of working upsets what I shall call, for want of a better phrase, those articulate or rhetorical systems we are accustomed to, even in modern films." We

3. See Kaplan, "A Biography for Monique Wittig" in this volume.

4. Wittig, "Lacunary Films," *The New Statesman*, July 15, 1966. Recently translated into French by Theo Mantion and republished in *Libération*, September 28, 2022 under the title "Éloge de la discontinuité. Jean-Luc Godard par Monique Wittig." Barthes, "Littérature et discontinu" first appeared in *Critique* no. 185, October 1962. The article was collected in Barthes, *Essais critiques* (Paris: Éditions du Seuil, 1964) and can be found in the *Œuvres complètes*, tome 2, 528. *Critique*, a key locus for the first deployment of the ideas we are parsing in the present contribution, was the journal published by Éditions de Minuit, the publisher where, well before coming out with her first novel, Wittig had found work as a copy editor. It is highly likely she had access, in this professional connection, to all the *pièces du procès* (trial documents) of the author.

can read Barthes and Wittig in perfect parallel here: the theoretical and aesthetic options are identical, and their points of contact with their objects of analysis (Godard's *Le Mépris* [*Contempt*], or Michel Butor's *Mobile* [*Mobile*]) are the same: privileging the detail over the overarching plot, neutralizing hierarchies, breaking down the principles of unity and homogeneity that hold narrative, book, and movie under the thumb of a subject (an identifiable focus of action and meaning). Wittig's "Lacunary Films" reads like a miniature of Barthes's "Littérature et discontinu."

10. None of this should surprise us. The influence of Barthes reverberated widely across the many circles of the Parisian intelligentsia, be it through the seminars he held at the École Pratique des Hautes Etudes or through his publications in major journals, such as *Critique*, *Tel Quel*, or, in a more academic vein, *Communications*. It has also been reported, in oral histories and published recollections of key actors of the French feminist movement, that Wittig attended Barthes's seminar around the year 1968.[5] It would have been the seminar,[6] spread over two years, that Barthes devoted to a structural analysis of the Balzac short story *Sarrasine* and would turn into his 1970 book *S/Z*.
11. The sessions of the seminar held on February 8th and February 29th of 1968 laid the groundwork for what would become the key polemical argument of Barthes's famous article, "The Death of the Author."[7]
12. Again, we would need a biography to corroborate the fact and the extent of Wittig's attendance at the seminar, to gather the traces it left in her archive, and its place in her intellectual trajectory.
13. But we can already safely say that Wittig became a writer in a moment and a milieu (the Parisian 1960s) in thrall to a particular idea, a particular speech act, a tenet or mantra enunciating, in

5. See for example Josiane Chanel, "Janvier 1968, j'ai présenté Monique Wittig à Antoinette Fouque," *Génération MLF* (Paris: Éditions des Femmes, 2008), 29. There is no mention of Wittig in the list of participants acknowledged by the editors of this seminar, nor in the index of the *Œuvres complètes*.

6. Barthes, *Sarrasine de Balzac. Séminaires à l'École pratique des hautes études (1967–1968 et 1968–1969)*, ed. Éric Marty (Paris: Éditions du Seuil, 2016).

7. First published in English as "The Death of the Author" in the avant-garde magazine *Aspen* no. 5–6, *The Minimalism issue*, Fall/Winter 1967. See a description of this volume on the Ubu web site: http://www.ubu.com/aspen/aspen5and6/index.html and collected in Barthes, *Image/Music/Text*, trans. Stephen Heath (New York: Hill and Wang, 1977), 142–8. The French version appeared in *Manteia*, no. 5, in 1968 and can be found in *Œuvres complètes*, tome III.

various forms and guises, the Death of the Author (and that of his siblings, Man and Subject), in a belated echo of the Nietzschean proclamation of the death of He Who Shall Not Be Named. This is well documented, has been the object of an endless stream of exegesis. Still, the speech act itself (or the family of speech acts) remains enigmatic.

14. Death of G** and Author are perfectly synonymous: with the demise of the Creator goes that of the Creature, be it Man or Book. And since literary interpretation was built on the ruined foundations of sacred hermeneutics, transferring the presuppositions of consistency and figurability that used to undergird the word of G** to modern prose, Critique could not fail to dispose of the fate of that latter-day prophet, the writer of post-Romantic inspiration.

15. "The narrative is a subject-less predicative fabric, with a migrating, evanescent subject. What speaks is neither the author nor the character (it is therefore not the 'subject'), it is meaning [. . .] When I speak, I deny the existence of what I am saying, but I also deny the existence of the person who is saying it [. . .] Here we find ourselves facing a gap that for a long time has remained invisible to us: the being of language appears for itself only in the disappearance of the subject." Who speaks here? Blanchot, Barthes, or Foucault?[8]

16. Does it matter who, precisely, speaks here? To quote Beckett quoted by Foucault in his February 22, 1969 remarks at the Société française de philosophie: "Qu'importe qui parle, quelqu'un a dit qu'importe qui parle" (What does it matter who is speaking, someone has said what does it matter who speaks). Notice the contradiction here: the indifference is carefully referred to a source or origin, to a signature bearing authority. It is not anyone or *n'importe qui*, who could apodictically but paradoxically assert such a thing (or rather, its negation). Notice the aporia or loop at the origin of both the trace and its retraction.[9]

8. The three preceding quotes are excerpted from Barthes's *Sarrasine* seminar. Maurice Blanchot, "La Littérature et le droit à la mort," first published in *Critique* in 1948, collected in *La Part du feu* (Paris: Gallimard, 1949); reprised in *L'Écriture du désastre* (Paris: Gallimard, 1980); translated by Lydia Davis as "Literature and the Right to Death," in *The Work of Fire* (Stanford: Stanford University Press, 1995). Foucault, "La pensée du dehors," first published in *Critique* in 1966, and collected in Foucault, *Dits et Écrits*, vol. I (Paris: Gallimard, 1994).

9. Foucault, "Qu'est-ce qu'un auteur ?" *Bulletin de la Société française de philosophie*, 63e année, no. 3, July-September 1969, 73–104. (Société française de philosophie, 22 février 1969; débat avec M. de Gandillac, L. Goldmann, J. Lacan, J. d'Ormesson,

17. But what kind of speech act was it that Blanchot, Beckett, Barthes, Foucault were supposed to have performed? Was it: a description, an objurgation, a conjuring, a consummation devoutly to be wished, a vital records entry, a prayer, a self-fulfilling prophecy, an axiom, a hypothesis, an inference, a fantasy, a requiem, a *stabat mater. . .*?
18. And what could the conditions of felicity or infelicity of such a speech act, whatever its nature might be, have been and shall be in each potential (re)iteration, or performance of the mantra?
19. I will venture that the trope of the death of the author, or the equation of language, writing, with negation and dispersion of the subject, is among other things, a contrecoup, or aftershock of a tectonic subsidence in the grounding of signature, authority and subjectivity, a tectonic shift in the political economy of sex. Textually and metaphysically, in both Blanchot and Barthes, the moment of the death of the author is preceded by the annihilation of either (a) woman or arises from the (mis)recognition (materialized by the slash so famously cut in the title *S/Z*) of castration.
20. "For me to be able to say, 'This woman,' I must somehow take her flesh-and-blood reality away from her, cause her to be absent, annihilate her. The word gives me the being, but it gives it to me deprived of being."[10]
21. "In his story *Sarrasine,* Balzac, describing a castrato disguised as a woman, writes the following sentence: 'This was woman herself, with her sudden fears, her irrational whims, her instinctive worries, her impetuous boldness, her fussings, and her delicious sensibility.' Who is speaking thus? Is it the hero of the story bent on remaining ignorant of the castrato hidden beneath the woman? Is it Balzac the individual, furnished by his personal experience

---

J. Ullmo, J. Wahl.); collected in Foucault, *Dits et Écrits* tome I, text no. 69. Translated as "What is an Author?" in J. V. Harari, ed., *Textual Strategies* (Ithaca: Cornell University Press, 1979), 141–160. (This is the version of the conference given at SUNY-Buffalo in 1970) and reprinted in *The Foucault Reader*, ed. P. Rabinow (New York: Pantheon Books, 1984). The quotation is from Samuel Beckett, *Nouvelles et textes pour rien* (1958) (Paris: Éditions de Minuit, 2003), 129. On Beckett's particular take on the trope, see Joseph Long, "Samuel Beckett: le sujet en exil," in Alain Goulet, *Voix, Traces, Avènement: L'écriture et son sujet* (Caen: Presses universitaires de Caen, 1999), 157–165.

10. Blanchot, "Literature and the Right to Death," *The Work of Fire*, 323. For elucidation of the context and political stakes of this text see James Swenson, "Revolutionary Sentences," *Yale French Studies*, 1998, no. 93, *The Place of Maurice Blanchot*, 11– 29.

with a philosophy of Woman? Is it Balzac the author professing 'literary' ideas on femininity? Is it universal wisdom? Romantic psychology? We shall never know, for the good reason that writing is the destruction of every voice, of every point of origin. Writing is that neutral, composite, oblique space where our subject slips away, the negative where all identity is lost, starting with the very identity of the body writing."[11]

22. The post-WWII philosophical fiction of the death of the author is a slash(er) tale as well as a fantastic horror story of dead/undead. From his 1967–69 seminar, Barthes will derive not only *S/Z*, and "The Death of the Author," he will also excerpt, refine, and produce "Masculin, féminin, neutre" ("Masculine, Feminine, Neuter") written during the summer of 1967 for a volume of essays in honor of Claude Lévi-Strauss.[12]
23. At the exact moment Wittig signs her first publication, becomes an author, and gains admittance to the circle of high-modernist writers, the ground of authority subsides, signature dissipates as a mirage, writing disperses subject.
24. To the question, "how did you become a feminist?" Wittig replied in 1979: "I remember I made a conscious decision at age twelve: I would escape women's dependence; I would not have the life of a woman who serves a man and has no life of her own. I read the Civil Code, and there were articles in it which deprived married women of juridical capacity [. . .] and I have wondered ever since why women would marry [. . .]."[13]

11. Original citation in French may be found in Barthes, "La mort de l'auteur," *O.C.*, III, 40. This translation comes from "The Death of the Author," collected in *Image, Music, Text*, trans. S. Heath (London: Fontana, 1977), 142.

12. *Échanges et Communications. Mélanges offerts à Claude Lévi-Strauss* (Paris: Mouton, 1970). Text collected in *O.C.* tome V, 1027–1045. Éric Marty, the editor of the *Sarrasine* seminar and Barthes's collected works, will claim that "one of the deep interests of the seminar is that it perhaps constitutes *in vivo* the first theoretical and hermeneutical reflection by which the concepts of 'gender' and 'sex' are dissociated, anticipating by many years the discoveries of gender studies that appeared in the United States in the 1980s, as indicated by the title of the text 'Masculine, Feminine, Neutral' written in the course of the seminar, and which draws the first conclusions" (my translation).

13. Interview with Josy Thibaut published [abridged] in *Prochoix* no. 46 (December 2008), 63. The original quote in French reads: "Je me souviens que j'ai pris une décision consciente à l'âge de 12 ans: j'échapperai à la dépendance des femmes, je n'aurai pas une vie de femme qui sert un homme, qui n'a pas de vie à elle. J'ai pris connaissance des lois et il y avait des clauses sur la tutelle qui ne frappaient que les femmes mariées [. . .] et je me suis toujours demandé pourquoi les femmes se mariaient [. . .]."

25. And indeed, one wonders with the twelve-year-old Wittig what it took to turn women into wives, what kind of social pressures, incitements, and constraints, what system of overt, covert, imaginary and material, subtle and brutal incentives (negative and positive) had to be deployed to manufacture the consent to alienate so thoroughly one's life and will.
26. In French, *une femme est une femme* (a woman is a woman). What the apparent tautology conceals and contains is that, by default, in the language, a woman is a wife, or that womanhood and matrimony are ideally coextensive. Thus, Wittig's scandalous declaration—"les lesbiennes ne sont pas des femmes" (lesbians are not women)—has to be heard, in French, as a quasi-analytical truth and warrants a double translation: Lesbians are not wives and lesbians are not women. (Or more radically, lesbians are not women because lesbians are not wives. To be a lesbian is to annul the foundational, axiomatic tautology of heterosexuality as a political regime: that *une femme est une femme*).
27. *Une femme est une femme* (*A Woman is a Woman*) is also the title of a 1961 movie. During the production, the director (Jean-Luc Godard) did marry Anna Karina, the female lead, making of the woman his wife and fulfilling the program of the title.[14]
28. Wittig turned twelve in 1947, that is, two years after women were first able to exercise their newly-granted right to vote, and right around the time the Preamble to the Constitution of October 27, 1946 stated that "the law grants to women, in all domains, rights equal to those of man."[15] Still, this is, strangely, the precise moment at which Wittig claims to have discovered the particular, subordinate, status of women and decided she would not be one.
29. And indeed, Wittig was not mistaken in suspecting the exactness, truthfulness, or completeness of the claims to equality or indifference of the Constitutional proclamation. It would be twenty years before crucial articles of the Civil Code, which belied the lofty principles of 1946, would be modified. When Wittig first published *L'Opoponax* (*The Opoponax*) and was awarded the Prix

Translation mine. I chose to hear and translate Wittig's decision as a conditional mood rather than a future tense.

14. On Godard's *Une femme est une femme*, and the sexual politics of the New Wave, see Geneviève Sellier, *Masculine Singular: French New Wave Cinema*, trans. Kristin Ross (London: Duke University Press, 2008).

15. In French, the language states "la loi garantit à la femme, dans tous les domaines, des droits égaux à ceux de l'homme." Translation mine.

Médicis, married women in France still could not open a checking account without the authorization of their husband, nor could they freely pursue their profession, or dispose of their property and money. Matrimony and its default regime (the *communauté des biens* or shared ownership of assets) placed all decisions concerning the household—the administration of the property held in common, the responsibility for signing the household's income tax declaration, the establishment of the abode and residence of the family, the education of the children—into the hands of the husband, a husband onto whom, as if to claw back some of the powers granted to women in the course of successive reforms of the Code, the law of 1938 had deemed expedient to confer the title of *chef de famille* (head of family).[16]

30. The 1804 (Napoleon) Civil Code, amended again and again, was (and still is) the foundational text organizing personal rights, family law, property and contracts, and the legal framework, or principles of law (their conditions of application). It had initially, and famously, enshrined the juridical incapacity of women and organized their dependency, on top of their political nullity. The nationality of a woman derived from that of her husband (until 1927). She could not obtain a passport and travel (until 1937), could not work without her husband's authorization (until 1965). In 1881, married women were allowed to open savings accounts and deposit money, but again the husband's authorization was needed to cash out the funds. It is not until 1897 that (married) women could bear witness and sign *actes d'état-civil* (vital records) and *actes notariés* (deeds and other notarized transactions). They owed their husband obedience (until 1938).
31. The 1965 law accomplished something of great import. Not only did it, in the bemused words of one law professor, "reveal in a quite remarkable way, the modern tendencies to *hisser* (raise, lift up) the married woman to the level of her husband," it also

16. See Florence Rochefort, "Laïcisation des mœurs et équilibres de genre. Le débat sur la capacité civile de la femme mariée (1918–1938)," *Vingtième Siècle. Revue d'histoire* 87, no. 3, 2005, 129–141: "The law of 1938 does not however establish equality between the sexes within matrimony nor within the family. [. . .] Under pressure from Catholic groups, the husband obtains a right of veto upon his wife's exercise of a profession, and he is referred to as *"chef de famille"* [head of the family] for the first time ever in the *Code civil*. [. . .] This mention is of great import and can be read as a first step on the path to the Code de la famille [Family Law] project which will animate the gender ideology of the late '30s, of the Vichy Régime and of the post-war order. The notion of *chef de famille* will persist in the *Code civil* until 1970."

granted her the full power of signature. To quote the *Revue internationale de droit comparé* in 1966: "the married woman will be able to manage her checking account under her sole signature, and without needing to produce any specific justification."[17]

32. Be it checkbooks or be it books, a woman's signature did not hold the same authority in the public square as a man's. By the time Wittig published *L'Opoponax* in 1964, her first book, only four women had been awarded the distinction of a Goncourt prize in the space of sixty years. The first female recipient was Elsa Triolet in 1944, the same year women recovered their political capacity. Twenty years later, as Wittig publishes *Virgile, non* (*Across the Acheron*), the number had risen to eight. By the time Wittig died in 2003, only two more women's signatures had been added to the Goncourt roster. As of prize year 2022, thirteen women in all have received this recognition in the space of 120 years.
33. Does it truly not matter *qui parle* (who speaks)? Someone said it did not matter.
34. Barthes famously transferred the privilege of meaning-making from author to reader. Does it then matter who reads, *qui lit*? The Femina prize, the twin and rival of the Goncourt, has been awarded since 1904 by an all-female jury, and originally intended to supplement the Goncourt, to fix its most glaring oversights. The ladies of the Femina (as they are known) had only recognized seventeen women authors by the time Wittig came out with her first novel. The list of winners today counts thirty more, but it is notable that in the entire decade of the 1970s, both the Goncourt and Femina were awarded only once to a woman. It is even more remarkable that the Prix Médicis, founded in 1958 to bypass the resistance of literary institutions to the *nouveau roman*, and which consecrated *L'Opoponax* in 1964, did not do better in later years than the Femina with regard to the gender distribution of its awards. After the four women who were distinguished in the 1960s (Colette Audry, Wittig, Marie-Claire Blais, and Hélène Cixous), the Médicis jury (which at some point counted among its members both Barthes and Foucault) bestowed its awards to

17. André Colomer, "Le nouveau régime matrimonial légal en France [Loi n° 65–670 du 13 juillet 1965]," *Revue internationale de droit comparé*, Année 1966 (18–1), 61–78: "la femme pourra, d'après les principes généraux, gérer ce compte comme n'importe quel autre compte sous sa seule signature et sans avoir de justification particulière à produire" (translation mine).

an all-male cast from 1969 till 1988, and by the time of Wittig's death in 2003, had only honored, in its forty-five years of existence, eight women's signatures, a barely higher proportion than the Goncourt in the same time span.

35. Need we mention that it was not until 2018 that the Baccalauréat would inscribe the signature of a woman (Madame de Lafayette) on its reading list (Bac de Lettres)?
36. All this accounting and ascertaining of who has signature and authority in the civil and literary field is but the material basis for what becomes, in the transcendentalized and rarefied plane of high theory, the trope of the death of the author, or his assumption into an impersonal architectonic function. It is rather curious, to say the least, that the attempt against the figure of the author and the proclamation of its demise should have followed (rather than heralded or merely coincided with) the successive legal reconfigurations of women's rights and the consecutive levelling of male authority in the civil realm.
37. The claimed equality of all subjects, the indifference to the origin of speech acts, the neutrality or the neuter toward which Blanchot or Barthes gestured, did however veil a continued polarity. Blanchot's negative dialectics transferred the author's signature to absence, silencing in the process, again, a woman's voice. The murdered woman, object of speech, figuration of the Muse, never seemed in the Blanchotian account to be granted the resurrection promised to the subject from the empty, sonorous tomb of the Œuvre.
38. The attempted *attentat* (if it was that) against author and subject must have been thwarted or was never truly meant to be executed. Was it meant in jest? Was the description of this state of subsidence of the signature anything other than a delusion or the sacrifice of a pawn? Were the theorists of the French 1960s merely the unreliable narrators of a cheap crime novel, or metaphysical *polar* (detective fiction)?
39. In *Le Chantier littéraire*, the thesis Wittig defended in 1986 at the EHESS, she objects on strikingly materialist grounds to this erasure which she describes as a classic process of alienation and mystification of labor: "The focus put purely on the work, on the product (of a labor), has cleared the space and eliminated the writer from the writing. [. . .] [T]he literary work has evacuated the worker (the writer) just as speech (discourse) has been voided of its speaker by the linguists [. . .] [in an] irresistible assumption of writing which, from product of a labor or process of work has

become the only active agent, to the detriment of the real agent of that labor, the writer."[18]

40. And a mystification it might very well have been. By the 1980s, the author, undead, returned. This was the return of the subject, or at least of the *moi:* for who else could be paraded weekly on TV, if not the effigy or imago of the author? And by now, how many biographies of those thinkers who called for the voiding of signature, who toyed with "qu'importe qui parle" (what does it matter who speaks) have we been given to consume? The Barthesian fantasy of dispersion (in *biographèmes*), the Foucauldian fantasy of the nameless *philosophe masqué* (masked philosopher), the Beckettian dereliction of subjectivity—these have been fully documented and referenced, firmly anchored in historical time and literary space. Foucault's entire body of archives, officially deemed a *trésor national* (national heirloom) and thus barred from export, was purchased by the Bibliothèque Nationale de France in 2012 for close to four million euros.[19]
41. No biography ever strategically attacks the patriarchal principle of Authority. But the cult of the impersonal functions like a Trojan horse, depriving all signature, allegedly, of authority. But both the Impersonal and Authority functioned and keep functioning differentially. Literary history is all too happy to do without acknowledging women's signatures. Checks will bounce. Books will fall out of print. Archives will remain homeless, fragmented. Lives unrecounted and unaccounted for. There will be no clamor for biographies of dead women. No thesaurizing or national treasure.
42. Why should feminists and readers of Monique Wittig collaborate in this process of selective erasure? Shall we remember Wittig's deliberate decision: "I would escape women's dependence, I would not have the life of a woman who serves a man and has no life of her own."
43. Wittig deserves, post-death of the author, a Life of her own.

18. The original citation reads: "A force de s'en tenir à l'œuvre, au produit (d'un travail), on a fait place nette, on a éliminé l'écrivain de l'écriture. [. . .] le travail littéraire a évacué le travailleur (l'écrivain) tout comme la parole (le discours) a été vidée de son locuteur par les linguistes. [. . .] irrésistible assomption de l'écriture qui de produit d'un travail ou de procès de travail est devenue le seul agent actif au détriment de l'acteur réel du travail qu'est l'écrivain." *Le Chantier littéraire*, only published posthumously in 2010 at the Presses universitaires de Lyon in an edition prepared by B. Auclerc, Y. Chevalier, A. Lasserre and C. Planté, 41. Translation mine.

19. See https://www.livreshebdo.fr/article/les-archives-du-philosophe-michel-foucault-classees-tresor-national.

SUZETTE ROBICHON

# Monique Wittig's "Reading Worksites"

"'Literary worksite' is what I call the chaotic space where books are created . . ." Monique Wittig wrote in her final work, published seven years after her death in 2010. She went on: "So that's how writers appear to me, as creators of Trojan horses . . ."[1] These Trojan horses enter through the various "reading worksites" that are created once the books are published: bookshops, articles, readers, translations, talks, events. Wittig's books have had a rather peculiar reception: honored in 1964 with the Prix Médicis for her debut novel *The Opoponax*, she was eventually given the cold shoulder by literary institutions after the publication of *Les Guérillères* (1969), *The Lesbian Body* (1973), and *Across the Acheron* (1985). Especially in France, engagement with her work happened through other, less conventional channels, which has clearly sparked the robust interest she now commands.

Everything begins with coming across and falling in love with a text. To hold a book in one's hands, to touch it, turn the pages, run one's eyes over the words, that raw material for a writer—these actions that foster intimacy and arouse feeling and fervor for these texts. In this way, my "constant journey" with Wittig's work began. It is clear that others in my generation undertook this personal journey as well. Later came the desire to share it with other readers, to set off on publishing ventures and to make her work more widely known.

1. Wittig, *Le Chantier littéraire* (Lyon: Presses universitaires de Lyon; Donnemarie-Dontilly: Éditions iXe, 2010), 77. Quotation translated by Jeffrey Zuckerman.

**YFS 142,** *Lesbian Materialism: The Life and Work of Monique Wittig,* ed. Cadieu and Kim, 

## 1964 *L'OPOPONAX* (*THE OPOPONAX*)

While I was in *hypokhâgne* in Toulouse, I dreamed of being able to take in all literature. I was reading the books columns, and I discovered Monique Wittig through Marguerite Duras's article in the November 5, 1964 issue of *France Observateur* and Jacqueline Piatier's piece in the November 14th issue of *Le Monde* a few weeks later. I kept an eye on the prizes; only one went to a woman in 1964—Wittig for *The Opoponax*. Her book had pride of place at the bookshop by the university on rue des Lois and it was published by Éditions de Minuit which I knew for its political and literary stance. I'd read titles such as Vercors's *Silence of the Sea* (1946), Henri Alleg's *The Question* (1958), and Micheline Maurel's *An Ordinary Camp* (1957). The university programs at the time were centered more on Claudel than on Beckett or Sarraute. I bought *The Opoponax*.

I read, and as I sank into those pages, I returned to my own childhood, feeling anew the gravel on the playground, the chalk on the blackboard, and this love for a little schoolgirl. I knew that love well, and I was haunted by the final line, which would remain untranslated in Helen Weaver's English version: ". . . On dit : tant je l'aimais qu'en elle encore je vis." As I repeated that line in my head, I forgot that it was drawn from Maurice Scève, but what I could never lose was its meaning—"It is said: So much did I love her that still in her I live"—which amounted to a secret confession of deep-buried love.[2]

Haunted because this indefinite pronoun, "on," included me. In making "on" the subject of this first book, Wittig did strike at the core of what happens in childhood, but if, as a young adult, this "on" especially strikes me it's because it signposts being among the "still ungendered," with no identity, and with no community. It was a moment where saying "I" was difficult because the pronoun's antecedent was still seeking out its place, its space, and for the time being lived in a hazy landscape where literary points of reference were few and far between, where identification was difficult. The "on" means exactly that: the subconscious sense of an ill-defined collective, of a still-marginal subjectivity with no definite name, that *The Opoponax* led off the beaten track.

2. Wittig, *The Opoponax*, trans. Helen Weaver (Plainfield, VT: Daughters, 1976), 256.

## 1969 *LES GUÉRILLÈRES* (*LES GUÉRILLÈRES*)

A year after May '68, the title immediately spoke to me. I was involved in the Vietnam War protests, supporting the guerrilla movements in Latin America and elsewhere, so the neologism didn't raise any eyebrows. I hadn't read a single line and I'd already been won over. No feminist group had made a name for itself and so many of us were bewitched by the words that opened up other vistas: "The women [Elles] say . . ."[3] "THE WOMEN [ELLES] AFFIRM IN TRIUMPH THAT ALL ACTION IS OVERTHROW"[4] ". . . They [Elles] say that a new world is beginning . . ."[5]

And by this truly essential line: "They say, if I take over the world, let it be to dispossess myself of it immediately, let it be to forge new links between myself and the world."[6]

Two years later, this theme of the guerilla came to the fore in an anthem of the feminist movement rumored to be composed by Wittig.

*La Guerilla*
Words: Les Petites Marguerites
To the tune of "Chant des marais"
1971

| | |
|---|---|
| Nous on fait l'amour et puis la guérilla | We made love then guerilla warfare |
| L'amour entre nous c'est l'amour avec joie | Love among us is love with pleasure |
| Mais pour faire l'amour il n'y a pas d'endroit | But there's no place to make love |
| Partout y'a des hommes et partout on se bat | Everywhere there's men and everywhere we fight |
| On prendra les villes, on prendra les jardins | We'll take the towns, we'll take the gardens |
| On cueillera les fleurs avec nos petites mains | We'll gather flowers with our little hands |
| Et sur nos poitrines on aura du jasmin | And in our bosoms we'll place jasmine |
| Et on dansera en mangeant du raisin | And we'll dance while eating grapes |

3. Wittig, *Les Guérillères*, trans. David Le Vay (Boston: Beacon Press, 1985), 256.
4. Wittig, *Les Guérillères*, 5.
5. Wittig, *Les Guérillères*, 85.
6. Wittig, *Les Guérillères*, 107.

| | |
|---|---|
| On prendra les zoos, on ouvrira les cages | We'll take the zoos, we'll open the cages |
| Vivent les oiseaux et fini le ménage | Long live the birds and long gone the chores |
| On se balancera au cou des girafes | We'll swing from giraffes' necks |
| L'amour entre nous, aux hommes la guérilla | Love among us, and to men the guerilla |

Only later did I realize that Wittig had to have written *Les Guérillères* while, or right after, translating Herbert Marcuse's *One-Dimensional Man*.

In May 1970, a year after *Les Guérillères* was published, *L'Idiot international* ran the foundational text, "Combat for the Liberation of Woman" (and not "For a Women's Liberation Movement"; in changing the title, the editor removed the plural.)[7] The article was signed by Monique Wittig, her sister Gille Wittig, Marcia Rothenburg, and Margaret Stephenson. The latter was also present at the Arc de Triomphe in 1970, and, under the name of Namascar Shaktini, would become one of the premier specialists on Wittig in the United States.

On August 26, 1970, Wittig was one of the nine women who tried to lay a wreath at the Arc de Triomphe with the dedication: "There is someone more unknown than the unknown soldier—his wife." The media took this gesture as the birth of the Women's Liberation Movement in France.

## 1973 *LE CORPS LESBIEN (THE LESBIAN BODY)*

Before even the shock of the words was the shock of the title. Such a simple title was still a slap in the face of a literary and social landscape hidebound in full-fledged heterosexuality.

The title was frank, the first edition bore a splendid jacket with an all-caps reproduction of the lists on two pages inside. I bought it immediately, compulsively, and I dove in. The first lines heralded the end of a literature "which has no name as yet" . . .

> In this dark adored adorned gehenna say your farewells m/y very beautiful one m/y very strong one m/y very indomitable one m/y very

7. Shaktini, Namascar, "Introduction to 'For a Women's Liberation Movement'" in *On Monique Wittig: Theoretical, Political, and Literary Essays*, ed. Namascar Shaktini (Urbana: University of Illinois Press, 2005), 15.

> learned one m/y very ferocious one m/y very gentle one m/y best beloved to what they, the women, call affection tenderness or gracious abandon. There is not one who is unaware of what takes place here, which has no name as yet, let them seek it if they are determined to do so, let them indulge in a storm of fine rivalries, that which *I* so utterly disown, while you with siren voice entreat some woman with shining knees to come to your aid.[8]

I discovered that the "*I*" here was just as nonexistent. No characters, no narrative, just a text that grabbed the reader, sunk in its claws, and demanded multiple rereadings to reveal itself fully.

The writer who in 1964 had been hailed in numerous articles as the last best hope for the nouveau roman was now barely noticed by the press. Newspaper reviews were less frequent and more likely to focus on the lesbian theme than on the form, which sometimes remained misunderstood by this larger, feminist, and lesbian readership that her work was now attracting.

As for me, it was through rereading it over the years that I slowly came to understand her work. Namely, how her words managed to shock, and how her Trojan horse needed space and time to do its work. It took almost fifty years for her texts to breach so many layers of silence and become a source of inspiration and energy for younger readers today.

### 1976 *BROUILLON POUR UN DICTIONNAIRE DES AMANTES* (*LESBIAN PEOPLES: MATERIAL FOR A DICTIONARY*)

This volume, written by Wittig and Zeig, is a masterpiece of lesbian peoples rewriting the world. It gives words meaning again, draws dreamed-of landscapes anew. The reader is pulled from one page to the next, as if from one island to another on a wholly unpredictable voyage where only trees for idleness offer any respite.

This avalanche of definitions puts paid both to the that-goes-without-saying of the straight mind and to particular myths that were rife among feminists then. It's a marvel of humor, lucidity, and love. Wittig and Zeig opened the doors of creative thought for us, and many of us took flight from these pages to invent other contents. I'm reminded of various writing collectives, one of which produced a

8. Wittig, *The Lesbian Body*, trans. David Le Vay (Boston: Beacon Press, 1986), 15.

six-handed book, *Le Jukebox des Trobairitz* (The Jukebox of Female Troubadours) and came up with new entries for the *Lesbian Peoples: Material for a Dictionary*.[9]

### 1980 *THE STRAIGHT MIND AND OTHER ESSAYS* (*LA PENSÉE STRAIGHT*)

Wittig was now living in the United States and was still aligned with the group of materialist feminists who had founded the *Questions féministes* journal: Christine Delphy, Colette Guillaumin, Nicole-Claude Matthieu, and Monique Plaza. They were a group of friends, and a working group for intellectual exchange.

After "One Is Not Born a Woman" came "The Straight Mind" in issue 7 of *Questions féministes*—that text concluding with the (in)famous and debated lines: "It would be incorrect to say that lesbians associate, make love, live with women, for 'woman' has meaning only in heterosexual systems of thought and heterosexual economic systems. Lesbians are not women."[10]

At the time I was also part of the editorial committee for the *Masques* journal, which we'd started in May 1979 to unite politics, activism, and culture.[11] I was fascinated by the feminist groups, the songs, the laughter, the fits of rage, the pleasure that emerged. I went to protests, to rallies of every sort, but how could I find my rightful place as a lesbian? How and where could I talk about my daily experience if not in private and eventually in the weekly meetings of the group of lesbians that took turns with the Lyon group publishing a magazine, *Quand les femmes s'aiment* (When Women Love Each Other)? To be lesbian was also to say no to the patriarchal order, to refuse the place women, wives, mothers, and so on were said to belong . . . but, while saying no was easy, framing it as a yes, beyond any circumlocution, was hard.

When Wittig's *The Straight Mind* came out, my delight was evident in issue 6 of *Masques* in fall 1980. I wrote: "I am not a woman, I am lesbian . . . I fully agree with these excerpts, it's a relief, a delight that at long last a lesbian, what's more one who calls herself feminist, should say so plainly what so many of us had of course silently

9. Clara Pacotte, Esmé Planchon, and Helena de Laurens, *Le Jukebox des Trobairitz* (Paris: RAG Éditions, 2022).

10. Wittig, *The Straight Mind and Other Essays* (Boston: Beacon Press, 1992), 32.

11. *Masques*, 1979–1986. *http://www.revuemasques.fr/*

thought, that we are not women. How nice it would be to fight for 'the destruction of heterosexuality.' We're feminists in that sense . . ."

Yes, it was a relief, all of a sudden, I felt lighter, after "on" and after "elles," now "we" and "us" were the subjects being conjugated. Wittig's analysis opened a door, brought walls crashing down, cleared a path, and gave us meaning and legitimacy.

For many of us, ("us" being "us lesbians"), her consideration of heterosexuality as a political regime was a break with the past. This conclusion was a welcome surprise, giving legitimacy and visibility to lesbian groups, initiatives, and arguments. Legitimacy in being the "fugitives" of this heteronormative world. Pride in being outside the norm.

Wittig furnished us with the theoretical tools to allow us to see why it might be difficult for us to recognize ourselves in the word "woman." She made what had been opaque and implicit suddenly intelligible and perceptible. She lay bare the political force of words.

A theoretical and emotional upheaval ensued, which became and remains the subject of many studies. The '80s were pivotal years. Wittig was in the United States, and it was also as a translator that she would continue carrying out her work.

## WITTIG, TRANSLATOR-WRITER

Reading and translating were part of her literary worksite from the outset. Translating, certainly for financial reasons, but also, apparently, out of kinship with the source. In 1968 Herbert Marcuse's *L'homme unidimensionnel* (*One Dimensional Man*) came out from Minuit, her publisher. She was the translator and her name was on the cover, which was uncommon. How could one not wonder about the influence this translation work might have had on her when it was known that this book had fostered the 1968 student protests, and was sometimes seen as its theoretical avatar?[12]

Wittig was translating from English, and from other languages. In the early days of this burgeoning feminist movement, translating texts by other feminist groups felt necessary.

In 1972, *New Portuguese Letters* came out in Portugal: a volume written by three woman who, in this tract, denounced patriarchal society, the Salazar dictatorship, and colonialism. The book was

12. See the article in this volume by Sandrine Sanos, "Monique Wittig's *One-Dimensional Man*: Translation Work and Post-'68 Feminist Utopian Thought."

banned, and a trial played out. In Paris, the feminists rallied in support of the "Three Marias": Maria Isabel Borreno, Maria Teresa Horta, and Maria Velho da Costa. Monique Wittig was an active participant. Even though she didn't speak Portuguese, she was involved in the book's translation with Evelyne Le Garrec, a fellow Frenchwoman, and Vera Alves da Nóbrega, who was Brazilian. The translation came out from Éditions du Seuil's "Combats" imprint in 1974.

Shortly after, she translated Andra Medea and Kathleen Thomson's *Against Rape*, the first book in the United States to break the silence around this subject. Her name, however, did not appear in the French edition, *Contre le viol*.[13] The only evidence of her translation is to be found in documents from her literary agency.[14] This work of translating a text that unambiguously frames rape as a crime against women, analyzes patriarchal society, and contains valuable advice on defense, would give Wittig the arguments, should she need any, to underpin her theoretical analysis. How remarkable that archives alone alerted us to the fact of this translation.

In 1982, the translation of two of Djuna Barnes's books came out from Flammarion in French: *Ladies Almanack*, translated by Michèle Causse as *L'Almanach des Dames*; and *Spillway*, translated by Wittig as *La Passion*. We can retrace a portion of the correspondence around these translations through the translators' letters to Bernard Noël, then editor at Flammarion, which are held at the Bibliothèque littéraire Jacques Doucet (BLJD).[15] Getting to read the letters between these two writers who knew each other could reveal further details; one can only hope that they might one day be made available to researchers.

For Wittig, translating Barnes was an opportunity to clarify her perspective on writing, as she does in a preface that is essential to understanding her own literary endeavor:[16]

> Writing a text which has homosexuality among its themes is a gamble. It is taking the risk that at every turn the formal element which

13. Andra Medea and Kathleen Thomson, eds. *Contre le viol: un livre pour les femmes* (Paris: Pierre Horay, 1976).

14. Monique Wittig papers, Beinecke, GEN MSS 1359.

15. BLJD, fonds Bernard Noël. Paris, France.

16. Preface to Djuna Barnes, *La Passion* (Paris: Flammarion, 1982). This text was published in English under the title, "The Point of View: Universal or Particular" in *Feminist Issues* 1, no. 1 (1980). It was reprinted under the same title in Wittig, *The Straight Mind and Other Essays* (Boston: Beacon Press, 1992), and then in the French edition of that book under the title "Le Point de vue, universel ou particulier."

is the theme will overdetermine the meaning, monopolize the whole meaning, against the intention of the author who wants above all to create a literary work."[17]

Even if Djuna Barnes is read first and widely by lesbians, one should not reduce and limit her to the lesbian minority. This would not only be no favor to her, but also no favor to us. For it is within literature that the work of Barnes can better act both for her and for us.[18]

Djuna Barnes cancels out the genders by making them obsolete. I find it necessary to suppress them. That is the point of view of a lesbian.[19]

A text by a minority writer is effective only if it succeeds in making the minority point of view universal, only if it is an important literary text.[20]

This poet generally has a hard battle to wage, for, step by step, word by word, she must create her own context in a world which, as soon as she appears, bends every effort to make her disappear. The battle is hard because she must wage it on two fronts: on the formal level with the questions being debated at the moment in literary history, and on the conceptual level against the that-goes-without-saying of the straight mind.[21]

Researching Wittig the translator is a worksite worth setting up, especially since she also undertook translations of her own work. When Wittig returned to a text of hers to ferry it from one language to another, she often made changes both big and small. This can be seen, for example, in the French version of the Barnes preface in the French edition of *La Pensée straight*[22] (which was first published in English as *The Straight Mind* with Beacon Press in 1992). Such comparisons are a worthy object of future research.

## PIONEERING "READING WORKSITES"

How Wittig's works are perceived and received is both implicit in and enabled by this gamble: taking the risk that at every turn the theme might overtake the formal element. The preface to her translation of

17. Wittig, *The Straight Mind*, 62.
18. Wittig, *The Straight Mind*, 63.
19. Wittig, *The Straight Mind*, 61.
20. Wittig, *The Straight Mind*, 64.
21. Wittig, *The Straight Mind*, 65.
22. Wittig, *La Pensée straight* (Paris: Éditions Balland, 2001); 2nd ed. (Paris: Éditions Amsterdam, 2018).

*Spillway* sparked little debate upon publication because at that point the entirety of Wittig's work had fallen into obscurity. Breaking this silence seemed necessary to us—Michèle Causse, Sylvie Bompis, and myself. Wittig's spirit directly inspired *Vlasta* magazine, which we began in 1983 as a journal of Amazonian utopias and fictions. In the wake of our work with *Masques*, a journal of homosexualities, we started the magazine to circulate texts by lesbians. The title was symbolic: under Vlasta's guidance, an army of women in eighth-century Bohemia had, as Wittig described in *Les Guérillères*, created the first independent female state.[23] With the pen as our sword, our goal was put simply in the editorial note: "to write what exists and was never expressed . . ."

So we decided to devote a full issue to Wittig, to demonstrate our support for the totality of her literary and theoretical work and make it more widely known. Wittig trusted us and entrusted us with the publication in our magazine of the text *Paris-La-Politique* which was intended to make waves among those of whom she wrote: "all that's left is for me to see in those splendid traitors the *guérillères* I once extolled . . ."[24] And we would publish, for the first time in French, the essential text, "The Trojan Horse."

In 1985, along with the journal, we also staged the play *Le Voyage sans fin* (*The Constant Journey*) which had a one-month run at the Théâtre Renaud Barrault in Paris.

Readers glancing at the table of contents might be amazed that nearly all our contributors were American, and that not a single contribution was francophone. The explanation was simple: not until 1999 did Catherine Écarnot defend the first thesis in France on Wittig's work.

The collective undertaking to put out this magazine was intense and driven by a belief that it was essential to foreground Wittig again. The texts, translations, and layout were all done without remuneration; printing (ink and paper) was done at cost by our friends at the women's printer Voix Off. The audacity was palpable, as was the excitement.

1985 was also the year *Across the Acheron* was published in French and it ought to have been the year of Wittig's literary comeback. But there was little media coverage of this new book and her play. Clearly this has to be assessed in a context where the narration of *Across the*

23. Wittig, *Les Guérillères*, 114.

24. Wittig, *Paris-la-politique et autres histoires* (Paris: P.O.L, 1999), 49. Quotation translated by Jeffrey Zuckerman.

*Acheron* was at odds with prevailing literary output and her literary project was little-understood. This silence also held sway in feminist spaces and in their publications—one exception being Christine Delphy's excellent 1985 article that contrasted with her total opposition to Wittig in 1980.[25]

## WITTIG IN TRANSLATION

*The Opoponax*, winner of the Prix Médicis in 1964, was snapped up by major international publishers. In German, the book came out from Rowohlt, one of the biggest houses. It was translated by Elmar Tophoven, the renowned translator of Sarraute and Beckett. Later, in the same country, it would be another story: a love story between translator and text.

Gabrielle Meixner remembers fondly how she became Wittig's translator and publisher. On a trip to Lyon to see her partner at the time, she went into a bookstore:

> Front and center was a book titled *The Lesbian Body*, with Éditions de Minuit's plain design. I don't remember any other book. My eyes were riveted to that white cover with blue and purple letters and those three words that were a slap in the face. I was thrilled, it was like love at first sight, with the small difference that I didn't feel one bit insecure, the way I might when obsessed with someone. The words 'the lesbian body' summed up my desires and my existence, as if my whole being were encapsulated in those three words: that was me, that was everyone I loved. With none of the shame I'd previously felt when I bought a book with lesbian content, I brought the volume to the cash register. Marie-Françoise said: 'I'm paying, it's my gift to you.' We walked out of the bookstore carrying the book like a trophy. All my old fears were gone. And that, precisely, is the remarkable power of books.[26]

With her colleagues she established the Amazonen Verlag, which in 1977, published *The Lesbian Body*,[27] then, in 1980, *Les Guérillères* came out from Frauenoffensive,[28] and finally, in 1983, the translation

25. See also Christine Delphy, "La Passion selon Wittig," in *Nouvelles Questions Féministes* 11/12 (1985), 151–186.

26. Benoît Auclerc and Yannick Chevalier, eds., *Lire Monique Wittig aujourd'hui* (Lyon: Presses universitaires de Lyon, 2012), 150. Quotation translated by Jeffrey Zuckerman.

27. Wittig, *Aus deinen zehntausend Augen Sappho* (Berlin: Amazonen Frauenverlag, 1977).

28. Wittig, *Die Verschwörung der Balkis* (Berlin: Frauenoffensive, 1980).

of *Lesbian Peoples: Material for a Dictionary* from the American version that Wittig and Zeig had done. The cover of the two latter titles reproduced a painting by the artist Lena Vandrey, then a friend of Wittig and involved in the 1985 issue of *Vlasta*.

In Italy, *The Lesbian Body* was translated in 1976 by a writer, Elisabetta Rasy. It was unfortunate that the translator and the publisher, Edizioni delle donne, were connected to the Italian wave of differentialist feminism, which is evident in the translation. But the book was widely read.

Years went by. Two decades on, another, younger Italian woman, Ana Cuenca, discovered *Les Guérillères* in France, brought it back to Italy, and, with a collective of aficionadas of this text, carried out a form of piracy by translating and publishing it in 1996 without acquiring the rights. In 2019 this version was republished—this time legally—by the same feminist and lesbian association.[29]

Additionally, an anonymous lesbian collective undertook a "rogue" translation of *The Straight Mind,* meant to be more faithful to the original, and Wittig's intentions, than the one put out by the publisher that had officially acquired the rights.[30] Books certainly can lead unconventional lives! What is clear is that it was thanks to the work of devoted Wittig scholars (including Eva Feole, Sara Garbagnoli, and Rachele Borghi) that new publications saw the light of day and that regular gatherings took place.

In 2020, a collective enabled the Italian translation of *Lesbian Peoples: Material for a Dictionary*.[31] Deborah Ardilli, who ran a notable materialist feminist blog, undertook a new, more faithful translation of *The Lesbian Body* slated for publication in 2023.[32] An endeavor to translate *Le Chantier littéraire* into Italian is also underway.

In Spain, the first translation of *Les Guérillères* was published in 1971.[33] But several passages were "overlooked." Whether it was of-

29. Wittig, *Le Guerrigliere*, trans. A. Cuenca (Bologna: Lesbacce Incolte, 1996); republished 2019.

30. Wittig, *Il pensiero straight e altri saggi*, trans. Collettivo della Lacuna, s.l. 2019. Available online at https://pensierostraighthome.files.wordpress.com/2019/04/il-pensiero-straight-e-altri-saggi.pdf. *Il pensiero eterosessuale*, trans. F. Zappino (Verona: Ombre Corte, 2019).

31. Wittig, *Appunti per un dizionario delle amanti*, trans. Onna Pas (Milan: Meltemi, 2020).

32. Wittig, *Il corpo lesbico*, trans. Deborah Ardilli (Rome: VandAedizioni, 2023).

33. Wittig, *Las Guerrilleras*, trans. Josep Elias and Juan Viñoly (Barcelona: Seix Barral, 1971 [1969]).

ficial censure or self-censure remains unclear. In Argentina, a new and complete translation of *Les Guérillères* was published in 2019 by Hekht Libros, and *The Lesbian Body* came out in 2021, both translated by Natalia Ortiz Maldonado.[34] A new generation of feminist and lesbian South American researchers, artists, and activists are discovering Wittig. *Lesbian Peoples: Material for a Dictionary* was translated into Spanish in 1981 by Christina Peri Rossi, the famous Uruguayan poet exiled in 1972 to Spain. She worked from the French version, not the American one, as the German translators had done.

The English-language version is no mere translation; it was done by Wittig and Zeig who added and deleted various entries and modified particular definitions. For example, the entry for "Lesbian" reads, in French:

> Lesbienne : celle qui vit dans un peuple d'amantes, celle dont l'intérêt est dirigé plus que toute autre chose vers ses amantes, celle qui a un désir violent pour ses amantes, celle qui « ne vit pas dans le désert », qui n'est pas perdue.

And in English:

> Lesbian: before the night of the vanishing powder, lesbian meant she who was interested by 'only' half of the population and had a violent desire for that half. A lesbian is a companion lover, or a companion lover is a lesbian. The lesbian people had been called such after Lesbos, the most beloved center of their culture. The word is still used in the Glorious Age, despite its geographical meaning.

## HOW SHOULD WITTIG BE TRANSLATED? WHAT SHOULD BE DONE WITH THE PRONOUNS?

At a 2013 event in Berlin honoring Wittig, an aging Erika Tophoven recalled the discussions with her husband who had translated *The Opoponax*: what was the best way to translate the "on" which would become, in German, "man"? There was no good solution.

Not to mention the "elles" of *Les Guérillères*. How could this universalization of "elles" be conveyed if, in the target language, the third-person plural made no difference between masculine and feminine? This was the case for such languages as German and English; as such, in German, an afterword was written to explain the author's

34. Wittig, *El Cuerpo Lesbiano*, trans. Natalia Ortiz Maldonado (Buenos Aires: Hekht_libros, 2021).

perspective, and, in the text proper, "Die Frauen" ("The women") sometimes appeared. Other questions of different sorts arose. How should "mon guide Manastabal" in *Across the Acheron* be translated? "Mein Führer Manastabal" was unthinkable; another solution had to be found.

Several translations will need to be revised or redone from scratch because they were originally done without the translators' full knowledge of Wittig's literary project, a project she develops in *Le Chantier littéraire*, published in French after her death. Translations of this volume are essential. One into English by Annabel Kim and Lynne Huffer is forthcoming from Verso. As mentioned above, an Italian translation, too, is in the works.

These translations serve as the basis of essential "reading worksites" which have slowly enabled Wittig's œuvre to circulate in other languages, making it possible for her to return, haunt, and inspire a whole new generation. Her work is circulating in Russia and soon will in Slovenia. A map of these translations would reveal where Wittigian thought circulates.

## *THE CONSTANT JOURNEY* IN FRANCE

In 1992, Monique Wittig published a collection of texts with Beacon Press under the title *The Straight Mind and Other Essays*. In France, Colette Guillaumin furnished a commendable overview of it.[35] Minuit refused to bring out a translation of this work and so Wittig had to find a different publisher. That turned out to be Éditions Balland, in its "Modernes" imprint, which was run by Guillaume Dustan, and which released the collection in 2001 under the title *La Pensée straight*. Wittig was deeply involved in this edition, and she herself reworked the title essay for its French-language publication. It was more than just a translation of the English. The book's success was undeniable, and Éditions Amsterdam, which now publishes the book, regularly orders new print runs.

Didier Eribon organized a colloquium on Gay and Lesbian Studies at the Centre Pompidou from June 23 to 27, 1997, and Wittig gave her talk "About the Social Contract" there.[36] In 1999, Éditions P.O.L pub-

35. Colette Guillaumin, "Monique Wittig, The Straight Mind and other essays" in *Mots / Les langages du politique*, no. 49 (December 1996), 127–130.

36. Wittig, "A propos du contrat social" in *Les Études gays et lesbiennes*, ed. Didier Eribon (Paris: Éditions Centre Pompidou, 1998), 57–64.

lished *Paris-la-politique et autres histoires*, collecting writings that had appeared in various outlets.

The Wittig resurgence was also rooted in the growing debates around queer thought, in the wake of the publication of Judith Butler's *Gender Trouble* (1990). With Marie-Hélène Bourcier's collaboration, *The Straight Mind* was prepared for publication in French and the two of us organized the first French conference on Wittig in June 2001.

This singular colloquium on Wittig's work, with her present, was done on a shoestring budget. Fortunately, Columbia University in Paris offered its space free of charge. The conference proceedings were published in 2002 under the title *Parce que les lesbiennes ne sont pas des femmes. . .* (Because Lesbians Aren't Women), allowing readers to engage with the talks given by Teresa de Lauretis, Simonetta Spinelli, Catherine Écarnot, Namascar Shaktini, Marie-Hélène Bourcier, Beatriz Preciado, Françoise Armengaud, Diane Crowder, Louise Turcotte, and Dominique Bourque.[37] Wittig herself read a still-unpublished portion of *Le Chantier littéraire* onstage.

The 2009 conference in Lyon organized by Yannick Chevalier and Benoît Auclerc revealed a growing interest in academic contexts, made clear by the conference proceedings titled *Lire Monique Wittig aujourd'hui*.[38] This event forged essential future connections that would result in the posthumous publication of *Le Chantier littéraire*. Little by little and thanks to these various initiatives, Wittig was reintegrated into the academic and activist realm.

*The Straight Mind* is widely read, studied, and cited, but Wittig's literary work remains less well-known. It feels necessary to change that. In 2013, declaring that words have to be "reactivated," we called for readings on January 3, 2013 in various countries and cities in every language. In France, in 2014, the Association of Friends of Wittig was created for the simple purpose of circulating her work. It is essential for the poetry of her language to be heard, for her words to be made flesh. And these networks, these circles kept on expanding with the numerous public readings we organized.

And so, in 2014, at the Maison de la Poésie in Paris, on the fiftieth anniversary of the Prix Médicis being given to *The Opoponax*, we

37. Marie-Hélène Bourcier and Suzette Robichon, eds., *Parce que les lesbiennes ne sont pas des femmes* (Paris: Éditions gaies et lesbiennes, 2002).

38. Auclerc and Chevalier, eds., *Lire Monique Wittig aujourd'hui*.

organized a reading with other writers who had won the Médicis. In 2019, with two evening readings for the fiftieth anniversary of *Les Guérillères*'s publication, we made it possible for a younger generation to understand what a true literary work was. It was touching and striking to behold the shock of Wittig's words in the room, laying bare a text that had been little or poorly known—if at all—for so many. The Trojan horse had entered and done its job. Making these texts palpable and heard gave them heft, furthered this spirit of *Les Guérillères* or of *The Constant Journey*; for a few hours, a community had been created. This traffic of texts, these transmissions to other listeners, makes it possible to forge further connections, to breathe life into what she inspired.

## "ALL ACTION IS OVERTHROW"

In April 2021, during the Paris Dyke March, big black letters drawn on cardboard placards echoed *Les Guérillères*: "They say that they will shake the world like thunder and lightning."[39] Other handwritten slogans announced different versions of "The women [elles] say. . ."[40] These Wittig texts repurposed in public spaces, like "Wittig m'a sauvée" (Wittig saved me) as a *cri du cœur* spray-painted in big black letters on a French city wall in 2019, evince the vitality and immediacy of Wittig's work. They speak to how Wittig's œuvre is received individually, and how the resulting readings only multiply. The woman writing on a wall and the women drawing inspiration from her œuvre to create art—choreography, fine arts, and music—are all part of the same movement, the same sentiment: of being inhabited, carried by Wittig's spirit and rhythm, by the gaze she holds and the revolution in language she has brought about.

To answer countless questions and broaden the field of research, the website for Wittigian studies was launched; it also houses the Association of Friends of Wittig. Its aim is to be a clearinghouse of resources and tools, a town square, and meeting place. The pages were made by, and for, others; readings can diverge or converge.

Each day, new readers discover Wittig's work, and translations are undertaken: *Les Guérillères* is forthcoming in Slovenian in 2023, for

39. Wittig, *Les Guérillères*, 120.
40. Wittig, *Les Guérillères*, 120.

Sentence from *Les Guérillères* at the Dyke March, April 25, 2021, Paris. (Photo Suzette Robichon)

example—yet another ever-widening ripple. To enable and encourage these readings is our challenge.

The republication of *The Constant Journey* in 2022 and its live reading at the Maison de la Poésie spurred new readings and rereadings of the book.[41] This little-known play was discovered by nearly 600 people during the three nights of June 24, 25, and 26, 2022. The voices, the presence of four readers in the middle of a stage set also occupied by some of the audience members, gave the text an immediate political weight. Wittig the Guérillère was there with us in all those moments following the performance: the discussions, the conversations, the laughter and smiling, expressing the delight of simply being together, to share and savor these back-and-forths between Quixote and Sancho Panza for a little longer. These adventures, journeys, paths, translations, visualizations, and other creations are just

41. Wittig, *Le Voyage sans fin* (Paris: Gallimard, 2022).

Sentence from *Les Guérillères* at the Dyke March, April 25, 2021, Paris. (Photo Suzette Robichon)

as much research worksites that we offer and make possible through the site for Wittigian studies, especially in 2023, the fiftieth anniversary of *The Lesbian Body* and the twentieth of the death of the one who led us on this constant journey in our readings.

—Translated from the French by Jeffrey Zuckerman

Other signs at the Dyke March, April 25, 2021, Paris. (Instagram: Trashbutkawai)

**SANDE ZEIG**

# Wittig's Way: *The Constant Journey*

> PANZA: Quixote, you don't seem to see that they all think you're mad.
> QUIXOTE: Even if the whole world thinks that I am mad, and not only those half-wits in the village who have not seen anything, I will say the whole world is crazy and that only I am right.[1]

The play *Le Voyage sans fin* (*The Constant Journey*) is Monique Wittig's satire based on the satire written by Cervantes about Don Quixote. The play utilizes the well-known episodes from its predecessor but reframes the injustices as social injustices and brings them to light through a lesbian perspective, with humor and panache. Wittig's Quixote dedicates all her exploits in the name and honor of her beloved Dulcinea del Toboso with her faithful companion, Panza, at her side.

Quixote's voluminous readings about the exploits of Amazons like Orithyia and Antiope, Clete and Penthesilea, Myrina and Libya, Anna and Artemis, as well as Tarina and Tula, are what inspire her to defend the oppressed. Panza, infatuated with Quixote, follows her, leaving her husband and children behind. Quixote's mother and sister do not understand her at all. Only her aunt defends Quixote's temerity as she tries to explain that the books they have stacked to throw out the window and burn are not books but manuscripts that Quixote has written. And even if they burn them, Quixote will write them again.

*The Constant Journey* is one of the lesser well-known works of Wittig and since I was involved in its creation from the outset, I

1. Monique Wittig, *The Constant Journey: An Introduction and Prefatory Note*, trans. Barbara Godard (Toronto: Modern Drama, 1996), 42.

**YFS 142,** *Lesbian Materialism: The Life and Work of Monique Wittig,* ed. Cadieu and Kim, © 2023 by Yale University.

would like to reflect on the process of its composition and its relevance today. I see Wittig as this Quixote character, the one who exposes heterosexuality as a political regime; the one who denounces the exploitation of women through the marriage contract; the one who refuses the category of sex as natural; the one who denounces these abuses to which everyone else turns a blind eye. Motivated by idealism, Wittig's lesbians become the knights errant of their day. They are the only ones able to take up the lance of chivalry and fight the oppressors.

Take this scene as an example:

> QUIXOTE: I tell you that it is the might of this world who are hostile to knights errant. They persecute us because we are their only obstacles to absolute power.
>
> PANZA: But who are they? When did you meet them? At least give me a name.
>
> QUIXOTE: Well, I call them giants and you call them monsters. I tell you, Panza, we must put to death the arrogance in the giants.[2]

In Wittig's *The Constant Journey*, Quixote is the one who has the final word and, in the end, teaches Panza, who is not only her squire but her companion, the art of weapons for battle. Quixote's aunt tries to explain Quixote's actions in the scene titled "The Books That Combat Injustice":

> AUNT: It is ridiculous in the world to have pity for the oppressed, and the world dictates what a person must think. For the world, fighting injustices is called fighting against windmills or thrusting a sword into water.
>
> SISTER 2: But Quixote has physically fought against real windmills. She destroyed a battalion of real puppets.
>
> AUNT: Quixote has sworn to combat injustice wherever she encounters it. Now the reparation of injustice appears to the world much more embarrassing than the injustice itself. It makes the injustice visible which, for the world, is in perfectly bad taste. When the victims want to find mercy in the eyes of the world they must disown, denigrate and ridicule those who defend them. All of Quixote's misadventures stem from that and not from the nonexistence of what she is fighting.[3]

2. Wittig, *The Constant Journey*, 9.
3. Wittig, *The Constant Journey*, 14.

*The Constant Journey,* as it was aptly titled, for the journey is far from over, was one of my three main collaborations with Wittig. We worked together on a book, a play, and a movie, each one expanding our creative collaborations into different forms.

This play was not Wittig's first foray into theatre. She had previously written four plays starting in the 1960s, and several were produced on British and German radio. These include *L'Amant vert (*The Green Lover) in 1967, *La Recréation* (Recreation) (translated into English by Barbara Wright and produced by Martin Esslin in 1971), *Le Grand-cric-Jules,*[4] and *Dialogue pour les deux frères et la sœur* (Dialogue for two brothers and a sister) (radio plays produced by Werner Spies, Radio Stuttgart, 1972). *The Constant Journey* was, however, the first time Wittig had written a play for, and with, someone.

When we first met in 1974, I was a young actor studying mime in Paris, unwilling and unable to play traditional women's roles. I was determined to write and create my own. Wittig was already an internationally renowned writer. I could not imagine that Wittig would write a role specifically for me or that together we would explore what was fundamental to us both, eliminating the category of sex in literature and in theatrical gestures and, at the same time, trying to think beyond it.

Our first collaboration was *Brouillon pour un dictionnaire des amantes* (*Lesbian Peoples: Material for a Dictionary*), which we started writing in Oia, Santorini, Greece. We were building a lesbian utopia word by word, concept by concept. And we defined the word "dictionary" accordingly: "The arrangement of the dictionary allows us to eliminate those elements which have distorted our history during the Dark Ages, from the Iron Age to the Glorious Age. This arrangement could be called lacunary. The assemblage of words, and what dictated their choice, and the fiction of the fables also constitute lacunae and therefore are acting upon reality. The dictionary is, however, only a rough draft."[5]

*The Constant Journey* was our second collaboration and a perfect vehicle for us. It allowed us to explore Wittig's interest in the theatre

4. Editor's note—The title of *Le Grand-Cric Jules* does not have a translation provided, for, as Yannick Chevalier explained, the title derives from the proper name of one of the characters, Le Grand-Cric being his first name, and Jules the family name. Email correspondence with Sande Zeig, February 25, 2023.

5. Wittig and Sande Zeig, *Lesbian Peoples: Material for a Dictionary* (New York: Avon, 1979), 43.

and film and my interest in physical comedy, including mime, clowning, and acrobatics. Through the play, we could reimagine and recreate the characters of Quixote and Panza as lesbian characters, righting the wrongs so clearly visible in society, at least for Quixote.

Wittig explains the endeavor:

> All theatre works with the same themes, endlessly repeated. Sophocles rewrote Aeschylus; Shakespeare took his themes from Greek and Roman antiquity, as did Racine; Brecht, continuing this tradition, rewrote Shakespeare. Without necessarily referring to these illustrious examples, we can see the same sort of rewriting everywhere in contemporary French theatre. This way of working informs us about the imaginary and is relevant here only as justification for my venturing to recreate Quixote and Panza once again in the theatre. In this case, the project requires a double justification, since the actors playing these roles are women. This is not, as some have charged, simply a matter of transposition. If the spectators of *The Constant Journey* are convinced when the curtain falls by these new characters Quixote and Panza, it is because they have been present scene by scene at the remaking of heroes of a new sort. Indeed, the success of this play depends on active spectators, capable of recreating a complete fable from nothing. As always, it's a fable they know by heart because each episode is faithfully repeated from Cervantes, including the scene of the puppet show, and even including Quixote's rewriting since in the second part of Cervantes's novel Quixote knows about his own adventures and takes the place of the author.[6]

Wittig began writing the play in French in the Anchor Bay area of Northern California in 1979, and that is where I started improvising the action on stage. We lived in a cabin called High Tor on Highway 1 just across from the Pacific. At the time, Wittig was also working on the translation of Djuna Barnes's book, *Spillway and Other Stories* and writing a screenplay, which remains unproduced, called "Jeanne d'Arc or Rather Jeanne Rommée: Since in my Country Girls Take Their Mothers' Names." During this period, she was also writing her early political articles which were later published in *The Straight Mind and Other Essays.*

Wittig was enthusiastic about the process of improvisation in theatre. We read Viola Spolin's book *Improvisation for the Theater*, and I

6. Monique Wittig, "*The Constant Journey*: An Introduction and a Prefatory Note," trans. Barbara Godard, *Modern Drama* 39, no. 1 (1996), 156.

practiced her method that utilizes a series of exercises that encourage spontaneity and expressive body language. At the top of my reading list were also Augusto Boal's *Theatre of the Oppressed,* Erving Goffman's *Gender Advertisements,* Paolo Freire's *Pedagogy of the Oppressed,* Peter Brook's *The Empty Space,* Henri Bergson's *Laughter: An Essay on the Meaning of the Comic* and Antonin Artaud's *The Theater and Its Double.*

We were interested in Bertolt Brecht's idea of epic theatre and how it differs from dramatic theatre, as he notes that "dramatic theatre implicates the spectator in the stage situation and wears down the capacity for action. Epic theatre turns the spectator into an observer but arouses the capacity for action. . . . In dramatic theatre the spectator is involved in something. In epic theatre the spectator is made to face something."[7] In terms of dramaturgy, in epic theatre, each scene is for itself, in contrast to dramatic theatre, where one scene leads to another. And finally, instead of invoking feeling, epic theatre provokes reasoning. All of these ideas were also part of what we wanted to explore theatrically, as well as experimenting with Brecht's "alienation effect," where familiar content is presented in unfamiliar ways. Wittig introduced me, during this time, to Viktor Shklovsky's theory of *ostranenie* ("making strange," or defamiliarization),[8] which can be found in much of her work, including her humor, an aspect of her writing which should not be overlooked.

Utopia was always part of Wittig's work. She speaks about it in her essay, "Some Remarks on *Les Guérillères*":

> My goal was to make *elles* come as a shock for the reader, as a surprise; since *elles* holds the whole story, a sort of disorientation should follow from it. The reader enters the book and finds her/himself confronted with an *elles* that is not familiar, not ordinary and that is new and heroic. In any case it's what guided me along with the hope that this *elles* could situate the reader in a space beyond the categories of sex for the duration of the book. (This is perhaps the utopia.)[9]

7. Bertolt Brecht, *Brecht on Theatre,* trans. and ed. John Willet (New York: Hill and Wang, 1964), 3.

8. Viktor Shklovsky, "Art as Device," in *Theory of Prose,* trans. Benjamin Sher (Elmwood Park, IL: Dalkey Archive, 1990).

9. Wittig, "Some Remarks on Les Guérillères," *On Monique Wittig,* ed. Namascar Shaktini (Champaign: University of Illinois Press, 2005), 42.

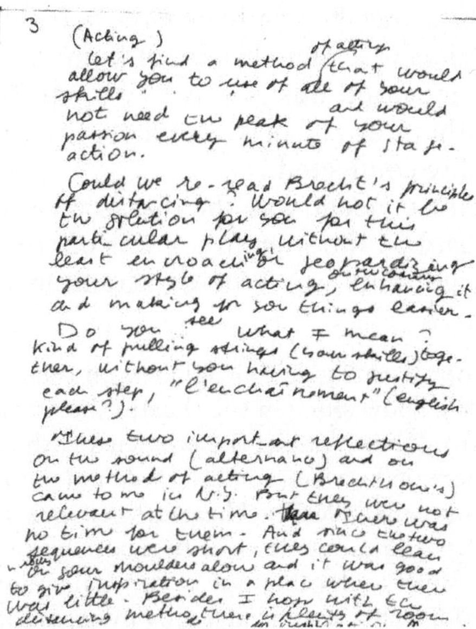
3

(Acting)

Let's find a method of acting that would allow you to use of all of your skills and would not need the peak of your passion every minute of stage action.

Could we re-read Brecht's principle of distancing? Would not it be the solution for you for this particular play, without the least encroaching or jeopardizing your style of acting, enhancing its dimension and making for you things easier. Do you see what I mean? Kind of pulling strings (your skills) together, without you having to justify each step, "l'enchaînement" (english please?).

These two important reflections on the sound (alternance) and on the method of acting (Brecht's own's) came to me in N.Y. But they were not relevant at the time. There was no time for them. And since the two sequences were short, they could lean on your shoulders alone and it was good to give inspiration in a place where there was little. Besides I hope with the distancing method, there is plenty of room [illegible]

Fig. 1. Monique Wittig's handwritten note to Sande Zeig

We created a utopia while writing *Lesbian Peoples: Material for a Dictionary*. We were writing it and we were living it. *The Constant Journey* follows Quixote and Panza's chivalric utopian desires.

Through my theatre and movement work, I was investigating gestures from the point of view of gender. Wittig had written in an unpublished paper, "Feminine gender is sex in language." I saw this as applicable to the body as well, in that feminine gestures are sex in movement. Our intention was to remove any remnant of feminine gestures, which are so predictable, and replace them with heroic gestures that were unexplored up until then. My work was to show that through gestures, lesbians were able to create new characters onstage.

We developed a working process where I would go to my studio to work on movement improvisations for Quixote and Panza, who were the only two actors on the stage, and Wittig would write the text. Sometimes the text would already be written, and then I would improvise a movement scene around it or related to it. The text has a great deal of humor which is highlighted with elements of physical comedy. After this type of rehearsal, I would reenact the improvisations for her, and she would give me valuable feedback. We had a shared aesthetic and a shared sense of humor, which underlies both the text and the action onstage. And we interwove the words and movement together into the play. Our daily lives and our creative lives were inextricably connected.

Another important concept was the disassociation of sound and action. What was heard on the soundtrack was not in sync with what was seen on the stage. This was Wittig's intention from the beginning. She wrote:

> The work carried out with Sande Zeig focused on the movement and displacements of the body, since in the theatre the physical presence of the actors is central. Now, one of the problems with theatre for me relates to the connection between actors' words and their movements. In what Peter Brook calls "Deadly Theatre," gestures and words are connected on the basis of convention, so that both become moribund, and in some way cancel each other out. . . my realization that, at the present time, a performance could exist only by separating words and gestures in some way, treating them independently as often happens in cinema.[10]

In addition, the entire soundtrack was whispered to eliminate traces of gender. We discovered that voices lost their "feminine" traits in a whisper. The whispered scenes created a soundscape above the spectators. Every character was located in a different area above the theatre space, including Quixote, Panza, and the secondary characters of Quixote's mother, aunt, and sisters, along with the Galley Slaves and Puppet Show Narrator, who never appear on stage. The whispering created a fantastic atmosphere and an auditory field which required the audience's full attention to the dialogue.

Our intention for staging was always guided by minimalist theatre. The idea was to use only essential set elements, props, and costumes. One of the most influential theatrical gestures I had experienced was in a performance of *Ubu Roi*, directed by Peter Brook. Jarry's play was set outdoors in freezing Livonia. Père Ubu tossed a handful of confetti above his head, and as it fell on him, he shivered, and we understood it was snowing. Wittig and I also envisioned this type of simplicity and a highly physical, acrobatic approach to using props. Both Quixote and Panza needed to be athletic actors with skills

10. Wittig, *"The Constant Journey,"* 156.

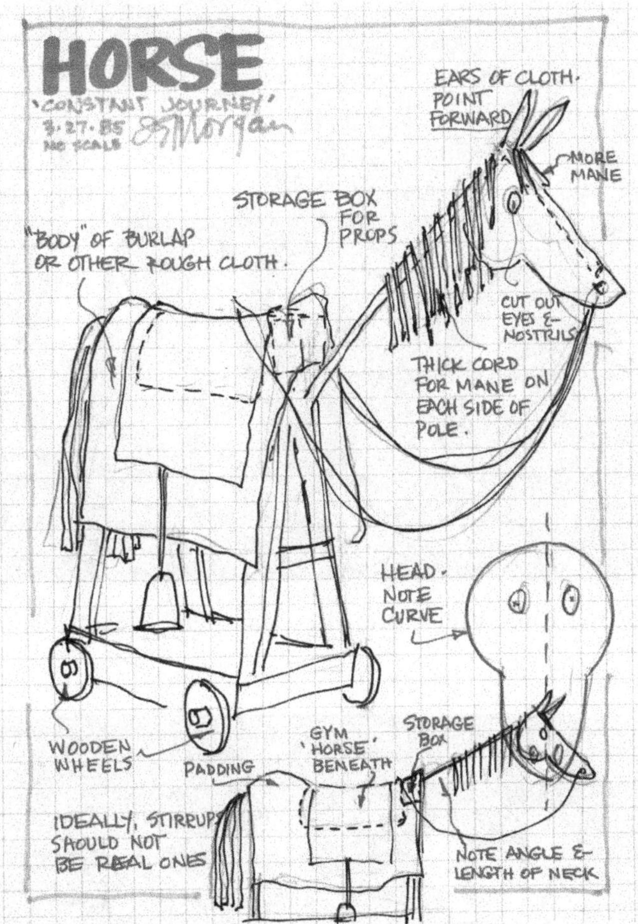


Fig. 2. Early design for Quixote's Rocinante

in mime, gymnastics, martial arts, and clowning. For the set, we created Quixote's horse, Rocinante, and Panza's donkey on wooden sawhorses with sticks for necks.

There was a table which served for the chin washing scene with candles reminiscent of Jean Cocteau's *Beauty and the Beast*, a silhouette of a windmill behind a scrim, Quixote's library with books stacked on the floor, a cage/throne for Quixote, and metal marionettes.

The costumes for the play developed over the years. From the outset, Quixote wore red American football shoulder pads and kneepads

Fig. 3. Zeig and Paule Kingleur in the scene "The Books" (Photo: Colette Geoffrey)

Fig. 4. Zeig in the scene "The Books Must All Be Burned" (Photo: Colette Geoffrey)

and high-top shoes. Panza wore a linen shirt, short pants with a sash and was barefoot. The props consisted of a lance, a wine jug, and some books. There were also magical props, including a book that burst into flames and a pitcher with endless water. Additional costumes and props were created by the painter Lena Vandrey for the Paris production, including Quixote's Rocinante, Panza's donkey, and the marionettes.

Judith Harding played the first Panza, I played the role of Quixote, and we performed scenes at Ubu Repertory Theatre in May 1983 and at the first Clown Theatre Festival in June 1983, both in New York City. Louise Smith was the second Panza. In January 1984, we held auditions for the role of Panza at the Perry Street Theatre and cast Pam Christian in the role. Then we workshopped the play and performed scenes at the Haybarn Theatre of Goddard College in Plainfield, Vermont, in March 1984 and performed scenes at the Women and Theatre Pre-Convention preceding the American Theatre Association's Annual Convention in August 1984.

During this time, we worked with John Townsen, Syn Guerin, and Jill Dolan, creating the style and characters. Phil Lee was the sound

Fig. 5. Zeig and Wittig, Goddard College opening performance, 1984

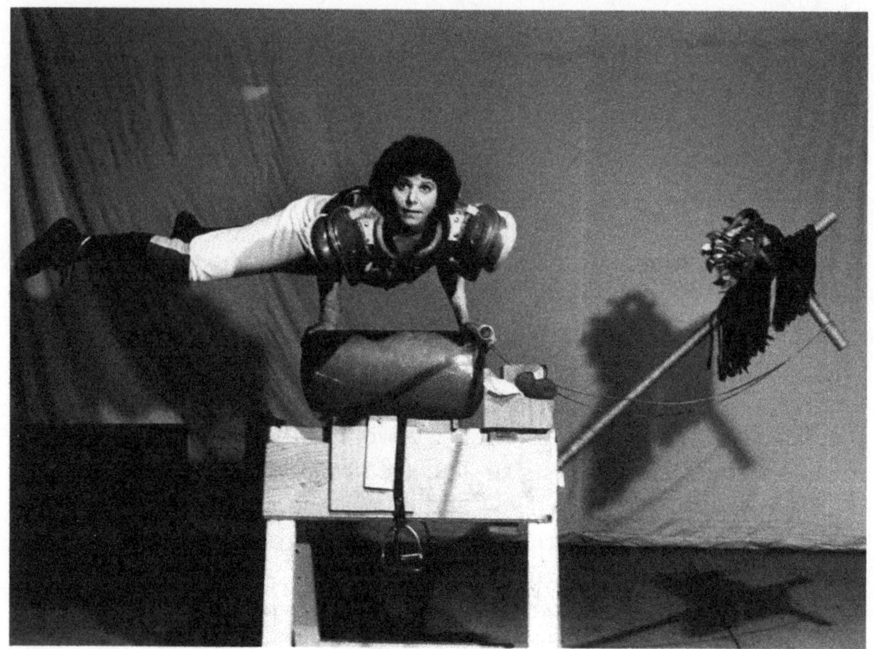

Fig. 6. Zeig as Quixote, Midwest tour

Fig. 7. Zeig as Quixote and Pam Christian as Panza in the scene "The Books Must All Be Burned," Midwest tour (Photo: unknown)

engineer on the audio track. Louise Turcotte was our constant companion and stage manager throughout all the stages of development and production.

In March-April 1984, we completed a Midwestern tour including Chicago, Wisconsin, and Minneapolis. In May-June 1985, we performed the play in Paris with the director Paule Kingleur and the Compagnie Renaud-Barrault at the Théâtre du Rond-Point, for a monthlong run, through the support of the Ministry of Culture, the Ministry of Women's Rights, and Simone Benmussa, who was the theatre director at the time, along with her partner, Erika Kralik.

The actress Delphine Seyrig came to see the play in Paris and arranged for it to be filmed by the Centre audiovisuel Simone de Beauvoir. A videotape of the production of *Le voyage sans fin* is in the New York Public Library (previously the Theatre on Film and Tape Collection at the Lincoln Center Library for the Performing Arts) and at the Centre audiovisuel Simone de Beauvoir. The video was directed and edited by Anne Faisandier with the audio track comprised of the following people and their roles: Lucienne Hamon (Aunt), Christiane Fey-Desbois (Mother), Lilo Politsky (Sister 1), Babelle Donnet (Sister 2), Valerie Bezançon (Narrator), Hélène Arié, Michèle Amiel, Cyrille Goudin, Sohailla Khodabandeh, and Delphine Edet (The Galley Slaves).

The original manuscript was composed of eighteen scenes. The final manuscript, which was performed at the Théâtre du Rond-Point and published in French by Vlasta, was edited by Suzette Robichon, and comprised fifteen scenes.[11] The scenes omitted were "The Fulling-Mills/Panza's Blanket Tossing," "The Wine Skins/Rocinante's Enchantment," and "Quixote Encaged II/Quixote Encaged with Honor."

I started translating the play into English in 1981 and finished the final version at Goddard College. The play was filmic in that it was composed of short sequences that opened and closed with a blackout. The order of the sound and action on stage are noted in the accompanying illustration (fig. 8).

One of my favorite scenes is "The Galley Slaves." With pointed humor, Wittig transposes the scene of the galley slaves who are

11. *Le voyage sans fin* was republished by Gallimard in the Collection "L'Imaginaire" in April 2022.

Sound: Music and voices. Works like the sound track of a film.

Image: A mime and a clown. Bright colors

Complete dissociation of sound and image. The play is presented as follows:

| SOUND (Sound Track) | IMAGE (Action on Stage) |
|---|---|
| 1. The Books Must All Be Burned | 1. Quixote Reading |
| 2. Approach to the Fortress | 2. Approach to the Fortress |
| 3. The Giants | 3. The Vigil |
| 4. Quixote's Books | 4. The Books |
| 5. The Books That Combat Injustice | 5. The Windmills |
| 6. The Windmills | 6. Panza's Meal |
| 7. The Forest | 7. Rocinante's Enchantment |
| 8. Silence | 8. The Chin Washing |
| 9. The Galley Slaves | 9. Panza's Blanket Tossing |
| 10. Silence | 10. Penance |
| 11. In Search of Dulcinea | 11. Mad of Love |
| 12. Back to the Village | 12. Back to the Village |
| 13. Quixote Encaged | 13. Encaged with Honor |
| 14. The Books | 14. Quixote's Armour |
| 15. Madness | 15. Presentation of Characters |

Fig. 8. *The Constant Journey*, notes for sound and image

assumed to be villains into righteous victims and the perceived madness of Quixote is, in fact, the madness of the injustice.

A number of writers who discuss *The Constant Journey* in books and articles on Wittig's work include Catherine Écarnot, Dominique Bourque, and Janelle Savona. One of the earliest articles about the play was published in *Trivia*:

> . . . How could Quixote played as a lesbian represent the secret heart of my experience? She did. I too am a voracious reader. I too take books for reality and emulate them to the shame of my family. I too appear absurd to others, if not always to myself. I too live with the sense that other, better socialized, "straighter" women whisper about me behind my back. I too have the feeling that I am perceived as a clown. I too discover in myself a desire to "win fame around the world by redressing wrongs with weapons." (And, like the foolish Panza, I would follow another such woman anywhere, "riding an ass.") Thus,

THE GALLEY SLAVES

| | |
|---|---|
| Quixote | Panza, did I not tell you that my assistance soon would be needed? Look at those poor unfortunates who walk bound in chains. |
| Panza | They're going to the galleys, criminals, prostitutes, maybe even murderers. |
| Quixote | Whatever their crime, they alone can judge them. And whoever dares to put them in chains, do not call them judges. In all honesty I cannot shut my eyes while passing by human creatures who obviously need my help. Let us approach and ask each prisoner the reason for her arrest. |
| Panza | If they had the strength, the courage and the intelligence of Gina de Pasamonte, they wouldn't be here. |
| Quixote | You, the one with such gentle manners. I assume some injustice has brought you here? Allow me to carry your ball and chain. |
| Prisoner 1 | Poverty is my only crime, my knighthood. After I spurned the advances of the master, he declared I was a prostitute and I was arrested. My name is Angela. |
| Quixote | Angela, the well named, angel of these poor unfortunates, you suffer great injustices because of your virtue. |
| Prisoner 1 | Knight, I wasn't sentenced for my virtue but for my firm stand. |
| Panza | May Gina de Pasamonte help you. |
| Quixote | And you, poor old woman, do tell us, is this where you belong? |

24

Fig. 9. "The Galley Slaves" scene manuscript page

> my attention was captured at the very beginning of *The Constant Journey* in a way it had never been captured before in a theatre.[12]

In the first published book on Wittig's work, Erika Ostrovsky commented on what motivates Wittig's journey: "A continual quest for renewal . . . has led her to abandon known territories, established traditions, past discoveries, and even domains successfully conquered, in order to push on to other explorations, and to further new ventures."[13]

12. Harriet Ellenberger, "The Dream Is the Bridge: In Search of Lesbian Theatre," *Trivia: A Journal of Ideas,* no. 5 (Fall 1984).

13. Erika Ostrovsky, *A Constant Journey: The Fiction of Monique Wittig* (Carbondale: Southern Illinois University Press, 1991), 167.

| | |
|---|---|
| Prisoner 2 | Poor without a doubt since I'm here. But old! I'm no older than your knighthood who carries a shield and a lance like a young fool. Attend to staying in your saddle and keep your pity for yourself. That's all I have to say. |
| Quixote | I have used the wrong words. Forgive me and tell me your story. There is not time for politeness. |
| Prisoner 4 | Leave her alone. She's furious because she confessed to several crimes. There's no greater shame for a prisoner. |
| Panza | May she be born again in the form of Gina de Pasamonte. |
| Quixote | And you, with the sad face and the brisk walk, is it not by some error that you find yourself here? |
| Prisoner 3 | I aborted an undesirable child, I was arrested as a murderer. |
| Quixote | Here is one of your murderers, Panza. Look at her face and her expression, what do you have to say? |
| Panza | Has she killed or not? |
| Prisoner 3 | Yes, I did, and I'd do it again. |
| Quixote | There is no murder, there is no crime so long as what we kill has no soul. And while an infant is unborn it cannot have a soul, otherwise we have to assume that a pregnant woman has two souls. And believe me, that is a theologically insurmountable problem. |
| Panza | I know nothing about souls. I don't feel mine until I stay too long without eating. |
| Quixote | Go in peace, my friend, and have courage until your freedom which is close at hand. |

25

Fig. 10. "The Galley Slaves" scene manuscript page

For those of us who knew Monique Wittig personally, those of us who know her through her work, or those of us who are yet to discover her, may we travel with her on this constant journey for which she paved the way.

| | |
|---|---|
| Panza | There's another who isn't Gina de Pasamonte if I can judge by her appearance. |
| Quixote | Don't be afraid, come closer. What have you done to deserve such punishment? |
| Prisoner 4 | I killed a man. His act was so palpable and odious that they didn't dare demand my head. |
| Quixote | By the burning fire, I like you. There would not be any more victims if every victim were like you. |
| Prisoner 4 | Indeed, they'd all be in irons. |
| Panza | Are you Gina de Pasamonte? |
| Quixote | Are you going to tell me who this Gina de Pasamonte is with whom you are driving me crazy? |
| Gina de Pasamonte | It is I and I can see that I'm better known by your squire than by yourself. |
| Panza | Heavens, it's her. |
| Gina de Pasamonte | Your pity is misplaced since you can't do anything for us. But I will tell you why I am here. When my rich family decided to marry me off, I went away and became a highway robber instead. |
| Quixote | I will not lecture you, you will be saved along with the others. |
| Gina de Pasamonte | Don't think that I am unworthy of your good care: I stole only from the rich and with their riches, like Molly Cutpurse, I tried to rectify the injustices inflicted upon the poor. |
| Quixote | Really? |

26

Fig. 11. "The Galley Slaves" scene manuscript page

| | |
|---|---|
| Gina de Pasamonte | Really. You can ask Vera de Mirador. She is here on her own accord, even after I exacted ransom from her family. And now she is helping me write my memoirs. |
| Quixote | I would be curious to read them. |

27

Fig. 12. "The Galley Slaves" scene manuscript page

# INTERLUDE III

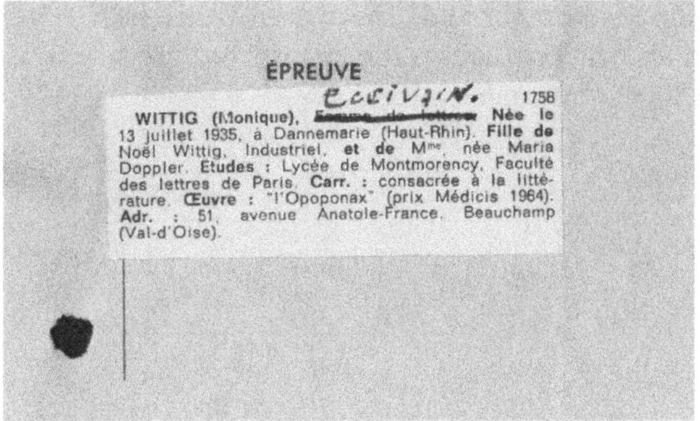

**ÉPREUVE**

1758

**WITTIG** (Monique), **Née** le 13 juillet 1935, à Dannemarie (Haut-Rhin). **Fille de** Noël Wittig, Industriel, **et de** M^me^, née Maria Doppler. **Études :** Lycée de Montmorency, Faculté des lettres de Paris. **Carr. :** consacrée à la littérature. **Œuvre :** "l'Opoponax" (prix Médicis 1964). **Adr. :** 51, avenue Anatole-France, Beauchamp (Val-d'Oise).

Proofs of the entry for Monique Wittig in *Who's Who in France* (Wittig Collection, Box 21, Beinecke Library, Yale University)

The double-meaning that "épreuve" has in French as being both proof (in this case, of a text) and trial (something to be surmounted, something taxing) can be seen here, in this brief biographical blurb. "Femme de lettres" (woman of letters) has been struck through in marker and replaced by "écrivain" (writer), the large period following the letter *n* calling attention to the way it serves as a full stop, cutting off any impulse to feminize the first and principal characterization of Monique Wittig here by adding an *e*, the mark of gender, of particularity. The heaviness of the writing, the thickness of the line, the lack of hesitation—these all bear witness to the trial, the *épreuve*, of gender being introduced into the privileged space of literature, which is where, through laboring on language, as Wittig knows

**YFS 142,** *Lesbian Materialism: The Life and Work of Monique Wittig,* ed. Cadieu and Kim, 

intimately, one might be able to shed the straitjacket of particularity and break free from the stranglehold that gender has outside literary space. Here, as in Wittig's novels, we have, in a few strokes of the pen, Wittig pursuing the project of universalizing the particular, the minority point of view, a project that was launched in *L'Opoponax* and would be sustained throughout Wittig's entire oeuvre. "Tout geste est renversement": all action is overthrow, announces *Les Guérillères*. This seemingly simple proof correction is overthrow, the refusal to be marked, the aspiration to seize the universal for oneself as embodied in the large **O** that will punctuate *Les Guérillères*, a text that is still in the *chantier* (workshop) at the time of this trial. The period, its ink thicker and darker than in the letters that precede it, is the **O**, the *guérillères'* cry, waiting to unfurl.

MORGANE CADIEU

# Afterword: Lesbian Atomism

Fig. 1. © Tarek Lakhrissi, Unfinished Sentence II (2020), 30 metal spears, chains, color filter, loudspeakers, performance. Soundtrack in collaboration with Ndayé Kouagou. Palais de Tokyo, Paris (FR). Courtesy of the artist and Vitrine Gallery. Photo: Aurélien Mole.

Tarek Lakhrissi's 2020 installation at the Palais de Tokyo (fig. 1) was inspired by *Les Guérillères*, but this photograph could also serve as an illustration of Monique Wittig's creative process: "I call the chaotic space where books are made the literary worksite."[1] Lakhrissi's

1. Monique Wittig, *Le Chantier littéraire* (Lyon: Presses Universitaires de Lyon; Donnemarie-Dontilly: Éditions iXe, 2010), 77. All translations cited here from this work are my own.

**YFS 142,** *Lesbian Materialism: The Life and Work of Monique Wittig,* ed. Cadieu and Kim, 

chaos is material *and* linguistic, too: the "Unfinished Sentences" of the installation's title are built out of metal scraps, forged into delicate lances and spears. As in *Le Chantier littéraire* (The Literary Workshop), the background (ceiling, lighting, walls, and poles here; archives there) is as important as the final work of art. It is hard to guess whether running into this suspended artillery would harm you, but you would certainly be touched by these round and rough edges that also look like disorienting signs, pointing in all directions. As a materialist writer and thinker, Wittig is often apprehended through this framework, in ways that expand the stakes of the field, as Lynne Huffer does in this very volume but also in *Foucault's Strange Eros*:

> Wittig's 'old' materialist 'lesbian body' returns to trouble the anti-linguistic turn that characterizes these new materialisms, [. . .] the mundane incommensurable *things* that we find in gutters and that new materialists like Jane Bennett offer us in the form of lists I can't help but hear as LESBIAN in the Wittigian mode: the list after list of word-body parts that comprise *The Lesbian Body*.[2]

The more I contemplate Lakhrissi's mobiles, the more I see Wittig's "lesbian bodies," their "word-body parts" covered in "iron nails" and "bristling with metal spikes."[3]

Strolling around the Yale Sterling Memorial Library in Fall 2022, I stumbled upon an exhibition curated by Gabrielle Colangelo, "We Are Everywhere: Lesbians in the Archive," in which I learned that the word "lesbian" became a Library of Congress subject heading in 1954.[4] If an enumeration can be, in Huffer's words, "LESBIAN in the Wittigian mode," what would it mean to envision the archives as lesbian?[5] In *Virgile, non* (*Across the Acheron*), the narrator's guide, Manastabal, calls Wittig a "paper lesbian." The annotated typescript of this novel, housed at the Yale Beinecke Rare Book and Manuscript Library, demonstrates that Manastabal's utterance was doubly right, in the fictional world and *on paper*; "une lesbienne," added by hand, came to replace "un jules" (a butch), stricken through (fig. 2).

2. Lynne Huffer, *Foucault's Strange Eros* (New York: Columbia University Press, 2020), 158.

3. Wittig, *The Lesbian Body*, trans. David Le Vay (New York: Avon, 1976), 55, 147.

4. https://onlineexhibits.library.yale.edu/s/we-are-everywhere/page/welcome.

5. Or, as Wittig's biographer Émilie Notéris puts it, "to amazon the archives." Émilie Notéris, *Wittig* (Paris: Les Pérégrines, 2022), 12. My translation.

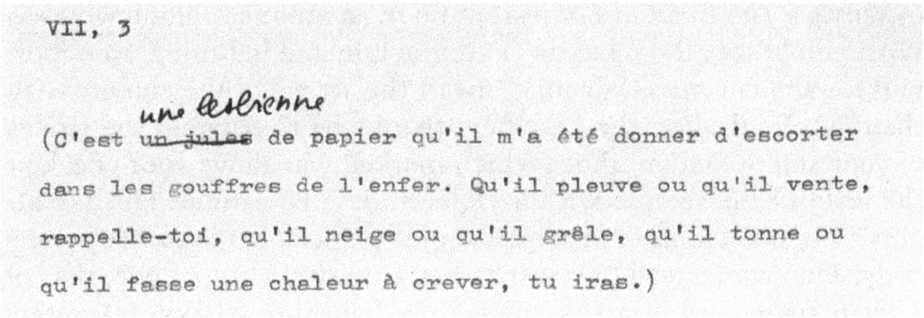

VII, 3

une lesbienne

(C'est ~~un jules~~ de papier qu'il m'a été donner d'escorter dans les gouffres de l'enfer. Qu'il pleuve ou qu'il vente, rappelle-toi, qu'il neige ou qu'il grêle, qu'il tonne ou qu'il fasse une chaleur à crever, tu iras.)

Fig. 2. Monique Wittig, annotated typescript of *Virgile, non*, formerly *La Cité*, GEN MSS 1359, Box 2. Beinecke Rare Book and Manuscript Library, Yale University. © Monique Wittig Literary Estate

The transition from "jules" to "lesbian" has broader implications for the materialist understanding of this keyword. In *Lesbian Peoples: Material for a Dictionary*, Wittig and Sande Zeig quote this invented song: "If you're poor / Then you're a dyke [*jules*] / If you're rich / you're sapphic // but if you're neither one nor the other / a lesbian, a lesbian, is what you'll have to be."[6] The fugitive figure of the lesbian thus points to an overthrow of gender *and class*. The French version goes even further. By chanting "lesbian," it transforms the noun into a pronoun-verb compound: "Si tu es pauvre / tu es une jules [. . .] mais si tu n'es ni l'une ni l'autre / lesbienne, lesbienne."[7]

Departing from Lakhrissi's installation—which translates the paper lesbian into other spaces and materials, revealing the many kinds of matter folded into Wittig's lesbian materialism—I would like to identify avenues for reading Wittig through a branch of materialist philosophy that is rarely studied in her work: atomism. I could certainly start with source critique and underline the possible references to Sappho's verses in Lucretius's landmark atomist poem, *De Rerum Natura* (*On the Nature of Things*). Critics have shown, for instance, how the two authors share a comparable "erotic compulsion" and "voluptuousness."[8] For that matter, a reference to Sappho

6. Wittig and Sande Zeig, *Lesbian Peoples: Material for a Dictionary* (New York: Avon, 1979), 47.

7. Wittig and Zeig, *Brouillon pour un dictionnaire des amantes* (Paris: Grasset, 1976), 143.

8. See Jeffrey Duban, *The Lesbian Lyre: Reclaiming Sappho for the 21st Century* (West Hoathly: Clairview Books, 2016), 304; and Laurel Fulkerson, "Lucretius and

in Wittig's *The Lesbian Body* crops up in an atomistic framework, as Wittig mobilizes the imagery of atomic rain and lightning, so important for ancient materialism: "*I* await the arrival of the comets with their smoky flashes, they are here thanks be to Sappho, the stones of your star are fallen, those which marked you above your cheek at the level of the temple with a violet seal."[9] The stones fall like atoms—tinier versions of Wittig's doodled planets—to mark the lover's body. The "violet seal" even matches Lakhrissi's color code, that of lesbian rights and of a sky snipped by lightning strikes. Like stars and comets, the intertwined lovers also tumble down in *The Lesbian Body*: "*I* fall *I* fall, *I* drag you down in this fall this hissing spiral"; "We descend directly legs together thighs together arms entwined."[10] To describe the chemistry between two bodies, the French even say that they have "hooked atoms," *des atomes crochus*. The use of the first-person pronoun underscores the drop: italicized in English as *I*, it is split in French, j/e. The use of the same cracked "j/e" activates the materialist dimension of Marie Darrieussecq's 2005 novel, *Le Pays* (The Country). It ushers the narrator—a pregnant, bi-national writer—into a world replete with swirling atoms, placental bubbles, oceanic molecules, and cosmic particles. In Darrieussecq as in Wittig, the two letters lean into one another via a slash, the way atomic corpuscles fell, tilted, and collided in antiquity. The detour at the origin of the world (Lucretius's coined *clinamen* in Latin; *swerve* in English) is at the core of Wittig's theory:

> There is a detour, and the shock of words is produced by their association, their disposition, their arrangement, and by each one of them as used separately. The detour is work, working words as anyone works a material to turn it into something else, a product. There is no way to save this detour in literature, and the detour is what literature is all about.[11]

The material aspect of language—the "shock of words" so often mentioned when it comes to Wittig—evokes the generative encounter between corpuscles, a material figuration of the "oblique point of view

---

Sapphic Uoluptas," in Thea S. Thorsen and Stephen Harrison, *Roman Receptions of Sappho* (Oxford: Oxford University Press, 2019), 61–76.

9. Wittig, *The Lesbian Body*, 57.

10. Wittig, *The Lesbian Body*, 50–51.

11. Wittig, "The Trojan Horse," in *The Straight Mind and Other Essays* (Boston: Beacon Press, 1992), 72–73.

on humanity" afforded by Wittig's "lesbian."[12] Nathalie Sarraute, abundantly quoted in *Le Chantier littéraire*, shares this atomistic outlook: her tropisms are "these subjacent movements, this incessant swirl, similar to the movement of atoms"; her texts are filled with shocks described as crashes, clashes, and frictions of words that attract one another and collide.[13] Quotes by Sarraute in *Le Chantier littéraire* incessantly describe "thin spurts," "sparkling sprays" and "arabesques," where words "flow," "erupt" and "cascade."[14] Words are "small cores surrounded by vast hazy expanses" and "small smooth and round pebbles that a thread crosses." In definitions reminiscent of Lakhrissi's suspended metallic cables, Wittig's words "float, [. . .] clinging to their visual forms, not yet crushed by their meaning."[15] The opening line of *Les Guérillères*, too, describes what happens "when it rains," and the book is interspersed with "O," as so many atoms, so many cores and pebbles, sprinkled on the typescript.[16] These large Os printed on the page find an equivalent in the archives, where I kept encountering round traces of Wittig's literary worksite: ink and coffee stains, shriveled flies, a piece of fluff that had been preserved between pages but disappeared in the process of putting together the exhibition "Drafting Monique Wittig" at the Beinecke.[17]

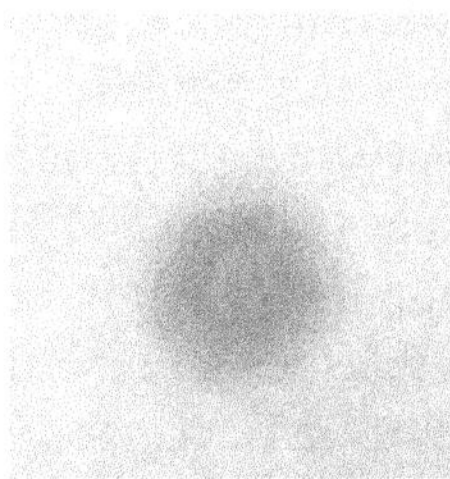
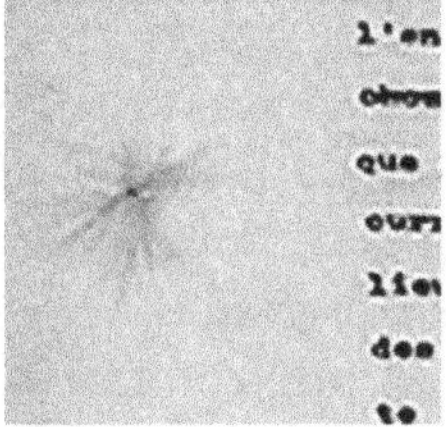

Figs. 3, 4, and 5. Stains and fluff on the annotated typescript of *Virgile, non*, formerly *La Cité*, GEN MSS 1359, Box 2. Beinecke Rare Book and Manuscript Library, Yale University. © Monique Wittig Literary Estate

12. Wittig, "Homo Sum," in *The Straight Mind and Other Essays*, 46.
13. Nathalie Sarraute, *The Age of Suspicion: Essays on the Novel*, trans. Maria Jolas (New York: Braziller, 1990), 30; Wittig, *Le Chantier littéraire*, 61–62.
14. Wittig, *Le Chantier littéraire*, 61, 104.
15. Wittig, *Le Chantier littéraire*, 62, 103, 104, 108.
16. Wittig, *Les Guérillères*, trans. David Le Vay (New York: Avon Books, 1985), 9.
17. Conference "Drafting Monique Wittig," co-organized with Annabel Kim, Beinecke Rare Book and Manuscript Library, Yale University, October 10–11, 2019.

The atomist, amorous, and creative rain of ancient materialism is further developed in *Across the Acheron*:

> The winged seeds of the ash descending in their flight, just like that, the words fall in thousands, the air is laden with them. Butterflies' wings gently beating, just like that, brushing against my eyes in thousands. Leaves coming away from the trees in one night, just like that, falling silently, their shapes enlarging or dwindling. Flakes of dissimilar density, obscuring the sky that is visible between them in long blue flashes, become heavy enough, just like that, to touch down. Never will their physical presence have caused me more perfect joy. [. . .] I perceive her only intermittently in the blue gaps created when the fall of the black masses is interrupted and their descent, at once slower and faster, at once speeds up and slows down. I see them meandering in flight and floating away at random.[18]

Black masses, words, leaves, flakes, flashes, and butterflies "meander" and "float away at random." They fall and are thereby joyfully felt by the flesh. Corpuscles hit the eyes, which is how sight was envisioned in ancient materialism: particles (*simulacra*) came away from atoms to touch the cornea. The paragraph is full of antithetical actions: "enlarging or dwindling"; "at once slower and faster, at once speeds up and slows down." These oppositions remind us that in an atomic world, creation announces its opposite: a future destruction and renewal. Here, in *Across the Acheron*, what falls (the seeds from trees) is meant to disseminate and germinate. Yet, they also announce a downfall, that of autumnal leaves. The translation reinforces such degradation because the tree in question, *un frêne*, is an "ash" in English, a word that also designates the residue after a fire.

Atomist notations underpin Wittig's understanding of creativity. In ancient materialism, the rain of atoms is a figuration meant to explain what happens before worlds are created, before atoms swerve from their fated fall, before bodies meet, or here, before books are completed and published. Because the world already exists, from time immemorial, this antediluvian rain stands as a fable, a fiction, a literary worksite where cards can be reshuffled, gender, class and subjectivities reconfigured, hierarchizing differences upended. I propose we read Wittig through the lens of "lesbian atomism," through what George Sand articulated in her autobiography: "I was no longer a lady,

18. Wittig, *Across the Acheron*, trans. David Le Vay (London: Women's Press, 1989), 108.

nor was I a 'gentleman.' [. . .] I was an atom lost in the immense crowd."[19]

The soundtrack of Lakhrissi's installation (*Buffy the Vampire Slayer*; *Xena: Warrior Princess*) points in the same direction. For critic Liz Millward, the latter series "is, in effect, a televised version of the myth making of lesbian origins through warrior poets, a tradition associated in particular with the works of Audre Lorde, Monique Wittig, Judy Grahn, and Paula Gunn Allen."[20] What we keep encountering in Wittig's works and archives are myth-making fables of origins, signaling the hope that words can reset or recast forms—bodily or societal— before they land, that language can forever be "unbecoming," that words can divert Lakhrissi's "unfinished sentences," understood as grammatical units, and as the judgments that fall onto people.[21] In that regard, Wittig's papers are an atomist worksite. Skimming through private and professional documents, the reader is bombarded by what Roland Barthes defines as "biographemes," that is, "a few details, a few preferences, a few inflections" that "come to touch, like Epicurean atoms, some future body, destined to the same dispersion."[22] References to Wittig in the twenty-first century are subject to a similar atomistic dispersion. She is indeed remembered in scattered fragments: Lola Lafon's 2014 novel *La Petite Communiste qui ne souriait jamais* (*The Little Communist Who Never Smiled*) starts with a quote from Wittig's *Les Guérillères*; Wittig's name appears in the margins of Maggie Nelson's 2015 work of autotheory, *The Argonauts*; a character from *L'Opoponax* crops up at the end of Anne Garréta's 2019 novel, *Dans l'béton* (*In Concrete*); Guillaume Lebrun turns Wittig's neological noun into an adjective in his *Fantaisies guérillères* (Guérillère Fantasies) (2022); and Léonora Miano's 2021 compendium of feminist citations is orchestrated by a reference to Wittig, as the book is entitled *Elles disent.*[23]

19. George Sand, *Story of My Life*, group translation edited by Thelma Jurgrau (Albany: State University Press of New York, 1991), 904–905.

20. Liz Millward, "Xena and the Warrior Poets: Audre Lorde, Monique Wittig, and the Myths of Lesbian Origins," *Feminist Media Studies* 14:1 (2014), 136.

21. See Annabel Kim, *Unbecoming Language: Anti-Identitarian French Feminist Fictions* (Columbus: The Ohio State University Press, 2018).

22. Roland Barthes, *Sade, Fourier, Loyola*, trans. Richard Miller (Baltimore: Johns Hopkins University Press, 1997), 176.

23. On how French anti-gay marriage militants tend to misspell Monique as Monica to underscore the alleged foreignness of her uncompromising feminism, see also

Ancient materialists thought of atoms as letters of the alphabet. If we pursue this analogy, we then start to see yet another form of atomistic rain at play in Wittig's archives: the typos, the alphabet sprinkled on paper, the letters arranged, scattered, diverted, and stirred on typescripts.

In this undated document typed for a seminar (fig. 6), Wittig couches on a single page her understanding of an entire literary genre. She defines the French novel without mentioning a single French novelist, except for Flaubert, whose name crops up between references to Baudelaire, Marx, Poe, Stein, and Kristeva. Wittig's improvised dictionary entry is everything but straight, as the short text zigzags from criticism to poetry and theory, from genre to time period, from French to German and American names. The celebrated proximity between prose and poem can be traced back to *Le Chantier littéraire*, in which a section on Sarraute is called "L'ordre du poème" ("The Order of the Poem"). In Wittig's reading of Sarraute, there are no "boundaries between the novel and poetry."[24] Referring to Poe or Mallarmé, Wittig and Sarraute agree that the poem can "demystify" creation, increase polysemy, and thus disorient readers from the everyday use of language.[25] More importantly, the poem is the material genre par excellence: "the poem is that form which lives closest to words in their raw state"; "the relation of the writer to language in its material form is that of poet."[26] As a poet-novelist herself, and an heir to Lucretius's atomist poem *On the Nature of Things*, Wittig highlights her multifaceted materialism by superimposing two words, "the matter" and "the subject," by jumbling together matter, material, substance, field, and subjectivity. The importance of poetry as a material genre is also present in one of the courses Wittig taught at the University of Arizona. In "Lesbians, Bisexual Women's theories, lives, and activism," she assigned the essay "Poetry is not a Luxury" (1985), in which Audre Lorde argues: "The farthest external horizons of our hopes and fears are cobbled by our poems, carved from the rock experiences of our daily lives."[27] Wittig shares Lorde's call for action

Camille Robcis, "Catholics, the 'Theory of Gender,' and the Turn to the Human in France: A New Dreyfus Affair?" *The Journal of Modern History* 87:4 (2015).

24. Wittig, *Le Chantier littéraire*, 92.

25. Wittig, *Le Chantier littéraire*, 82, 99.

26. Wittig, *Le Chantier littéraire*, 99, 118.

27. Audre Lorde, "Poetry is not a Luxury," in *The Collected Poems of Audre Lorde* (New York: Norton, 1997), 37.

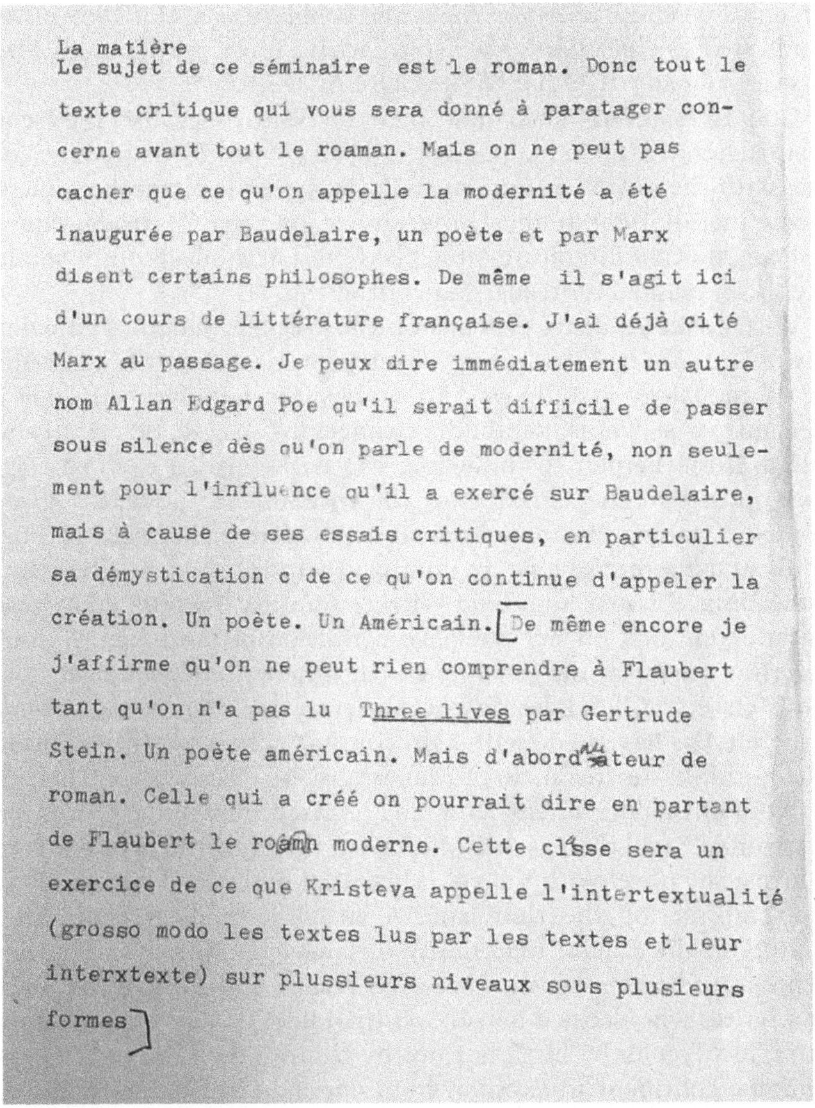

La matière
Le sujet de ce séminaire est le roman. Donc tout le texte critique qui vous sera donné à paratager concerne avant tout le roaman. Mais on ne peut pas cacher que ce qu'on appelle la modernité a été inaugurée par Baudelaire, un poète et par Marx disent certains philosophes. De même il s'agit ici d'un cours de littérature française. J'ai déjà cité Marx au passage. Je peux dire immédiatement un autre nom Allan Edgard Poe qu'il serait difficile de passer sous silence dès qu'on parle de modernité, non seulement pour l'influence qu'il a exercé sur Baudelaire, mais à cause de ses essais critiques, en particulier sa démystication c de ce qu'on continue d'appeler la création. Un poète. Un Américain. [De même encore je j'affirme qu'on ne peut rien comprendre à Flaubert tant qu'on n'a pas lu <u>Three lives</u> par Gertrude Stein. Un poète américain. Mais d'abord ateur de roman. Celle qui a créé on pourrait dire en partant de Flaubert le roamn moderne. Cette clsse sera un exercice de ce que Kristeva appelle l'intertextualité (grosso modo les textes lus par les textes et leur interxtexte) sur plussieurs niveaux sous plusieurs formes]

Fig. 6. Monique Wittig, notes for a class on the novel at the University of Arizona, undated, GEN MSS 1359, Box 25. Beinecke Rare Book and Manuscript Library, Yale University. © Monique Wittig Literary Estate

through a concrete poetry of rocks and cobblestones. Her 1969 novel-manifesto *Les Guérillères* even starts with a prose poem made of free verse as so many "GOLDEN SPACES LACUNAE."[28]

Course materials shed new light on Wittig because they constrained her to explain her poetics in just a few words, as we have just seen with the novel lecture notes. In the syllabus of another course, taught in Fall 1999 at the University of Arizona, "Introduction to Lesbian and Gay Literature," the class presentation's prompt sounds like a user manual for readers and critics (fig. 7).

Wittig asks students to focus on the "weight, length, and color" of words to study "how a text develops a meaning." She describes her methodology as follows: "To analyze the texts we will look at them in parts: words, sentences, paragraphs, pages. Practically we will go from the part to the whole. We will consider each part as a close-up in film and as reflecting the ensemble of the text." A very atomistic reading, during which students were encouraged to place words under a microscope, to atomize them into the smallest units of meaning. If I were to attend Wittig's seminar, I would do a "reading intervention" on her one-page definition of the novel. I would underline the misprints generated by the typewriter: "paratager," "ateur," "clsse," "Allan Edgard Poe," "interxtexte," "plussieurs." Many of these typos have to do with a drifting "a," a letter so important for Wittig; think, for instance, of Manastabal in *Virgile, non*. The very keyword of this document, "roman," is itself misspelled twice: first as "roaman," and then as "roamn." With this misprint, Wittig seems to invest the novel with the vocal hiatus of poetry and *poésie*, of creation and *création*, the friction of two vowels (*oé* and *éa*) that reminds locutors of the palatal materiality of language. Moreover, the typo seems to indicate a tension between France and the United States for a writer who defined herself, on the folder of *Virgile, non*'s typescript, as "French by birth but not by habit."[29] Her *roman* "roams" from one continent to another, from one language to another, from one genre to another, turning Wittig into "Un poète. Un Américain," "Un poète américain." The first person itself must be split in two: "je j'affirme." Misprints in French are called either *bourdon* when letters are forgotten (literally a stick, but also a lance and a bumblebee)

28. Wittig, *Les Guérillères*, trans. David Le Vay, 5.

29. Wittig, folder of the typescript of *Virgile, non*, formerly entitled *La Cité*, Box 2, GEN MSS 1359, Beinecke Library, Yale University. My translation.

**The University of Arizona**
**Fall 1999**
**ENGL/WS 351A: INTRODUCTION TO LESBIAN AND GAY LITERATURE**
**PROFESSOR MONIQUE WITTIG**

TUESDAY & THURSDAY
3:30PM-4:45PM
M LNG 205 [watch for changes]

OFFICE: Communication Bldg. Rm. 114C
OFFICE HOURS: W 3:00-6:00 PM and by appointment
PHONE: 621-3573
e-mail: wittig@u.arizona.edu

**COURSE TOPIC: HOMOEROTICISM IN EURO/AMERICAN LITERATURE**

**COURSE DESCRIPTION**: Homoeroticism refers to the subtle and delicate expression of something foreign to the strict heterosexual regime of reproduction [love]. Where can we find it? At the edge of the text, in the vocabulary, in the form of the sentences, in the depiction of the characters and their relationships, sometimes in the title of a novel, short story or poem.

**METHODOLOGY**:

To analyze the texts we will look at them in parts: words, sentences, paragraphs, pages. Practically we will go from the part to the whole. We will consider each part as in a close up in film and as reflecting the ensemble of the text. Each student will choose a fragment of each text, no more than a page and study it at home. The remarks and notes will be presented in what I call a "reading intervention". It's a short oral presentation, informal without prepared sentences. Thus everybody can comment and participate.

The methodology of our "reading interventions" can be summarized thus:

An approach to the text,

1] at the lexical level: vocabulary, all the words, their weight, their length, their colors

2] at the phonological level: alliterations, assonance etc.

3] at the syntactical level: contrasts, symmetry, oppositions, allusions, symbols, myths, ideology; how does a text develop a meaning [through the elements described here] and what is the meaning.

Fig. 7. Monique Wittig, syllabus of the course "Introduction to Lesbian and Gay Literature," taught at the University of Arizona in Fall 1999, GEN MSS 1359, Box 25. Beinecke Rare Book and Manuscript Library, Yale University. © Monique Wittig Literary Estate

or *coquilles* (shells) when letters are substituted, which recalls Sarraute's definition of words as *coquillages*, shells of shellfish. Readers must pay attention to the shells of words, their destructive power, their *bourdonnement* (buzzing), the way their "weight, length, and color" produce new transversal meanings across Wittig's archives. The shock—or shells—of words saps the ordinary use of orthography. The *c* of *coquille* (an atom sliced in two) even floats in the middle of the page.

In a letter dated September 30, 1985 (fig. 8), Wittig's thesis advisor Gérard Genette begs Wittig "not to change [. . .] quotation marks into brackets." What better misprint than a bracket, a punctuation mark that looks like a shell, like a letter upside-down. Half of Wittig's aforementioned definition of the novel is in brackets, added by hand in the second part of the text. Likewise, the transition from the typed "jules" to the written "lesbienne" in *Virgile, non* occurs in parentheses.

These papers teach us that Wittig's oeuvre originates in a typo. On the first page of her unpublished novel *La Mécanique*, either the typewriter jammed, or the writer made a happy mistake: a *shell* conceals the agreement of an adjective (fig. 9). Wittig indicates—albeit through a negative, hypothetical, and circumvoluted phrase—that her narrator is a man ("en admettant même que je ne sois pas encore réveillé"), but she then struggles with the next predicate: "je serais conttnt [happy] si je pouvais voir Jeanne tous les matins." As a result, the *e* of *content* or *contente* disappears altogether, forever blurred and hidden behind a forest of "t," behind the "TNT" of words as shells, both fragile receptacles (*coquilles*) and explosive ammunition (bombshells). The "content" (in the sense of *contenu)* roams between genders and languages, between past and future, dynamited and unbounded by its archival, atomistic, and lesbian materiality.

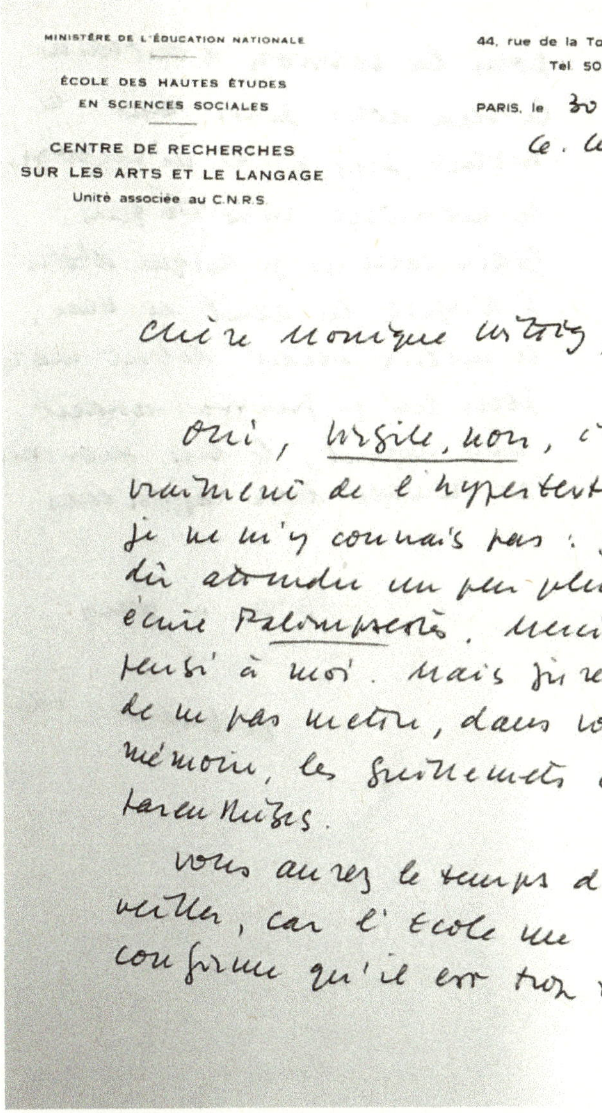

MINISTÈRE DE L'ÉDUCATION NATIONALE

ÉCOLE DES HAUTES ÉTUDES
EN SCIENCES SOCIALES

CENTRE DE RECHERCHES
SUR LES ARTS ET LE LANGAGE
Unité associée au C.N.R.S.

44, rue de la Tour, 75116 PARIS
Tel. 503-21-20

PARIS, le 30.9. 1985
G. Genette

Chère Monique Wittig,

Oui, Virgile, non, c'est vraiment de l'hypertexte où je ne m'y connais pas : j'aurais dû attendre un peu plus pour écrire Palimpsestes. Merci d'avoir pensé à moi. Mais dites-moi de ne pas mettre, dans votre mémoire, les guillemets en parenthèses.

Vous aurez le temps d'y veiller, car l'École me confirme qu'il est trop tard

Fig. 8. Letter from Gérard Genette to Monique Wittig, September 30, 1985, GEN MSS 1359, Box 20. Beinecke Rare Book and Manuscript Library, Yale University. © Monique Wittig Literary Estate

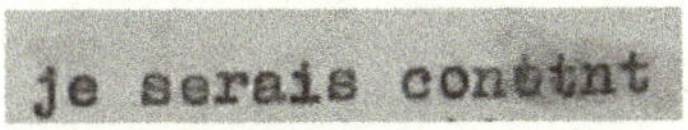

je serais conetnt

Fig. 9. First page of Monique Wittig's first, unpublished typescript, *La Mécanique*, circa 1960s, GEN MSS 1359, Box 10. Beinecke Rare Book and Manuscript Library, Yale University. © Monique Wittig Literary Estate

# Contributors

Morgane Cadieu is Associate Professor of French at Yale, author of *Marcher au hasard: clinamen et création dans la prose du XXe siècle* (Classiques Garnier, 2019), and co-editor of the special issue "Beaches and Ports" (*Comparative Literature*, 2021). Her second book, *On Both Sides of the Tracks: Social Mobility in Contemporary French Literature*, is forthcoming with The University of Chicago Press.

Katherine A. Costello is an independent scholar working at the intersection of U.S. and French feminist, queer, and transgender studies. She received her PhD from Duke University in 2016. She is also the author, with Ilana Eloit, of "Monique Wittig (ou le lesbianisme intraduisible)" (*Dictionnaire du genre en traduction*, 2021).

Ilana Eloit is Assistant Professor of Gender and Sexuality at the University of Geneva where she directs the Master's program in Gender Studies. Her interdisciplinary work brings together feminist and queer theories with historical and cultural analysis of feminist and LGBTQ+ movements in France. She holds a PhD in Gender Studies from the London School of Economics and she has taught, among others, at the University of Lausanne, Sciences Po Paris, Paris 8 University and the Paris School of Fine Arts.

Anne F. Garréta, a graduate of l'École normale supérieure, is Research Professor in the Literature Program at Duke University as well as co-founder and vice-president of the Association des Ami.e.s de Monique Wittig. Her first novel, *Sphinx*, hailed by critics, told a love story free from gender marks. She was co-opted into the Oulipo in 2000. She won the Prix Médicis in 2002 for *Pas*

**YFS 142**, *Lesbian Materialism: The Life and Work of Monique Wittig*, ed. Cadieu and Kim, © 2023 by Yale University.

*un jour* (*Not One Day*) and her latest novel to be translated into English is *Dans l'béton* (*In Concrete*).

LYNNE HUFFER is Samuel Candler Dobbs Professor of Philosophy at Emory University. She is the author of five books: *Another Colette*; *Maternal Pasts, Feminist Futures*; *Mad for Foucault*; *Are the Lips a Grave?*; and *Foucault's Strange Eros*. She is currently completing a book-length project called *The Ethics of Extinction: 99 Anthropocene Fragments*. She is also translating, with Annabel Kim, Monique Wittig's *Le Chantier littéraire*.

ALICE KAPLAN is Sterling Professor of French at Yale and author, most recently, of *Maison Atlas: roman* and, with Laura Marris, *States of Plague: Reading Albert Camus in a Pandemic*.

ANNABEL L. KIM is the Roy G. Clouse Associate Professor of Romance Languages and Literatures at Harvard University and author of *Unbecoming Language: Anti-Identitarian French Feminist Fictions* and *Cacaphonies: The Excremental Canon of French Literature*.

TAREK LAKHRISSI is a French artist and poet with a background in literature who explores sociopolitical narratives and speculative situations of transformation and magic through text, film, installation, and performance. Lakhrissi, based in Paris, has been exhibited internationally at galleries and institutions including Palais de Tokyo, Museum of Contemporary Art, 22nd Biennale of Sydney, Wiels, Centre Pompidou, Hayward Gallery, La Verrière, Fondation Hermès, Haus der Kunst, Auto Italia South East, Grand Palais, FIAC, Palazzo Re Rebaudengo/Sandretto, Manchester International Festival, Mostyn, Tinguely Museum, HKW, ICA, Shedhalle, Fondation Ricard, CRAC Alsace. Lakhrissi's artworks are part of different private and public collections such as Defares, Lafayette Anticipations, Sandretto Foundation and CNAP.

Paris-based SUZETTE ROBICHON is an essayist and longtime lesbian activist with a focus on archives and the transmission of lesbian memory. In 1985, she published an issue of *Vlasta* magazine dedicated to the writing of Monique Wittig, where Wittig's stage play *Le Voyage sans fin* was published for the first time. In 2001, Robichon was co-organizer of the first international conference focusing exclusively on Wittig's work. She is co-President of the Friends of Monique Wittig. The non-profit organization coordinates events around the work of Monique Wittig and maintains the website *https://etudeswittig.hypotheses.org*.

SANDRINE SANOS is a cultural and intellectual historian of twentieth- and twenty-first-century France. She is the author of *Aesthetics of Hate: Far-Right Intellectuals, Antisemitism, and Gender in 1930s France* (Stanford, 2013) and of a historical biography of *Simone de Beauvoir: Creating a Feminist existence* (Oxford, 2017), as well as articles on British and French cinema, French literature, and feminist theory, and the co-editor of *Le genre carcéral: pouvoir disciplinaire, agentivité et expériences de la prison, XIX-XXI siècle* (Éditions des maisons des sciences de l'homme, 2022). She is currently at work on *The Horror of History: Violence and Gender in Cold War France (1954-1967)* which examines how representations of the sex of violence shaped understandings of past and present wars, from the Holocaust to Algeria and Vietnam.

GINA STAMM is Assistant Professor of French at The University of Alabama, having earned a PhD in French from Emory University in 2016. Their research uses the frameworks of ecocriticism and gender studies to address twentieth- and twenty-first-century French and Francophone Caribbean literary avant-gardes, from modernism to contemporary science fiction.

SANDE ZEIG is a film director and producer. She was the life partner of Monique Wittig. Together they collaborated on a book, *Lesbian Peoples: Material for a Dictionary*, a play, *The Constant Journey*, and a film, *The Girl*. Zeig has directed six films and is currently working on two documentaries, *Firelighters: Fire Is Medicine* and *Wittig, Yes!*

JEFFREY ZUCKERMAN is a translator of French, including books by the artists Jean-Michel Basquiat and the Dardenne brothers, the queer writers Jean Genet and Hervé Guibert, and the Mauritian novelists Ananda Devi, Shenaz Patel, and Carl de Souza. A graduate of Yale University, he has been a finalist for the TA First Translation Prize and the French-American Foundation Translation Prize, and has been awarded a PEN/Heim translation grant and the French Voices Grand Prize. In 2020 he was named a Chevalier in the Ordre des Arts et des Lettres by the French government.

*Yale French Studies* is the oldest English-language journal in the United States devoted to French and Francophone literature and culture. Each volume is conceived and organized by a guest editor or editors around a particular theme or author. Interdisciplinary approaches are welcome, as are contributions from scholars and writers from around the world. Recent volumes have explored a wide variety of subjects, among them: *Claude Lanzmann after "Shoah"*; *Maryse Condé, a Writer for Our Times*; *North African Poetry in French*; and *Photography and the Body in Nineteenth-Century France.*

*Yale French Studies* is published twice yearly by Yale University Press (yalebooks.com) and may be accessed on JSTOR (jstor.org).

For information on how to submit a proposal for a volume of *Yale French Studies*, visit yale.edu/French and navigate to "Yale French Studies."